B E C —

POINT LEVI.

A Future Defined

Records of Our History

A Future Defined

Canada from 1849 to 1873

George Bolotenko

National Archives of Canada
Archives nationales du Canada

Canadian Cataloguing in Publication Data

Bolotenko, George, 1946-
A future defined: Canada from 1849 to 1873

(Records of our history)
Issued also in French under title:
Edifier l'avenir.
Includes index.
DSS cat. no. SA2-129/5-1992-E (bound)
SA2-129/5-1992-lE (pbk.)
ISBN 0-660-14410-7 (bound)
0-660-14411-5 (pbk.)

1. Canada — History — 19th century — Sources.
2. Canada — Politics and government — 19th century — Sources.
3. Canada — Social conditions — 19th century — Sources.
I. National Archives of Canada. II. Title. III. Series.

FC500.B64 1992 971.04 C92-099303-6
F1033.B64 1992

National Archives of Canada
395 Wellington Street
Ottawa, Ontario
K1A 0N3
(613) 995-5138

DSS cat. no. SA2-129/5-1992-lE
ISBN 0-660-14411-5

This publication is printed on alkaline paper.

Cover: House of Parliament, Ottawa, circa 1870s. (C-37874)
Back cover: Relieving the Guard in winter, Montreal, 1856. (C-111217)
Endleaves: A view from Point Levi. (PA-185572)

Table of Contents

Life in British North America/Canada (1850-1873) 65

Political Life, Confederation and the Northwest (1850-1872, 1899) 141

Foreword

A Future Defined is the fourth volume prepared by the National Archives of Canada in its major exhibition series titled *Records of Our History*. It illustrates many of the significant events and developments of the Confederation era when modern Canada, as we know it today, took shape.

Canada has a rich and varied past. The records of that past are preserved by the National Archives so that all Canadians have access to them. Through these records, which serve as windows into by-gone years, we can all savour the life of our ancestors, vicariously re-live their hardships and joys, delve into their minds and hearts: in brief, we can better understand how our country came into being and what forces and personalities shaped it. Knowing the past is of inestimable benefit to Canadians as they search for answers to many fundamental problems of modern life.

The maps and drawings, photographs, works of documentary art, rare printed items and manuscript material selected for this publication are all drawn from the fonds and collections of the National Archives, the repository of the nation's memory. Virtually all of the documents are contemporary to the years covered by this exhibition and catalogue (1849-1873). Most of them, as unique items existing in single copy, are beyond price; all of them, in their instructive value about Canada's past, are priceless. The documents are arranged broadly by theme and chronology, to provide the reader with an awareness of significant developments in Canada's history as they unfolded over time. The text that accompanies each item explains its creation, provides the historical context in which it was produced, and comments on its significance as an archival document.

Whether people read *A Future Defined* from start to finish, or browse through it, reading only what they choose, I sincerely hope they find the catalogue both interesting and stimulating. I hope, moreover, that the publication instills an increased awareness of the influence of the past upon our lives, and that Canadians from all corners of our vast country come to better appreciate and use our nation's archival legacy housed in the National Archives of Canada.

Jean-Pierre Wallot
National Archivist

Acknowledgements

Any large exhibition, and its accompanying catalogue, cannot succeed without the help and advice of colleagues. This is certainly so with this publication and the exhibition it represents — the contributions of many merit acknowledgement.

Several colleagues read and commented upon my early proposals for the scope and design of this catalogue and this exhibition. To Terry Cook, Bruce Wilson, Ian McClymont, John Bell, Brian Murphy, Loretta Barber, Doug Whyte, Andrew Rodger, Peter Delottinville and Edward Dahl I would like to express my thanks for their time and constructive advice. To Michel Wyczynski I am much indebted for a very large amount of technical research work, which immensely facilitated my search for exhibit material.

Patricia Kennedy was most generous with time and advice. She read the catalogue manuscript and her comments were extremely helpful. Others also read the manuscript either in whole or in part. To Ian McClymont, Christian Rioux, Lydia Foy, Andrew Rodger, Marg Mattson, Harold Naugler, Terry Cook, Bruce Wilson, Doug Whyte and Lewis Jackson — sincere thanks for their time, advice and help. Professor Chad Gaffield of the University of Ottawa offered to read the manuscript. Offers such as that come rarely, and to him also I would like to express my appreciation.

I would like to address special thanks to Ian McClymont who searched out much historical information for a number of exhibit descriptions; to Tim Dubé for his help with the military exhibits; to Brian Murphy for the knowledge he shared about postal history; to Anne Goddard for her generous help with literary documents; to Andrew Rodger for his advice and expertise on the photographs of this period; to Lydia Foy and Gilbert Gignac, who helped so much with their knowledge of documentary art; to Brian Hallett, who eased my work with maps and drawings; and to Larry McNally, who located required information on technological developments. Professor Norman Ball of Waterloo University helped immensely with his general commentary on exhibits reflecting mid-nineteenth-century technological developments, and Professor Michael Peterman of Trent University provided the background context for the C.P. Traill manuscript.

To reference staff in all divisions of the Historical Resources Branch, sincere thanks for their professional and kind response to all my research needs. None were more helpful than Paddy MacIntyre.

Brian Carey, Louise Blais, Micheline Robert, Wilma Macdonald and Tom Nagy also went far beyond the bounds of the expected in their help, while the quality of the reproductions in this catalogue attest to Karen Clack's photographic professionalism. I would also like to acknowledge the Public Programs Branch for its assistance in the production of the exhibition and publication.

Last, but far from least, I wish to express my gratitude to several clerks in Manuscript Division, without whose help my work would have been so much more onerous. Dave Ross and Jamie Louks saved me months of labour in various aspects of document and information search. And both helped with their good humour when it was most needed.

Acknowledgements generally fail to note all who helped in lesser, though not less important, ways. To others who contributed to this publication and exhibition — anonymous and undeserving victims of oversight — my gratitude is no less sincere.

George Bolotenko

Introduction

Historical processes are continuous. People, however, in their effort to better understand historical development, treat history in more manageable blocks of time, in historical periods marked off by outside dates which often reflect signal events.

The outside dates for this exhibition are 1849-1873. I have taken 1848 as the terminal year of the preceding era — the rebellions and struggle for responsible government — and hence commence this exhibition with the year 1849. Confederation was perhaps not inevitable with the coming of responsible government. But the increasing self-management of British North American colonial governments and Confederation did develop simultaneously, as if two sides of the same coin. Hence the closing date of the exhibition, 1873, by which time all former British colonies in North America except Newfoundland — which would join Canada only in 1949 — were in Confederation.

This pre-Confederation period is a time of remarkable and fundamental change. Were a traveller to have visited the British North American colonies in 1849, and then to have returned in 1873, he would have been struck by the sweeping changes that had occurred. From disparate political entities, the British colonies and the Northwest (formerly Prince Rupert's Land administered by the Hudson's Bay Company and territories beyond), had been federated into a new state entity, the Dominion of Canada. Much of the interior and peripheries of the British North American land mass had been known only to aboriginal inhabitants and voyageurs, unstudied and unsurveyed by European immigrants to the New World; by the early 1870s various expeditions had opened much of the interior, and the Dominion survey was laying out land for occupation and agriculture in the Northwest. New relationships between whites and aboriginal peoples were established through a treaty system that was based on land reserves and subsidies, and traditional Indian ways of life and well-being was subjected to forced change.

Agriculture, in the first half of the nineteenth century, was still largely characterized by traditional, manual operating methods; by the 1870s an agrarian revolution was well under way. And an industrial revolution was also in the making in the Montreal area and at the head of Lake Ontario, in the Hamilton-Toronto region, with factories employing up to several hundred persons. With industrialization, of course, urbanization quickened, and towns began to take on a more modern character, with gas-lighting, water-works and sanitation systems. Government-funded welfare institutions, regularized public education, labour legislation and organized sports — attributes of modern life as we know it — all appeared at this time.

The most significant development of this era, however, which changed the character of life, was the revolution in communications, behind which lay the development of technology. Telegraph lines snaked out from metropolitan centres to hinterlands and tied colonies together; in 1866 North America was joined to Europe through the trans-Atlantic cable. Better roads (macadamized, i.e. built of properly-layered, well-drained gravel of various sizes) appeared in this era; and many roads, especially colonization roads into areas newly-opened for settlement, were cut and laid down. Improvements to the Welland Canal and the St. Lawrence locks continued, raising the efficiency of water transport. The ubiquitous lake and river steamer came to ply interior waters. The postal system, transferred to colonial management in the 1850s, steadily improved. These critical developments in communications helped to overcome distance in the vastness of British North America — but none of them were as revolutionary as the railway.

This period is the era *sans pareil* of the railway. As the railway network began to burgeon, it tied towns to hinterlands and opened areas to settlement and development. The railways overcame distance and inclement weather; they expedited the movement of people; and they bound regions, and later colonies, into ever-larger economic units. They both fired economic development, and threatened urban and provincial governments with ruin as these overextended themselves to fund the colossal capital costs of railway building.

The railways were a significant factor in promoting Confederation. Merchants and politicians hoped that they would bind the colonies into a single economic entity, which spurred Confederation. But in a sparsely settled land, only the Dominion government could successfully underwrite their construction. Hence the prominence of railways in Confederation — New Brunswick and Nova Scotia both demanded completion of the Intercolonial, and British Columbia and Prince Edward Island called for railways, as conditions of entry into Confederation. Railways were the primary agency of the political conquest of geographic space.

A new political order, a great opening of the interior and peripheral lands elsewhere for occupation, an agrarian revolution, early industrialization, rising urbanization, a communications revolution — these and other developments of the pre-Confederation era support the notion that this period was a time of fundamental change when the shape of modern Canada, as we now know it, was drawn.

This exhibition seeks to convey this idea. It is not dedicated solely to the politicians of the era, nor exclusively to the political intricacies of achieving Confederation. Rather, it strives to reflect the life of the pre-Confederation era, and the signal developments in economic, social and cultural spheres of life in the British North American colonies. It also notes the influence of international factors upon the colonies, so important to the attainment of Confederation. These factors forced choices upon Britain's North American subjects and their politicians, choices about future directions.

The leaders of the colonies could choose to maintain the status quo, and some, particularly in the Maritimes, preferred this. Not so the leaders of the United Province of Canada, created in 1841 through union of Canada West (previously Upper Canada) and Canada East (formerly Lower Canada). The two halves of the United Province had learned accommodation to a degree. However, strained cultural relations between French and English, and resultant political paralysis, made a new order imperative. The French of Canada East sought a new way to secure their identity and customs; and the English of Canada West, with a more possessive and continental vision, feared American occupation and seizure of the Northwest. Both elements in the province were disposed to look for a new future, either through separation of the two halves or through a general Confederation of all British colonies in North America.

Many Maritimers, their views ably expressed by Joseph Howe, held to another vision — complete and unflinching loyalty to the motherland, full autonomy in the colony, and perhaps even representation in an Imperial Parliament. There was recurring talk of a Maritime Union. Other Maritimers felt the pull of American annexation, as did some of the Grits of Canada West, some of the merchants of Montreal and the Parti rouge of Canada East. To a significant number of inhabitants of the colonies, it was only a matter of time before the British colonies were drawn into the American union.

Separation, annexation, local union, general confederation — these various views were about, and people made and argued their choices. The choices that political leaders, merchants, capitalists and visionaries made, argued and fought for; the course of economic and technological developments in the colonies; and the key influences of outside players, of Britain and the United States — all came together in this era to produce Confederation, and to define the future of Canada.

Hence the title selected for this exhibition, *A Future Defined*. In both domestic and external developments it seems to best express the *zeitgeist,* the historical movement and character of the period 1849-1873.

The items selected for this publication and exhibition, as well as the mass of historical records and documents housed at the National Archives, reflect the above processes and events. Without such records, our understanding of our past would be gravely compromised, if at all possible. In this lies the significance of the National Archives of Canada, without which we could know ourselves only very imperfectly.

I

Responsible Government

The attainment of responsible government was a significant step in the maturation of the British colonies in North America. While it came peacefully to other colonies, this was not the case in the Province of Canada. There it was accompanied by anger and rioting, though the actual causes of these disorders lay elsewhere.

While in some ways the achievement of responsible government was the culmination of the pre-1849 period, in other respects it opened a new era in Canada's achievement of control over her own destiny.

Responsible government introduced British cabinet government into the colonies, and gave colonials fiscal responsibility. But it was not a grant of self-government. In international matters London continued to determine policy. All colonial acts required royal assent; any act deemed contrary to British interest or practices could be disallowed by the British Parliament. Only in 1865 did the *Colonial Laws Validity Act* provide that no colonial law could be challenged by the Home Parliament unless it contravened an Imperial statute made expressly for a given colony.

At the same time, though, the *Colonial Laws Validity Act* was the capstone of the British policy of devolution of self-management to the colonies throughout the 1850s and 1860s. The management of canals, the postal service, clergy reserves, Indian affairs, currency, crown lands, military reserve lands, immigration — these and other responsibilities were delegated by Britain to her colonies in British North America. Britain's support of Confederation was the culmination of this steady policy of devolution from the time of the granting of responsible government.

I

"Canada, New Brunswick and Nova Scotia"

This map, executed by Sydney Hall of Longman and Co., and later published in Hall's *General Atlas*, represents the mainland British North American colonies, Prince Edward Island and the far western coast of Newfoundland in 1849. It is striking how little territory was enclosed within colonial borders, and how vast a land mass was administered by the Hudson's Bay Company which, by its charter of 1670, exercised authority over all lands drained by rivers flowing into Hudson Bay. The Company, through later licenses, also came to manage lands drained by Arctic rivers, as well as the west coast. In fact, in 1849 the British Crown granted the colony of Vancouver Island to the Company, which in turn was to colonize and administer it.

The map reveals how thinly the colonies were settled; most occupied points hugging shorelines or river banks. The northern reaches of the two Canadas were largely unknown; even Lake Abitibi's shores are imperfectly represented. While the Maritime colonies were already organized into counties, this map reflects the old district structure of the United Province of Canada. A statute of 1849 introduced a county structure into the province (except in Quebec's seigneurial parishes) which, although modified by recent regional and metropolitan reorganizations, is still the basis of administrative divisions in both Ontario and Quebec.

There is a notable anomaly to this map. In 1849 the British colonies only had several short railway lines (such as the one from Montreal to Lachine). Hall's map represents the equivalent of the Great Western, Grand Trunk and Intercolonial railways as completed or under construction. Perhaps the mapmaker intended to designate these railways as intended. Misinformation is possible, even in "historical" documents.

Hall's colourful map reflects the general outlines of the British North American colonies at the dawn of responsible government.

Sydney Hall. ca 1849.

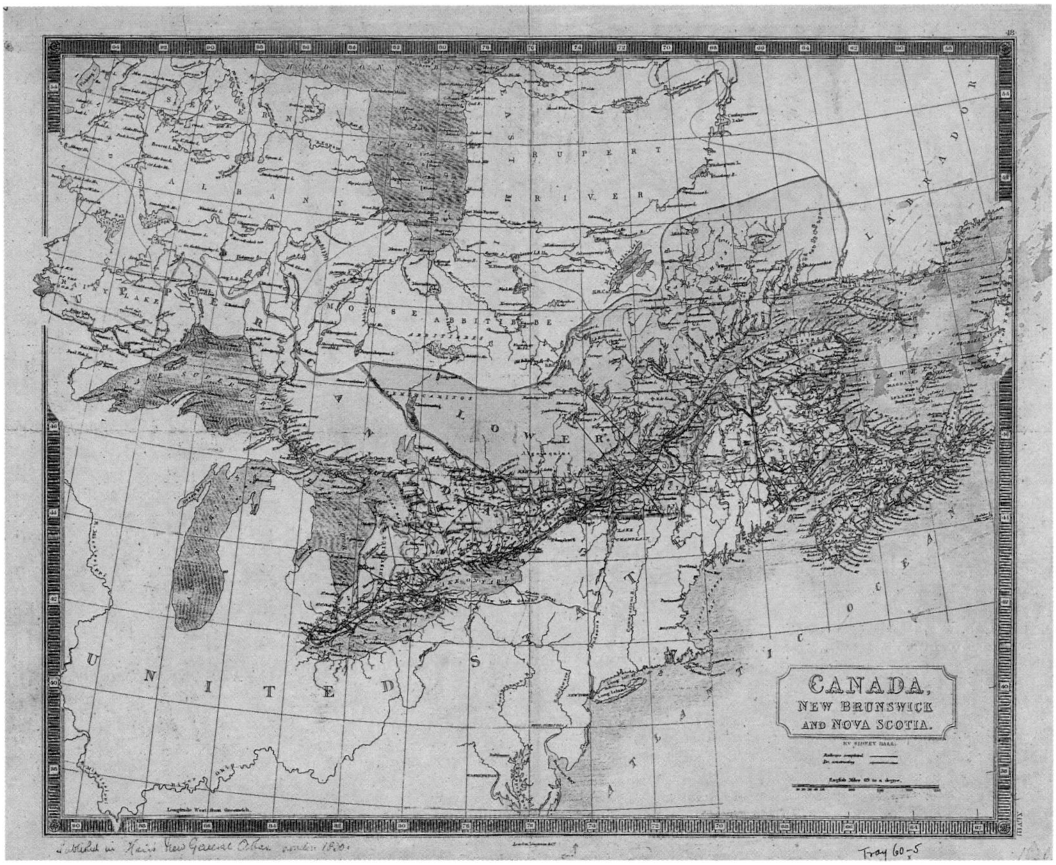

41.8 cm x 50.8 cm

National Archives of Canada,
Cartographic and Audio-Visual Archives Division,
NMC-10330.

"Destruction of the Parliament House, Montreal, April 25TH, 1849"

This handcoloured lithograph, based on an eye-witness sketch by E. Hides, was produced by George Matthews, a Montreal lithographer and is among the earliest prints made in Canada.

The burning of the House of Parliament in 1849 was a result of Britain's grant of responsible government to the North American colonies, first realized in Nova Scotia in 1848. Until the 1840s, the motherland-colonies relationship had been characterized by rather close political control of the colonies, and their economic integration into a closed mercantilist system. Significant economic changes in Britain rendered this arrangement obsolete and uneconomical. Free trade carried the day in Britain, and throughout the 1840s the British Parliament repealed various laws which inhibited free trade. A new Liberal administration, which came to power in Britain in the latter 1840s, was prepared to countenance a much looser political, as well as economic, relationship with Britain's North American colonies.

In 1848 the Crown instructed its governors in the British North American colonies to adhere to the principles of responsible government. Governors were to select to cabinet men who enjoyed the majority support of their legislature, and to approve legislation passed by such legislatures (insofar as it did not contravene existing British laws), regardless of governors' personal views. The first exercise of responsible government occurred with little difficulty in Nova Scotia in 1848; by 1855 all British colonies in North America were governed by responsible cabinets.

Responsible government came to the colonies peacefully, except in the Province of Canada. In 1848 the Governor-in-Chief of Canada, Lord Elgin, had confirmed the Baldwin-Lafontaine Reform ministry in office. That ministry pushed through the Rebellion Losses Bill in early 1849. The bill intended to compensate individuals in Lower Canada (some of them former *patriotes* of 1837) for property losses incurred during the uprising. The same had already been done earlier for victims of losses in Upper Canada. This act enraged the English merchants of Montreal. Then suffering through depressed times and the loss of protected commercial staples markets in Britain, they saw the passage of this bill as their final desertion by a motherland prepared to compensate former "traitors" for losses. Elgin adhered to the wishes of Parliament and assented to the bill on 25 April 1848, thereby demonstrating that responsible government had arrived. Riots followed, and in the evening an enraged English-speaking crowd sacked the Houses, tearing up gas mains in the process, which resulted in the conflagration.

The anger of the English merchant class of Montreal was the result of economic dislocation as metropolitan and hinterland relations were changing dramatically. They expressed this anger at a bill distasteful to them. The bill was possible only because of a new political relationship between the motherland and the colonies. It was indeed a time of root changes, during which the colonies of British North America would strive to define for themselves, singly or together, a new future.

E. Hides, artist; George Matthews, lith. 1849.

23.7 cm x 40.7 cm

National Archives of Canada,
Documentary Art and Photography Division,
C-10721.

"From Her Majesty's Secretary of State for the Colonies to the Right Honourable the Earl of Elgin"

The passage of the Rebellion Losses Bill, which led to the burning of the Houses of Parliament in Montreal, also disposed many Montreal merchants to openly champion annexation to the United States. On 11 October 1849, a broadside entitled *An Address to the People of Canada,* reflecting this new political direction, appeared in the streets of Montreal.

The address argued that Britain had taken from her North American colonies their protected market, and thus brought economic ruin upon them. Of six possible courses of future action available, only annexation to the United States made any sense. Annexation would open great markets for colonial staples. It would bring in American capital and, with waterpower and excess manpower available in Canada, manufacturing would develop along the St. Lawrence. The great waterway, now stilled by economic recession, would spring back to life. Piqued at Britain's desertion of her loyal subjects, the authors of the address expressed gloomily that the British population of the colony was far too small to allow for market development, and that sooner or later, by threat or blandishment, the colony would inevitably become part of the United States.

Within one week, approximately 1,000 persons, many of whom would later contribute significantly to the political and economic developments leading to Confederation, signed an annexation manifesto. Lord Elgin was swift in dismissing anyone who signed from government service. The dispatch shown here, from Lord Grey, the Colonial Secretary, approved of Elgin's measures, reaffirmed Britain's connection to Canada, and authorized Elgin to bring before courts of law any individuals guilty of treason.

The Annexation Manifesto did not find much support. The majority of Upper Canadian farmers, Grit in political inclination, approved of responsible government. The francophone mass of Lower Canada did not wish to lose themselves in an English-speaking sea to the south. But annexationism in principle did not die. After 1849, as before, the question of Canada's relationship with the United States would loom large. Self-management through responsible government, new trading relationships based on free markets, new political and economic relationships to be established among the colonies themselves, Britain and the United States — all these concerns manifested themselves in the year of 1849. How the British North American colonies would respond to these issues would shape the course of future events.

Henry George, Lord Grey. 1850.

Enclosure to 152.

152b
152 f

DESPATCH

FROM HER MAJESTY'S SECRETARY OF STATE FOR THE COLONIES

TO THE

RIGHT HONORABLE THE EARL OF ELGIN.

DOWNING STREET, 9th JANUARY, 1850.

MY LORD,

I have to acknowledge your Despatches of the dates and numbers quoted in the margin :

[Nos. 114, 19th Nov. 1849. — 127, 3d Dec. 1849. — 129, 3d Dec. 1849. — 134, 14th Dec. 1849.]

2. I have laid these Despatches before Her Majesty, and also the Address of the Warden and Councillors of the Municipal Council of the District of Gore : of the Lt. Colonel and Officers of Militia of the 1st and of the 8th Battalions of the Regiment of Dorchester : of the Officers of the 4th Battalion of the Regiment of Kamouraska, and the inhabitants of the Parish of Ste. Anne de la Pocatière : and of the Officers of Militia and Lieut. Colonel Commanding Battalions of the Regiment of Quebec, enclosed in the two first of these Despatches, which Her Majesty has been pleased to receive very graciously. It has afforded Her Majesty great satisfaction to receive these expressions of that loyalty and attachment to the British Crown which she trusts is generally felt by Her Canadian subjects.

3. With regard to the Address to the people of Canada in favor of severing the Province from the British Dominions, for the purpose of annexing it to the United States, which forms the subject of the third of these Despatches, I have to inform you that Her Majesty approves of your having dismissed from Her Service those who have signed a document which is scarcely short of treasonable in its character. HER MAJESTY CONFIDENTLY RELIES ON THE LOYALTY OF THE GREAT MAJORITY OF HER CANADIAN SUBJECTS, AND SHE IS THEREFORE DETERMINED TO EXERT ALL THE AUTHORITY WHICH BELONGS TO HER FOR THE PURPOSE OF MAINTAINING THE CONNECTION OF CANADA WITH THIS COUNTRY, BEING PERSUADED THAT THE PERMANENCE OF THAT CONNECTION IS HIGHLY ADVANTAGEOUS TO BOTH.

4. Your Lordship will therefore understand that YOU ARE COMMANDED BY HER MAJESTY TO RESIST, TO THE UTMOST OF YOUR POWER, ANY ATTEMPT WHICH MAY BE MADE TO BRING ABOUT THE SEPARATION OF CANADA FROM THE BRITISH DOMINIONS, and to mark in the strongest manner Her Majesty's displeasure with all those who may directly or indirectly encourage such a design.

5. And if any attempt of this kind should take such a form that those who are guilty of it may, according to such advice as you may receive from your Law Advisers, be made responsible for their conduct in a Court of Justice, you will not fail to take the necessary measures for bringing them to account.

I am, my Lord, your most obedient Servant,

Right Honorable *(Signed,)* GREY.
THE EARL OF ELGIN.

27.2 cm x 18.5 cm

National Archives of Canada,
Manuscript Division,
MG 26, A 10, Vol. 2.

II

Exploration and Communication

Exploration of the northern British half of the continent caught the imagination of both the public and the government of the Province of Canada. The British (and American) search for Sir John Franklin in the Arctic continued, and grew into a gripping saga. The government of the Province of Canada itself sent expeditions into Rupert's Land, desirous of accumulating evidence for its claim to the patrimony of the Hudson's Bay Company. The Geological Survey of Canada undertook exploratory activity and amassed information about the geography, geology and nature of the relatively unknown interior.

The acquisition of such knowledge about the vast expanses of land lying back of the thin pale of settlement along the St. Lawrence and what would be southwestern Ontario went hand-in-hand with the development of communications. Where good arable land and profitable timber stands were discovered, there went colonization and logging roads. Settlement and economic development followed, and often a railway.

Exploration, knowledge, surveying, settlement, communications, economic development — these were necessary and sequential steps in opening the interior. At the same time, colonial governments did not forget about water communications, developing both interior ports and canals, and coastal ports and navigational beacons and lighthouses.

"Noon in Mid-Winter (Pt.Leopold). H.M.S. Ships *Enterprise* and *Investigator* in Winter Quarters, Port Leopold, North Somerset — Noon in December. Last Plate in W.H.J. Browne's *Ten Coloured Views Taken During the Arctic Expedition of Her Majesty's Ships* Enterprise *and* Investigator, *under the Command of Captain Sir James C. Ross, R.N., K.T., F.R.S.*"

This coloured lithograph was published in 1850, when the Franklin search phenomenon was near its peak. William Henry James Browne served as second lieutenant on HMS *Enterprise*, a ship of Captain James C. Ross' squadron sent in search of Franklin in 1848-1849. During that winter, as the ships lay locked in the winter ice, Lt. Browne led a sledge party that traversed the sea-ice from Port Leopold to the coast of Prince Regent's Island. He made many sketches of what he saw during this sojourn through the Arctic.

Based on one of Browne's sketches, this lithograph is a dramatically effective representation of Arctic winter. From the right side comes a white-pinkish glow, the Arctic "noon," while light plays off jagged ice formations. The sheeted sails, the spars and rigging of the vessels, are all caked in ice, while the distant ship stands shrouded in an opaque blue. The lithographer (Charles Haghe), modelling his image upon Browne's sketch, captures the sense of isolation, desolation and numbing cold of the Arctic, and effectively conveys what winter meant to men who ventured into the distant Canadian North.

After Lieutenant William Henry James Browne. (London; Ackermann and Co., 1850).

15.9 cm x 23.7 cm

National Archives of Canada,
Documentary Art and Photography Division,
C-100191.

Journal of HMS *Assistance*

To the north and west of the British North American colonies stretched trackless expanses of land traversed by Indians, fur-traders and explorers, but unknown to most whites. Further beyond lay the Arctic extremity of the future Dominion of Canada. Inhospitable to all but the Inuit who knew it, the Arctic reaches drew explorers who sought the Northwest Passage, a variation on Columbus' original dream of finding the passage to India.

In search of this passage went the renowned English explorer, Sir John Franklin. He and his party disappeared in the Arctic in the winter of 1845-1846. The British admiralty launched one of its greatest search-and-rescue operations, sending four search missions to the Arctic over the next decade. In addition, Lady Franklin sent three missions, the Hudson's Bay Company participated in one, and the United States also sent three.

This journal was kept by Lieutenant Walter May of HMS *Assistance* and probably dates from when Sir Edward Belcher searched for Franklin in 1852-1854. The diary contains information about climate and weather, about American whalers who latched onto the expedition and their operations in the Arctic approaches, and about the rigours of navigation through ice. The entry for "Friday 16" recalls how an American whaler struggles to stay afloat, and how a crew member of the *Assistance*, having spotted a polar bear, attempts to shoot the animal. An interesting historical record, the diary brings home the adventure of Arctic exploration and illuminates the great search for Franklin which captured popular imagination over several decades.

Lieutenant Walter May. 1852-1853.

and found it to Answer admirably - The
average temperature about the Ship
being about 70° - Still getting water
from the wreck. ——

Friday 16th.

It has been indeed a beautiful day
which is cheering under the present circumstances as we are still fast and
as yet no chance of getting free -
~~[illegible]~~ Having finished with
the wreck of the American. It was
determined that she should be
blown up - therefore two 20lb charges
were placed in her hold
but with very little effect and ignited
other charges. [illegible] - Several
and tho the decks were also fired
several places by them, torn up in
floated having yet a quantity still the vessel
her. - a Bear came close to the North Star of oil in
this morning and a Veteran Sportsman
immediately pursued him - But un-
fortunately; when within 80 yards of
the Bear - his gun missed fire - and the
bear wished him good morning
and was off like a shot.

22 cm x 18.5 cm

National Archives of Canada,
Manuscript Division,
MG 24, H 31, Vol. 2.

"Arctic Seas Shewing the North-West Passage, the Coasts Explored by the Several Searching Expeditions, and the Spot Where the Remains of Sir John Franklin have been discovered"

Knowledge about the Canadian Arctic gained by various expeditions sent out in search of Franklin is perhaps best expressed in this attractive map published in 1854.

The search for Franklin drew many explorers and rescuers, as evidenced by this map's legend which names the various commanders leading whole expeditions or partial squadrons in search of the lost explorer and his party. As squadrons raced to locate the missing expedition, they explored and charted the Canadian Arctic coast and islands. With such new information, mapmakers could fill in many of the grey areas on maps of the Arctic.

This map reflects such new knowledge. There are virtually no blank or shaded regions left. Islands and coasts are clearly demarcated. The Northwest Passage has been determined (which Captain Robert McClure discovered, and for which he received an Admiralty prize of £10,000 sterling in 1854). An "X" on King William Island fairly accurately denotes the spot, as determined by Captain John Rae, where Franklin and most of his men perished (for this achievement Rae also received an Admiralty prize of £10,000 sterling).

The manuscript annotations on the map make it all the more valuable as an archival document, providing additional information on the Franklin expedition and naming native tribes on the mainland, evidence of how knowledge was acquired as men searched for Franklin and his crew.

The map is clean, legible and attractive, a visual summation of the exploration of the Canadian Arctic, and of a great drama played out in a cold and demanding climate as brave and curious men went in search of one of their comrades, of reward and of glory. The Arctic Islands came into Confederation in 1880, when Britain transferred sovereignty to the Dominion government in Ottawa.

William and Alexander
Keith Johnston.

1854.

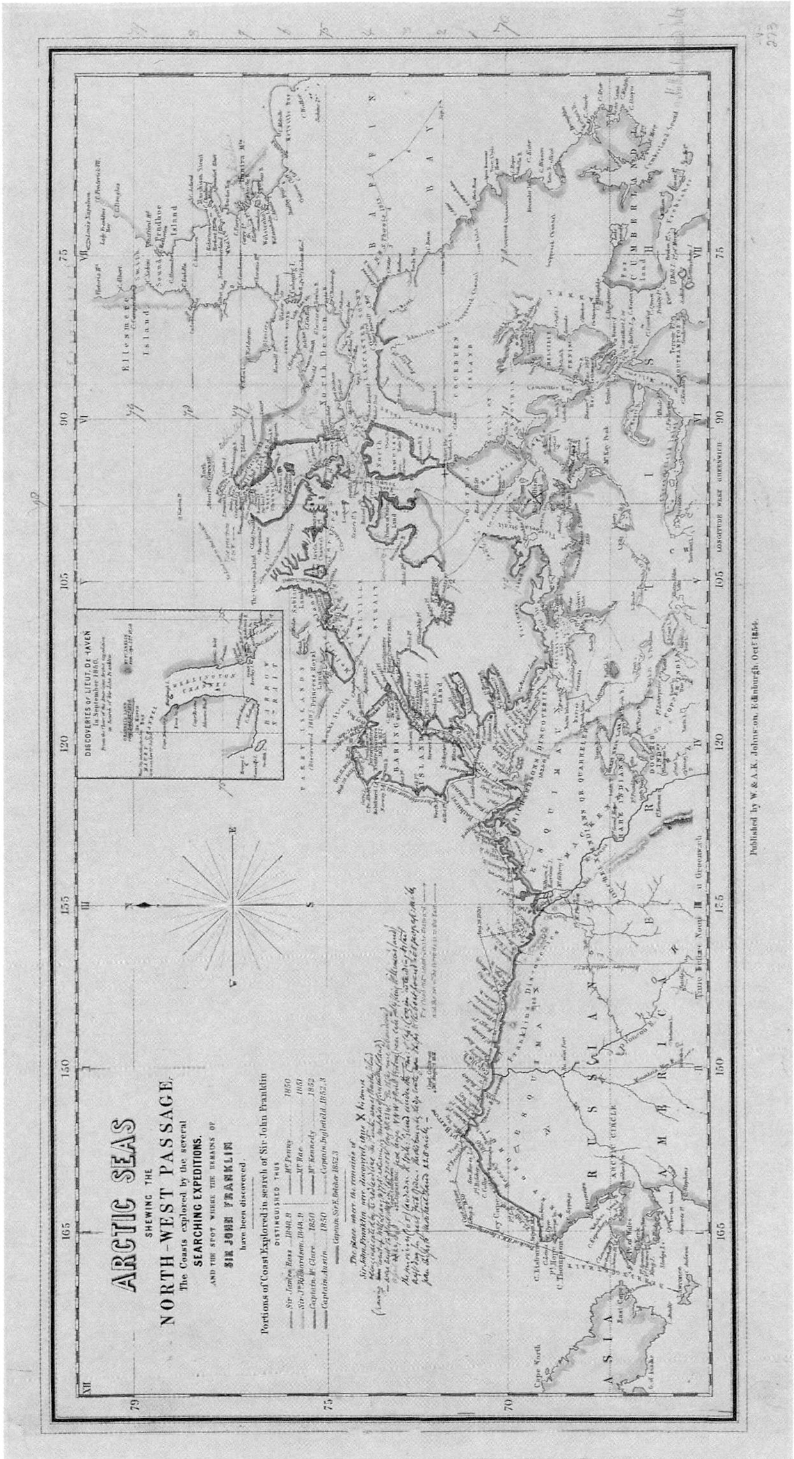

32 cm x 62.5 cm

National Archives of Canada,
Cartographic and Audio-Visual Archives Division,
NMC-6296.

"Encampment on the Red River [Henry Youle Hind Expedition, 1857-58]"

This photograph was taken by Humphrey Lloyd Hime, an Irishman born in 1833 who migrated to Canada in 1854. After settling in Toronto, he worked as a surveyor on the Bruce Peninsula survey in 1855-1856, and also took up photography. From the 1840s on, photography was used in expeditionary and exploratory work, to record in images the topography, flora and items of interest in unknown regions. By then, the medium had developed to the point where multiple paper copies could be made as illustrations of things seen, and assumed a greater significance in exploration. Hime was chosen official photographer for the Hind expedition into the Red River country.

The Hind expedition, sent by the Province of Canada, paralleled the Palliser expedition sent into Rupert's Land by the British government. While the Palliser expedition operated on a much broader mandate, the Hind expedition was instructed to explore the area from Lake Superior westward, and to lay out the best communications route traversing wholly British territory from Canada to the Red River settlements, and to arable land beyond.

The Hind expedition was preparatory to Canada's staking out her claim to Rupert's Land (roughly the future Prairie provinces), then administered by the Hudson's Bay Company under license from the British Crown. The license was due to expire in 1859, at which time hearings would be held on its renewal. Canada wished to extend its jurisdiction into Rupert's Land and so neutralize the threat of American expansion into this region. Also, with its best farmland already occupied, the colony wished to open up arable lands for settlement. The Hind expedition went westward to gather geographical, geological, meteorological and other data, on the basis of which Canada could better argue her claim.

This photograph was taken by Hime as part of the expedition as it camped along the Red River. The canoe is prodigious in size, the *canot du maître*, to allow for transport of extensive supplies. Along with the white men in the photo, there are several Metis, possibly local guides. The Indians in the photograph may very well be some of the 14 Caughnawaga Iroquois who were hired on as canoe men for the Red River journey.

The Hind expedition achieved its objective. Colonel Simon James Dawson laid out the famous "Dawson Road" from Lake Superior to the Red River; and Henry Youle Hind returned with proof that there were both tillable soil and an agreeable climate in Rupert's Land, stimulating in the Province of Canada an even greater interest in the region. Armed with this knowledge, a new, "confederated" Canada would, ten years later, successfully argue its case for Rupert's Land before an accommodating British Crown.

Humphrey Lloyd Hime. 1858.

13.9 cm x 17.2 cm

National Archives of Canada,
Documentary Art and Photography Division,
C-4572.

"A General Map of the Routes in British North America Explored by the Expedition Under Captain John Palliser During the Years 1857, 1858, 1859, 1860"

John Palliser, an Irish adventurer born in 1817, became intrigued by the New World as a result of several big-game hunting expeditions in 1847-1848 in Missouri. He persuaded the Royal Geographic Society to underwrite an expedition into Rupert's Land, to explore the territory from the Red River to the Rocky Mountains along the unsurveyed 49th parallel. The Society expanded this original design, and then applied to the British government for a subvention to help defray costs.

British governmental authorities responded keenly to the application. Britain was then very much concerned about American expansionism; the loss of the Oregon Territory in 1846 was a lesson well learned. American expansion northward could drive a wedge between the British colonies in the eastern half of the continent and the colonies west of the Rockies.

Britain realized as well that the amorphous authority exercised by the Hudson's Bay Company in Rupert's Land (granted to it by charter), and in the Northwest and British Columbia (by license), could neither restrain American expansion nor secure these regions through settlement. With hearings on renewal of the Company's license due in 1859, the Crown wished to inform itself as fully as possible about these lands. Thus it willingly co-sponsored the expedition and further broadened its mandate. The expedition was to explore not only the plains lying between the 49th to 54th parallels and to search for southern passes through the Rockies. It was also to examine the old Nor'westers' canoe route west of Lake Superior with a view to developing communications between western and eastern British colonies in North America, by which immigrants could settle the interior of the continent and thus assert British sovereignty.

The expedition was staffed by geologists, naturalists, astronomers and other scientists instructed to study the flora and fauna of the territory, its climate, its soil types, its forest and underground resources and so on.

This map, prepared to accompany the expedition's final report, is a visual summation of its most significant findings. There are comments on significant topographical and geological features, existing waterways and cart trails (land routes were measured out by odometers), timber and vegetation, and Indian tribes and their location. The map reflects a wealth of information about Rupert's Land and the Northwest. Along with the report it accompanied, the map for many years served as the definitive source of knowledge about this great expanse of British North America.

The expedition accomplished much. It flew the British flag throughout the vast Northwest. It determined that communication throughout wholly British territory was difficult and costly; but it also surveyed six passes through the Rockies, including the Kicking Horse Pass, through which eventually the Canadian Pacific Railway would go. It dispelled forever the contention that the Northwest could not sustain agriculture; beyond the semi-arid region (Palliser's Triangle) reaching northward across the border from the United States, there lay a very fertile belt suited for agriculture and stock raising. Both Britain and the British colonies learned the true wealth of the interior, and that it was worth keeping and settling.

Once Rupert's Land and the Northwest passed to the new Dominion, most government policy decisions regarding this territory — on the settlement and use of prairie land (*The Dominion Lands Act*), on the construction of a transcontinental railway, on the establishment of provincial and territorial boundaries, on the establishment of the North-West Mounted Police, on treaties with prairie Indians — all these fundamental decisions were made on the basis of the Palliser report and its maps.

Captain John Palliser. 1863 [1865].

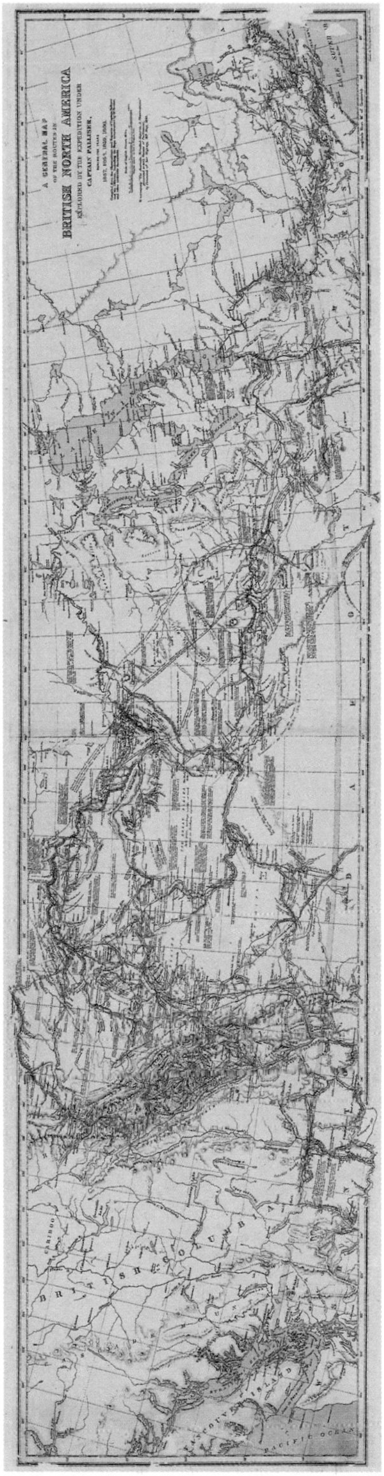

32 cm x 127.6 cm

National Archives of Canada,
Cartographic and Audio-Visual Archives Division,
NMC-11931.

"Manitoulin Island, Showing Portions Ceded"

Exploration, whether in the Arctic periphery, in Rupert's Land or closer to settled areas, had as one of its primary objectives the acquisition of knowledge about the physical nature of British North America. One of the most notable explorers of this era was Robert Bell, who prepared this manuscript map. Born in Toronto in 1815, Bell spent all his summers as a young man with field staff of the Geological Survey of Canada (GSC). He was interim professor of natural sciences at Queen's University, 1863-1867, and from 1869 onwards was employed full-time by the GSC, participating in a number of northern and western expeditions which mapped rivers draining into Hudson Bay, and reconnoitering routes for a transcontinental railway.

Because much of Canada's best farmland was already occupied, settlers from Canada West had begun to move westward, and to spill over onto Manitoulin Island. Hence, in 1862, the province purchased portions of Manitoulin Island from the Indians resident there, and dispatched Bell both to determine boundaries of the ceded portions, and to prepare analyses of the island's topography and soil conditions. Such information was necessary for legal and promotional purposes, so that settlement of the island could proceed in an orderly fashion.

Bell prepared this map for the GSC, established in the province in 1842 with a mandate to amass and disseminate knowledge about the geological base of the province with the intention of promoting mining. Headed by William E. Logan, later knighted for services, the GSC began operations with a questionnaire addressed to all farmers throughout the breadth of the province, from Niagara to Gaspé. By 1853 it had accumulated enough geological knowledge to publish Logan's *Geology of Canada.* Following Confederation, the GSC continued its work on a continental scale.

In this preliminary manuscript version of his map, Bell provides information useful to the government in directing settlement of the island. He describes the terrain, makes note of lines of communication, records peculiar geological formations and provides intriguing information on Indians and their agricultural practices. The map not only demonstrates the art of map-making, but tells us much about the era — about land-hunger and the pressure to migrate, about the drive westwards, and about the imperative of legal transfer of land title from aboriginal people to the Crown. These dynamics would remain central to Canadian growth well into the twentieth century.

Robert Bell. 1862.

57 cm x 94 cm

National Archives of Canada,
Cartographic and Audio-Visual Archives Division,
NMC-132507.

"Reports of Professor Bell For the Year 1865 on the Grand Manitoulin Island"

While a professor of chemistry and natural science at Queen's University, Robert Bell continued to work for the Geological Survey of Canada (GSC) in the summers. He continued his explorations and studies of Manitoulin Island. This document is a preliminary copy of his report to Sir William E. Logan, Director of the GSC.

In this report Bell provides a brief history of the settlement of the island which, until the 1830s, was only sporadically inhabited. At that time it became the centre of Indian administration in northern Upper Canada. Indians came there annually to receive their "presents" from the Crown, and so began to settle it and to remain permanently. By 1862, when the island was purchased from the Indians, white settlers were already present, having begun farming, as well as logging and commercial fishing operations.

Bell goes on to provide geographical and geological descriptions of the island, assessing its extent, describing its coasts, lakes and rivers, plateaux and highlands. While he explored and surveyed, potential economic development was foremost in his mind as he noted what rivers could drive mills, what timber was available and for what purposes it could be used, and what portions of the island could be cultivated. In this latter regard he drew on the experiences of the island's Indians, who had practised extensive farming there in the preceding twenty years. Perhaps surprisingly, given the island's geographical location, he found the "climate very well suited for growing all the usual crops of the other parts of Western Canada." Even melons, according to Bell's evidence, never failed to ripen before the frosts.

As this record demonstrates, Bell helped to open various regions for settlement (Manitoulin Island being only one of many theatres for him). He contributed vastly to knowledge about the future Dominion. He reported not only on the geography and geology of regions he explored and studied, but also on flora and fauna, on native ways and folklore, on agricultural potential and forest reserves. He was, in his time, a universal man — geographer and geologist, botanist and zoologist, ethnographer and historian, and much more. A prodigious writer and tireless speaker, he never wearied of explaining the natural and social history of a marvellous new land which, in his view, had before it a very promising future.

Robert Bell. 1865.

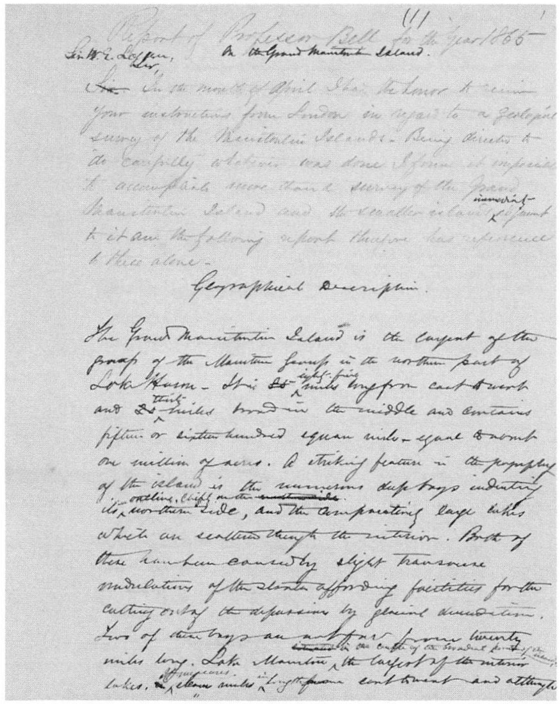
Report of Professor Bell for the year 1865 (1)
On the Grand Manitoulin Island.
Sir W. E. Logan,
Sir,
In the month of April I had the honor to receive your instructions from London in regard to a geological survey of the Manitoulin Islands. Being directed to do carefully whatever was done I found it impossible to accomplish more than a survey of the Grand Manitoulin Island and the smaller islands immediately adjacent to it and the following report therefore has reference to these alone.

Geographical Description.

The Grand Manitoulin Island is the largest of the group of the Manitoulin group in the northern part of Lake Huron. It is eighty-five miles long from east to west and thirty miles broad in the middle and contains fifteen or sixteen hundred square miles, equal to nearly one million of acres. A striking feature in the geography of the island is the numerous deep bays indenting its outline, chiefly on the northern side, and the corresponding large lakes which are scattered through the interior. Both of these have been caused by slight transverse undulations of the strata affording facilities for the cutting out of the depressions by glacial denudation. Two of these bays are upwards of twenty miles long. Lake Manitou, in the centre of the broadest portion of the island, the largest of the interior lakes, is upwards of eleven miles in length from east to west and although

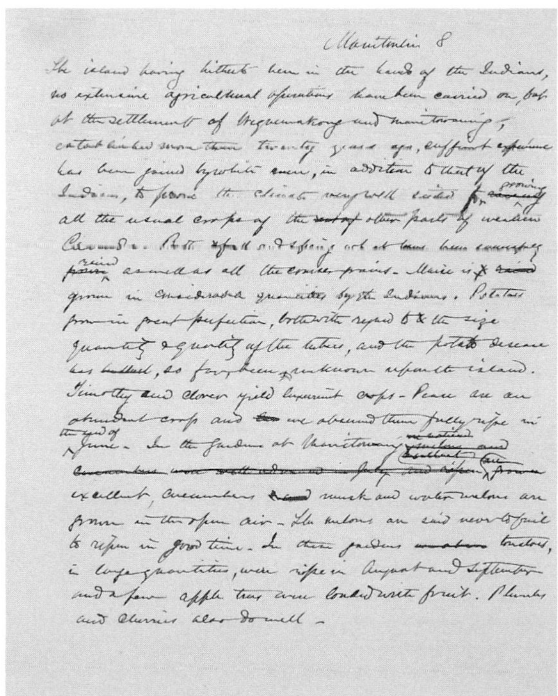
Manitoulin 8
The island having hitherto been in the hands of the Indians, no extensive agricultural operations have been carried on, but at the settlements of Wequemakong and Manitowaning, established more than twenty years ago, sufficient experience has been gained by white men, in addition to that of the Indians, to prove the climate very well suited for growing all the usual crops of the other parts of western Canada. Both fall and spring wheat have been raised as well as all the smaller grains. Maize is grown in considerable quantities by the Indians. Potatoes grow in great perfection, both with regard to the size quantity & quality of the tubers, and the potato disease has, so far, been unknown upon the island. Timothy and clover yield luxuriant crops. Pease are an abundant crop and we observed them fully ripe in the end of June. In the gardens at Manitowaning melons are excellent, cucumbers musk and water melons are grown in the open air. The melons are said never to fail to ripen in good time. In these gardens tomatoes, in large quantities, were ripe in August and September and a few apple trees were loaded with fruit. Plums and cherries also do well.

25.2 cm x 20.4 cm

National Archives of Canada,
Manuscript Division,
MG 53, B 181.

"Thunder Cape, Lake Superior"

A native of Dublin, William Armstrong emigrated to Canada in 1851 and settled in Toronto. He was a rather unusual mix of engineer and accomplished artist. With several partners (William M. Beere and Humphrey Lloyd Hime) he opened a photography studio and taught art at the Toronto Normal School. Very popular in his day, Armstrong captured in prints and paint the notable and newsworthy events of the day (such as the visit of the Prince of Wales in 1860), great engineering feats, sport boats on Lake Ontario and the life of natives, painted in the style of Paul Kane. He also painted scenes of the Canadian wilderness. "Thunder Cape" is one of his finest.

This depiction of "Thunder Cape" was based on sketches from Armstrong's trips to Lake Superior. It is a dramatic watercolour which expresses the spirit of the Canadian north. The sky is fired by a sun low on the horizon. Light plays about the rock and, through a break in the clouds, illuminates the soaring face of the cliff, while the rest of the rock mass recedes increasingly into shadow and darkness. Whether Armstrong so intended or not, his work is a paean to the sublime power and splendour of nature, emphasized by the smallness of man in the camp at the foot of the cliff, in the several minuscule canoes and the partially hidden vessel (probably a York boat) whose sail we see.

To the Ojibway the Cape was home to their Creator, to the Cree the residence of their chief spirit, the Thunderbird. In the shadow of this rock, which stood on the main communications route into the interior, passed Indians in their travels, voyageurs in search of furs, surveyors and explorers in the acquisition of knowledge, settlers on their way to new homesteads and Wolseley's expedition into the Red River in 1870. So much of the human energy of the era 1849-1873 was dedicated to Confederation, and one of Confederation's primary aims was to secure for Canada both Rupert's Land and the North-Western Territory, both of which lay beyond the rock. "Thunder Cape," painted by Armstrong in so masterly a fashion, could rightly be described as the symbolic geographical and historical hinge of Canada. It also reminds the viewer that, cities, towns and villages aside, Canada was powerfully conditioned by a majestic and demanding nature which never was — perhaps even now never is — very distant from us.

William Armstrong. 1867.

50.1 cm x 69.8 cm

National Archives of Canada
Documentary Art and Photography Division,
C-40358.

Explorations in The Interior of the Labrador Peninsula. The Country of the Montagnais and Nasquapee Indians

Not all exploration went into Rupert's Land; much remained to be done just north of the existing borders of the Province of Canada. Henry Youle Hind, after participating in the expeditions into the Red, Assiniboine and Saskatchewan River country (the expedition was named after him because he prepared the final report of findings), turned his attention to the Moisie River basin of Labrador.

Hind was born in England, and migrated to Canada in 1846. A geologist and naturalist, he became second master of science and mathematics at the Toronto Normal School, and in 1851-1863 served as professor of chemistry at Trinity College. Later, he worked as a consulting geologist in the Maritime provinces. Closely identified with the Canadian Institute, a loose association of engineers and scientists, Hind in 1852-1857 edited the institute's *Canadian Journal*, which reflected a growing sense of supra-colonial, if not national, spirit. He was a prolific publicist popularizing scientific knowledge about British North America, and in response to a popular market, wrote about his explorations. This work is of such a genre, appealing to people's sense of adventure and of the exotic.

Like Robert Bell, Hind was a universal man, a keen observer of nature and life. The record of his Labrador expedition, *Explorations in The Interior*, conveys to the reader a wealth of information. Scenery and vegetation, animal life, geological formation, topographical observation, river currents and speeds, communications routes, corrected maps of the area — the information is limitless. Like Bell also, Hind had an abiding interest in ethnography; his work is replete with observations on the lifestyle, customs and habits of Indians of the Moisie basin, including fascinating accounts of their natural forest medicines.

The book was illustrated by William George Richardson Hind, the author's brother, who accompanied the expedition and captured in pencil, watercolour and oil the grandeur of the Moisie River country.

Henry Youle Hind.

(London; Longman, Green, Longman, Roberts, & Green, 1863).

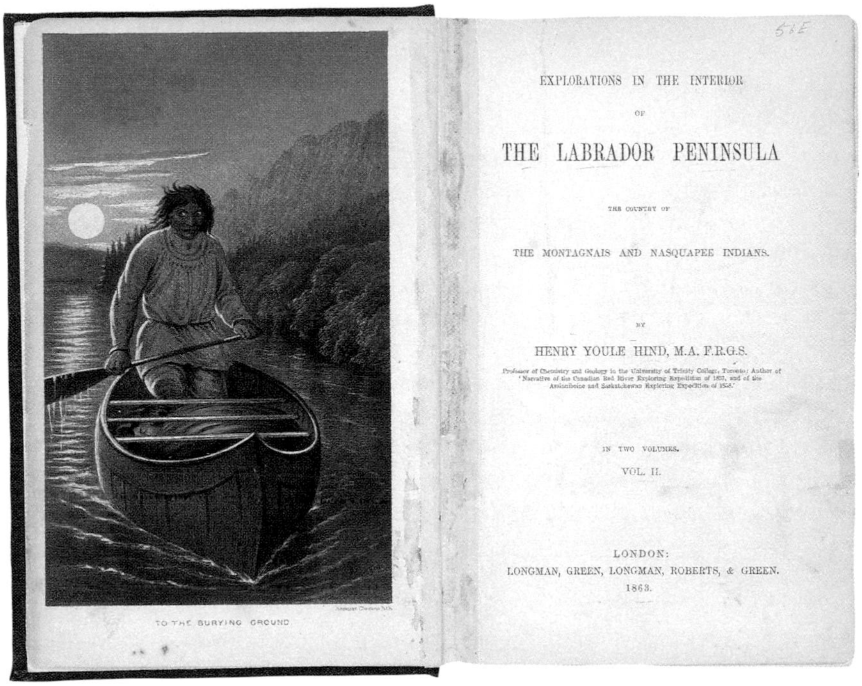

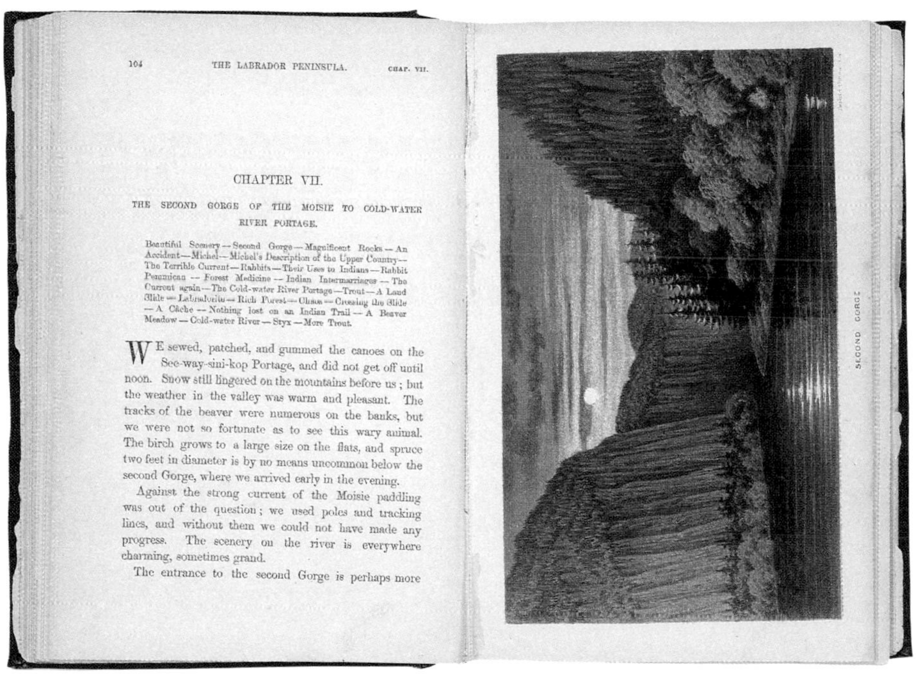

19.7 cm x 13.3 cm

National Archives of Canada,
Archival Community Programs Division,
Rare / F5398 / L3H5.

Geological Map of Newfoundland

This map was prepared by Alexander Murray and drawn by Robert Barlow of the Geological Survey of Canada. Geologists of that early time wore many hats. First and foremost, they were driven by the curiosity of the explorer, which took them into lands traversed by few except aboriginal inhabitants. Often knowledgeable in a range of subjects — geography, botany, zoology and anthropology, as well as in natural history — they studied British North America in the rough.

This map of Newfoundland reflects the achievements of the Geological Survey of Canada in its search for earth-sciences information about Canada. Alexander Murray, the map's author, worked at the Geological Survey of Canada from 1843 to 1864, at which time he transferred to the island's geological service; he later became the first director of the Geological Survey of Newfoundland. Despite the fact that Canada, following Confederation, forbade its geological service from dealings with its sister institution on the anti-Confederation island, the fact that the map was drawn by Robert Barlow of the Geological Survey of Canada indicates that professional interests and co-operation overcame political divides.

Until the production of this map, Newfoundland's geology was almost unknown. Anxious to promote mining and development, the island's government aimed for a map that was informative, attractive and easy to read. Colour coding distinguishes the soil types by geological era, while cross-sections across portions of "the Rock" explain geomorphological formation of the sub-soil base. The map comments on Newfoundland's topography: it bears notations such as "marshes and barrens," "innumerable ponds," and the somewhat whimsical observation, "desolate country." The map also shows a "line of railway survey" for future development, and notes the existing telegraphic line linking North America with Europe. While aesthetically pleasing, the map's utility lies in the information it holds on soil types and mineral reserves.

It is worth recalling that all this information was acquired by men of the Geological Surveys of Newfoundland and Canada who, under arduous and sometimes dangerous conditions, laboured in the field to inform the citizens of both the new Dominion and of Newfoundland of the riches which nature had bestowed upon them.

Alexander Murray. ca 1873.

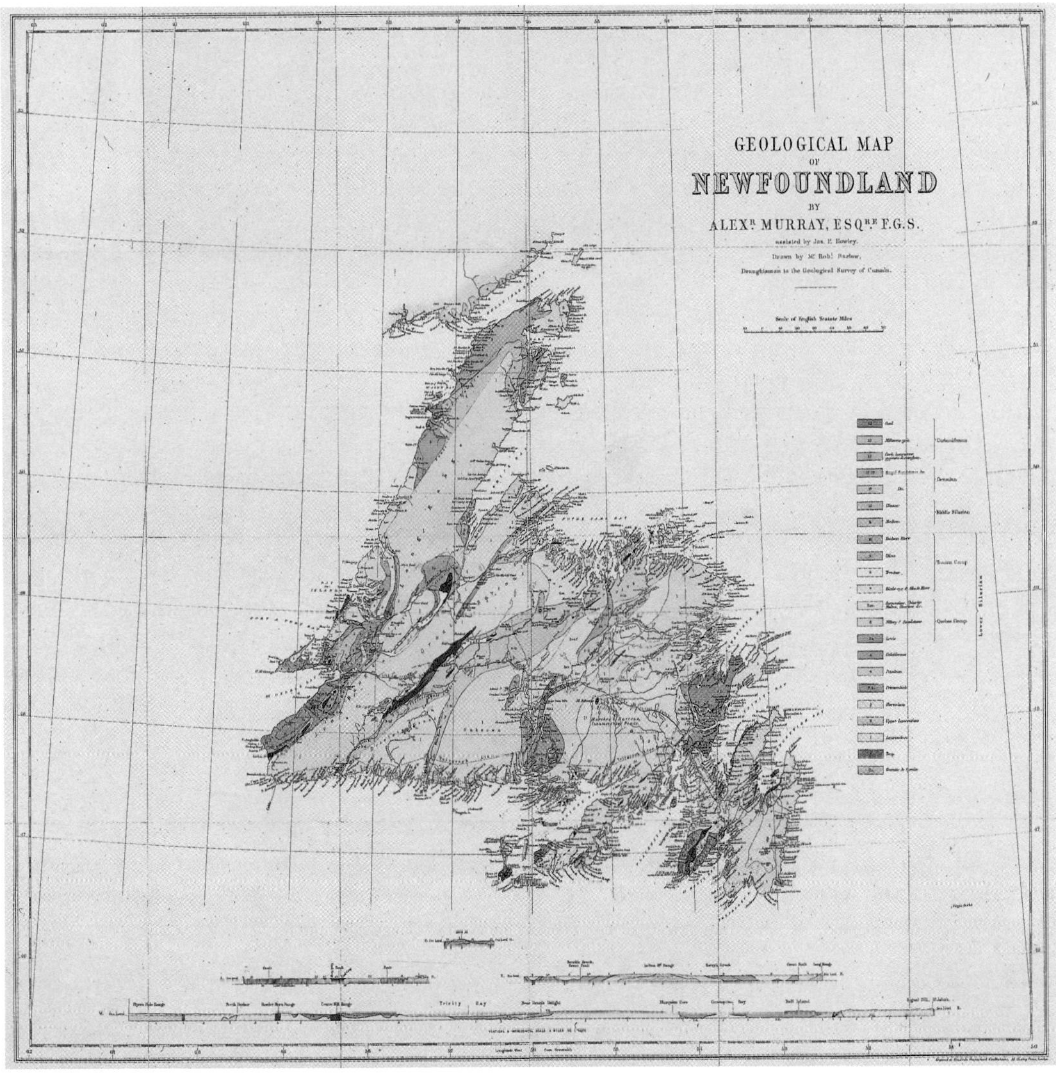

61.5 cm x 61 cm

National Archives of Canada,
Cartographic and Audio-Visual Archives Division,
NMC-17782.

II

Portaging

Cornelius Krieghoff's name is synonymous with depictions of French Canadian rural life in the 1850s and 1860s. Of German ancestry, he was born in 1815 in Amsterdam. He later studied at the renowned Academy in the city of Dusseldorf, where he mastered genre painting. In 1835 Krieghoff migrated to the United States; there he experienced the life of an adventurer, fighting in the Seminole Wars of 1835-1836. In the 1840s he lived, at various times, in Montreal, Rochester (NY) and Longueuil, and in this period he recorded on canvas and paper the life of the French habitants. His works occasionally are anecdotal, satirical and mischievous; they breathe mirth and humour, gossip and flirtation, wine and good times. But habitants are not his sole subject; Krieghoff painted everyone, from officers and gentlemen to aboriginal people.

In Quebec City from 1853 to 1863, he produced forest and hunting scenes, as well as many of his well-known scenes of merrymaking in the cold Canadian winter, of sleigh-riding and of frozen waterfalls. People, nature, life in all its celebration — all was fair game for his brush and pencil. He left Quebec City for Europe in 1863 or 1864, returning only in 1870. By then, however, his patrons were departed. Of the lumber barons, whose massive lumber deals had floated yearly down the St. Lawrence to Quebec City, very few remained. The British garrison officers had largely departed as Britain, following Confederation, hastened to withdraw her military establishment from Canada. In Krieghoff's time, French Canadians did not much care for his work, feeling that it was too patronizing, stereotyping them into simple, jolly folk in stage-set venues that were not true to life. Krieghoff died shortly after his return to Canada while visiting his daughter in Chicago.

In this pleasing watercolour over pencil, Krieghoff depicts several travellers portaging over a height of land between rivers. The bright colours and the almost jaunty step of the voyageurs do not convey the true burden of water travel and portage. It is important to recall that water transport was still by far the most significant mode of travel in this era. Corduroy, plank and macadamized roads, each in their turn, eased the burden of land travel. The railways, with all their conveniences, were appearing. However, only a few miles back from settled river frontages or developed concession roads, just in from main colonization roads and King's highways, it was the river-lake systems which carried people and freight, often by canoe. And travel by canoe almost always demanded the back-breaking toil of portage.

Attributed to Cornelius Krieghoff. ca 1865.

15.1 cm x 21.8 cm

National Archives of Canada,
Documentary Art and Photography Division,
C-13456.

"City and Harbour of Montreal"

James Duncan was born in Ireland in 1806, emigrating to Montreal in 1830. An artist who worked in oils and watercolours, he was a founding member in 1847 of the Montreal Society of Artists. He is best known for scenes of his beloved Montreal.

By Confederation, Montreal was a significant manufacturing centre. Its development had disproved the gloomy predictions of the Annexationists of 1849. Wheat and lumber mills, tanneries, household goods and furniture manufactories, textile and footwear shops, glass houses and iron foundries — such enterprises and more were producing various goods, giving employment to a work force coming out of agrarian regions that could not sustain the excess population produced by a high birth rate. Heavy machinery shops (locomotive works) in St. Charles pointed to future industrial development.

But Montreal, given its strategic communications location, remained also a great *entrepôt*, a commercial centre. The produce and goods of the interior came to it both by rail and water, and were then carried away, either by water down the St. Lawrence, or by rail into the Eastern Townships and on to Portland (Maine) and its ice-free port. This print captures the spirit of commercial Montreal. It should be noted that the print is a concocted scene, with artificial packing of waterfront activity, an early exercise in Canadian print-making of "boosterism." The print itself is poor in execution, perhaps because it is among the early products of a printing industry just getting under way in the British colonies.

These reservations noted, however, the print has much to tell about Montreal. In the foreground of this print floats a massive log raft, a reminder of the capital importance of the timber trade. Probably harvested in the Ottawa River Valley, the felled logs, lashed together, may well be on their way to Quebec City, there to be sold for shipment overseas. Tens of vessels are docked along Montreal's waterfront, while others are in motion, travelling both upstream and downstream. Interesting to note is the mix of vessels. To the left is a side-wheeler, the *Beaver*, to the right is a sailing vessel under tow by a side-wheeler. Duncan's print captures the sense of transition, with steam and sail both represented here, working busily in the harbour and waters of Canada's premier city.

After James Duncan, litho. by Roberts and Reinhold. ca 1867-1872.

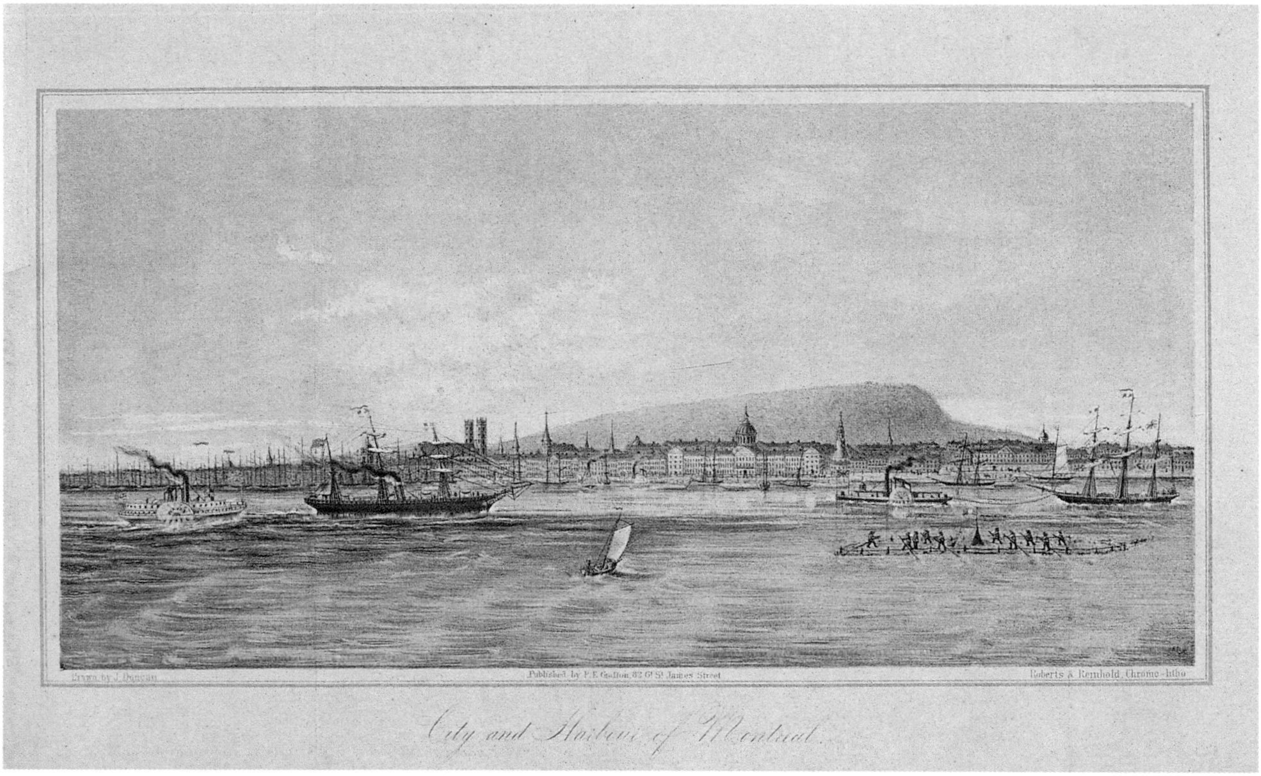

23.6 cm x 47.8 cm

National Archives of Canada,
Documentary Art and Photography Division,
C-121143.

II

"Plans of the Several Light Houses in the Colony of New Foundland"

Born in 1824 in Quebec City, George Frédéric Baillairgé was a member of a notable Quebec family which produced five generations of prominent architects, sculptors and painters. He joined the old Board of Works of Canada, became a surveyor, later an engineer, and finished his career as Chief Assistant Engineer of the Department of Public Works. Like Samuel Keefer, he symbolizes the solid achievement of native Canadian engineering.

These documents were prepared by Baillairgé for the Department of Public Works of the Province of Canada. Since Canadian shipping utilized the Gulf of St. Lawrence, the province, in an effort to improve the safety of water communications, shared the costs of proper navigational aids with the colony of Newfoundland. In connection with a new proposal to erect additional lighthouses at the south-western extremity of Newfoundland, the Canadian government sent Baillairgé to St. John's in 1865, to assess the need for new navigational lighting. While in St. John's, Baillairgé copied out for his department the records and plans of Newfoundland's lighthouses.

These documents describe the lighthouse at Cape Race, which stood at the southeastern extremity of Newfoundland. To travellers making their way to the British colonies, the Cape presented a desolate and stark image of flat-topped cliffs, hardly an inviting first glimpse of the New World. Baillairgé's record indicates that this lighthouse became operational in 1856, and that on a clear day its signal could be seen 17 miles out at sea. The drawings of the lighthouse, showing various elevations and floor plans, are classically elegant, typical of many of the working documents of this era.

Baillairgé's notes and drawings of Newfoundland's lighthouses reflect the imperative need felt by colonial governments to improve the safety of water communications, and to co-operate among themselves in necessary ventures.

George Frédéric Baillairgé. 1865.

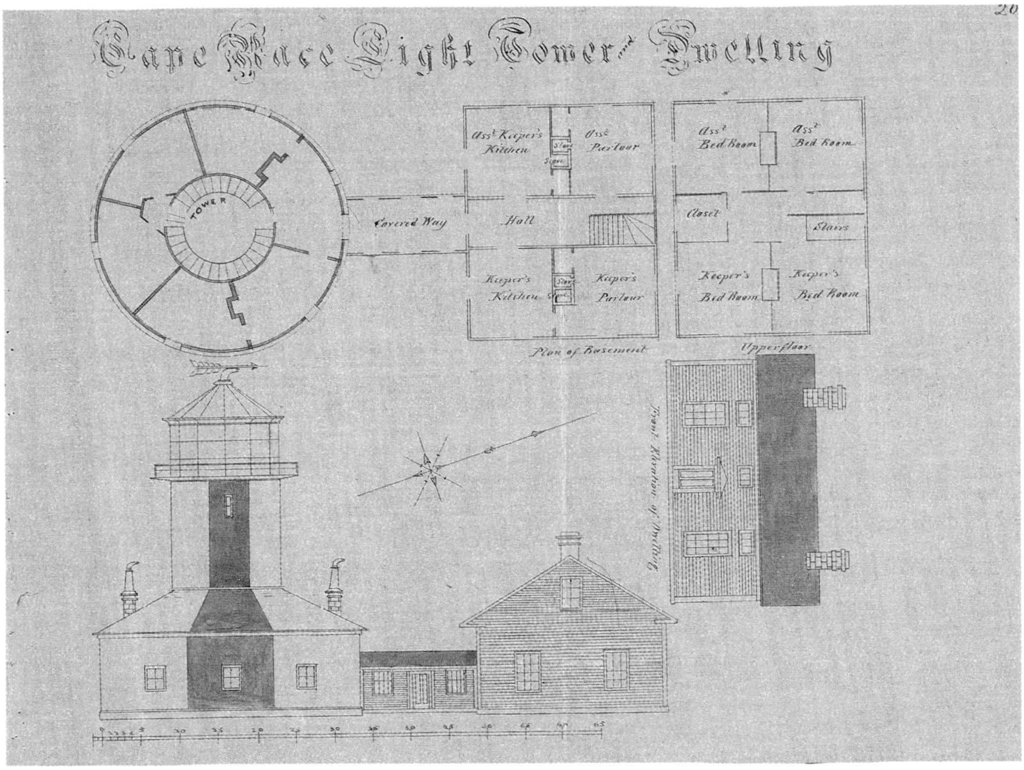

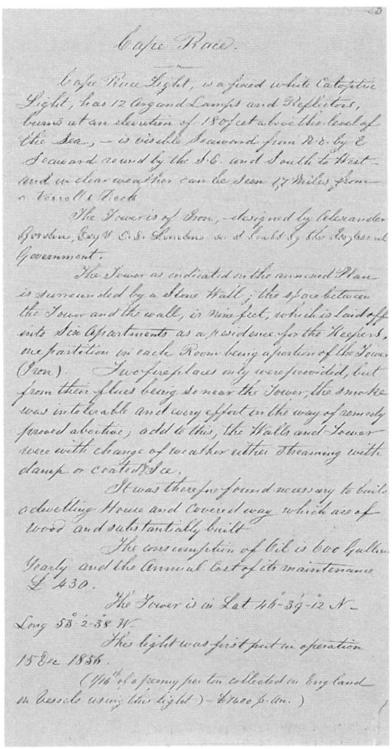

Cape Race.

Cape Race Light, is a fixed white Catoptric Light, has 12 Argand Lamps and Reflectors, burns at an elevation of 180 feet above the level of the Sea, – is visible Seaward from N.E. by E Seaward round by the S.E. and South to West – and in clear weather can be seen 17 Miles, from a Vessel's Deck

The Tower is of Iron, – designed by Alexander Gordon, Esq. C.E. London and built by the Imperial Government.

The Tower as indicated in the annexed Plan is surrounded by a Stone Wall; the space between the Tower and the wall, is nine feet, which is laid off into Six Apartments as a residence for the Keepers, one partition in each Room being a portion of the Tower (Iron). Two fireplaces only were provided, but from their flues being so near the Tower, the smoke was intolerable and every effort in the way of remedy proved abortive; add to this, the Walls and Tower were with change of weather either Streaming with damp or coated Ice.

It was therefore found necessary to build a dwelling House and Covered way which are of wood and substantially built

The consumption of Oil is 600 Gallons Yearly and the Annual Cost of its maintenance £ 430.

The Tower is in Lat 46°-39'-12 N – Long 53° 2'-38 W –

This light was first put in operation 15 Dec 1856.

(1/16th of a penny per ton collected in England on Vessels using this light) – £1400 p. An.)

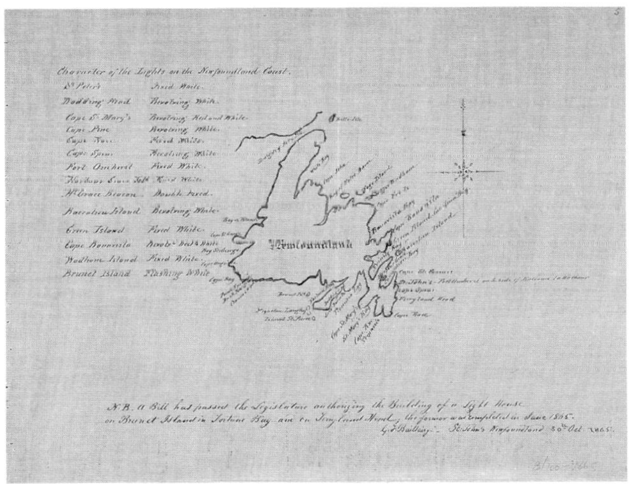

24.5 cm x 37 cm
42 cm x 29 cm
17 cm x 33 cm

National Archives of Canada,
Cartographic and Audio-Visual Archives Division,
[Cape Race Light Tower] NMC-13273,
[Cape Race Description] S/100-1865,
[Newfoundland Map] NMC-9718.

"Chimney Cove Harbour, County of Inverness... Cape Breton, NS"

As navigation developed, so did ports to accommodate water traffic. The 1850s and 1860s saw the flowering of many ports along the Great Lakes and along major rivers. Coastal ports as well were improved, with the addition of piers on which to handle goods and breakwaters to better protect anchorages from tides and storms.

Prepared by G.F. Baillairgé, this plan depicts such an improvement. Baillairgé probably prepared the drawing while working principally on the Bay Verte Canal project (1870-1872), intended to link the Bay of Fundy with the Gulf of St. Lawrence. In the vicinity of Chimney Cove harbour were important coal mines opened in the 1830s; an improved harbour would greatly facilitate the export of coal from Cape Breton.

This document consists of three units. There is a representation of the hydrographic surface of the bay, showing soundings contours based on actual measurements of water depths in the harbour, as well as the proposed location of a breakwater. The second unit is a subsurface profile along the proposed breakwater. Such subsurface profiles are analogous to surface elevation profiles prepared by railway engineers; unlike railway engineers, however, hydrographic engineers could far less manipulate existing surfaces at that time. The third unit locates Chimney Cove harbour in relation to other ports over a portion of the Cape Breton Island coastline, with indications of beacon and lighthouse placement, a responsibility of the federal government following Confederation.

The breakwater at Chimney Cove was never constructed. Of the four harbours which Baillairgé surveyed along that portion of Cape Breton Island, he finally recommended development at Cheticamp. This document represents visually the level of hydrographic engineering then achieved and the commitment to development of water communications.

George Frédéric Baillairgé. 1871.

17

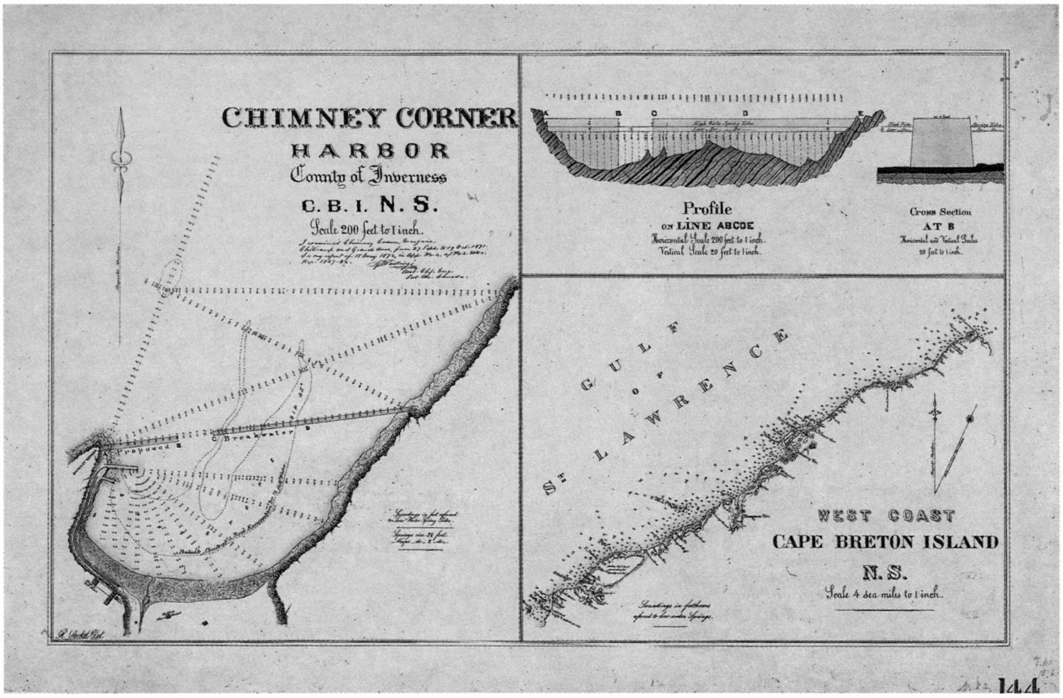

53.3 cm x 87 cm

National Archives of Canada,
Cartographic and Audio-Visual Archives Division,
NMC-96334.

“Landing the Atlantic Cable in Heart’s Content Bay, Newfoundland” *and also* “The Great Eastern From the Foot of Hammond Street [New York]”

This engraving, published in the *London Illustrated News* of 8 September 1866, is based on a drawing by Robert Dudley, official staff artist aboard the *Great Eastern* during the laying of the trans-Atlantic cable. In this depiction, while onlookers and several ladies on the pier and on the log scaffolding cheer, sailors just several feet from shore draw the cable to land. A first attempt to lay the cable in 1854, as well as several subsequent efforts, had failed. In 1865 a fourth attempt went awry; the cable snapped when the vessel laying it was just one day out of Newfoundland.

But the consortium led by the British financier Cyrus Field persisted in its efforts, and in 1866 it made the historic connection between Valentia in Ireland and Heart’s Content Bay in Newfoundland. From these two terminal points cables laid earlier in the 1850s linked back to continental mainlands. The Anglo-American Telegraph Company opened an operations office in Heart’s Content Bay, sending and receiving information at the rate of eight words per minute. By means of the telegraph wires strung throughout the colonies, which then linked into the cable, British North Americans could communicate almost instantaneously with the motherland and Europe.

The *Great Eastern*, depicted in the stereograph, was a ship of colossal proportions, four times as large as any ship then afloat. It was launched in Britain in 1858. Originally designed as a passenger vessel capable of carrying 4,000 persons, the ship was 210 metres in length. It was a vessel of the transitional period, powered both by sail (six masts) and steam (two side-wheels and a seven-metre screw). For the cable-laying operation shipwrights adapted its hold to contain almost 4,500 kilometres of a single, continuous cable, which was played out over a drum at its stern. Only when advancing technology had produced a vessel of such proportions could the trans-Atlantic cable be laid, and the transmission of information between continents reduced from weeks to minutes.

After Robert Dudley. 1866.

Anthony’s Stereoscopic Views. nd.

24 cm x 34.6 cm
7.2 cm x 15.3 cm

National Archives of Canada,
Documentary Art and Photography Division,
[Wood Engraving] C-66507,
[Photograph] PA-182058.

Postage Stamps

As early as the 1830s, recommendations were made for the transfer of control of domestic postal services to the individual colonies of British North America. For the colonies of Canada, Nova Scotia and New Brunswick that recommendation was realized in 1851, when Britain devolved the management of colonial postal services to local administrations. Newfoundland received this right in 1857, while British Columbia and Prince Edward Island were granted postal self-management in 1860 and 1861 respectively. Until Confederation, the colonies co-operated in the delivery of mails so effectively that the original intent of the devolution of postal control was realized — mail moved more efficiently at much reduced rates.

With control of their postal systems, the colonies all began to issue their own postage stamps, a selection of which is displayed here. The issues from the Province of Canada include the well-known three-pence "Beaver" (designed by Sandford Fleming), the colony's first stamp and one of the world's first pictorial stamps. The stamp was engraved by the security printing firm of Rawden, Wright, Hatch and Edson of New York; all colonial stamps were engraved and printed abroad.

Among the New Brunswick issues shown here are the interesting geometric pence issues (the colony's first stamps), and the one cent and twelve and one-half cent issues bearing images of a train and a steamship, reflecting key communications developments of the era. There is also the five-cent "Connell" stamp, which was never circulated. Postmaster Charles Connell of New Brunswick arranged for the printing of a stamp bearing his portrait. Public anger at such presumption forced him to resign, and most of these "Connell" stamps were destroyed.

The early Newfoundland stamps merit interest because of their geometric design, and for the first colonial triangle. The two-cent salmon and five-cent seal are among the earliest representations on stamps of fish and animals, while the thirteen-cent issue shows a sailing vessel, so central to the commerce and fishing industry by which Newfoundland lived.

At Confederation, provinces ceased printing their own stamps, which were replaced by the "Large Queen" issue shown here.

These colonial stamp issues are not only colourful and pleasing; they are also records of their time. They reflect important developments, such as the growth of communications in the colonies, the shift from British stirling to American-style decimal sytems in 1859 and increasing self-management in colonial life — a step on the road to colonial maturity and Confederation.

Colonial Postal Departments. 1851-1868.

National Archives of Canada,
Canadian Postal Archives.

Postal Covers

The first of the covers shown here is a steamboat mailing of 19 October 1855, from Montreal to Toronto. It was put aboard the Montreal steamer that day, and probably removed at Kingston for overland transport by rail to Toronto, where it arrived on 21 October. Mail was carried by steamboat from 1809 onwards. By the 1860s steamboats delivered mail all along the St. Lawrence River, on the Great Lakes, and along lesser rivers and lakes where there was a need for mail service. They interconnected with terminals from which mail was then shipped overland by coach, sleigh or train. Some coastal steam packets performed the same service in the Maritimes.

But the era of steamboat mail was fast coming to a close in the 1860s. From the late 1850s on, as a railway network began to establish itself, the postal departments in the colonies began to move mail by train. Trains were much less affected by weather, and so the mail moved with much more regularity and far fewer losses. As soon as railways reached areas serviced by steamboats, postal agreements with steamboat operators were terminated, and mail movement contracted out to railway companies.

The sorting and distribution of mail en route first occurred on the Niagara-London route in 1854. Within several years there were specially designed mail cars, mobile post offices in which mail to and from destinations along the route was processed by hand and stamped. In this and many other respects, railway delivery procedures were adaptations with minor changes from methods developed for mail steamboat operations. The second of the covers displayed was stamped aboard a train on the Montreal and Quebec Grand Trunk Railway line in 1858.

The third cover represents mail delivered overseas by contract with the Allan Line. The line was founded in 1819 by Captain Alexander Allan of Scotland; his sons developed a very successful shipping operation. Hugh Allan (1810-1882), one of the sons, settled in Montreal. He became president of Montreal's influential Board of Trade. Through this office and political connections, Hugh Allan convinced the government of the Province of Canada to subsidize regular trans-oceanic communication by the award of mail contracts to shippers. In 1856 his newly-incorporated Montreal Ocean Steamship Company won the government contract to carry the mails from Montreal to Liverpool. The line prospered and became legendary for its innovative ships and ever-faster movement of people, cargo and mails between the old world and British North America.

Colonial Postal Departments. 1855-1866.

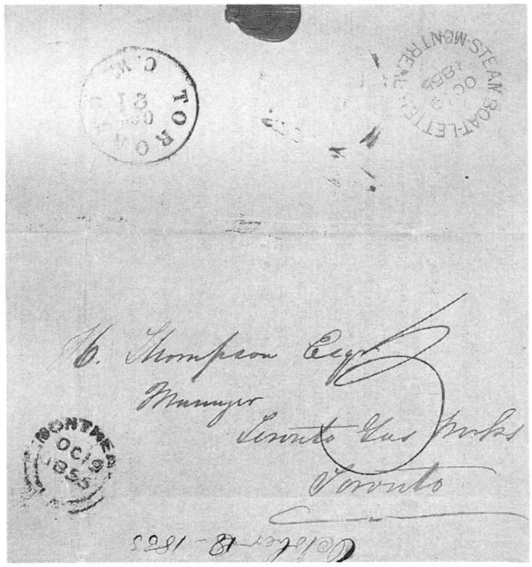

15.2 cm x 14 cm
5.7 cm x 10.2 cm
8.9 cm x 16.5 cm

National Archives of Canada,
Canadian Postal Archives,
[Stuhlberg Covers, Steamboat] POS-2494,
[Railway Cover] POS-2495,
[Allan Line Cover] POS-2626.

"Winter Mail"

The artist who painted this watercolour is unknown; the work is attributed to a member of the Ottawa branch of the Goode family.

The watercolour bears the inscription "Daniel Goode on the Road to Kingston, Dec. 16, 1851." It purportedly represents the first overland winter mail run from Ottawa to Kingston, which occurred on the date given in the inscription. By "first" is meant, of course, the first winter delivery of mail between these two centres following the assumption of responsibility for the mails by the colonial government. It is interesting to note that the sleigh is appropriately light, for fast travel, and the pair of horses drawing it of a finer breed than common farm horses.

In all likelihood the mail route ran through a number of villages and towns where the courier would stop at post offices or designated way stations, deliver and pick up mail, change horses, spend the night if required and then continue on his way. In this watercolour, the people in the back of the covered sleigh appear to be bundled in furs against the cold.

Like steamboat mail in the pre-Confederation period, overland bulk mail delivery by coach or sleigh faded away wherever the railway appeared.

Unknown Artist. 1851.

29.8 cm x 40 cm

National Archives of Canada,
Canadian Postal Archives,
POS-32.

Notice of Public Meeting to Discuss Building of Local Railway Line (Sorel-Drummondville)

Both Sorel and Drummondville were dynamic towns at this time. Drummondville, located on the St. François River as it flowed out of the Piedmont Appalachians on its way to the St. Lawrence, was founded in 1815. It was beginning to experience incipient industrialization, as sawmills, tanneries and forges opened. Sorel, founded in the mid-eighteenth century in the original seigneury of Saurel, stood on the south shore of the St. Lawrence, at the mouth of the Richelieu. By the mid-nineteenth century it had become a shipping terminal for vessels plying the Richelieu River, and benefitted from the Montreal-Quebec City river trade as a port-of-call.

The two towns, strategically located on commercial routes and experiencing an economic upturn, were caught up by the railway mania of the time. In the 1850s virtually every town of any consequence in the British North American colonies strove either to entice the larger railway companies to include their town on planned routes, or to build their own railways, to open up and develop their own hinterlands and to connect with commercial centres. This notice reflects the great enthusiasm aroused by the coming of railways, and the initiative demonstrated by citizens who sought to link their towns with the developments of the future.

Citizens of Yamaska Region. 1854.

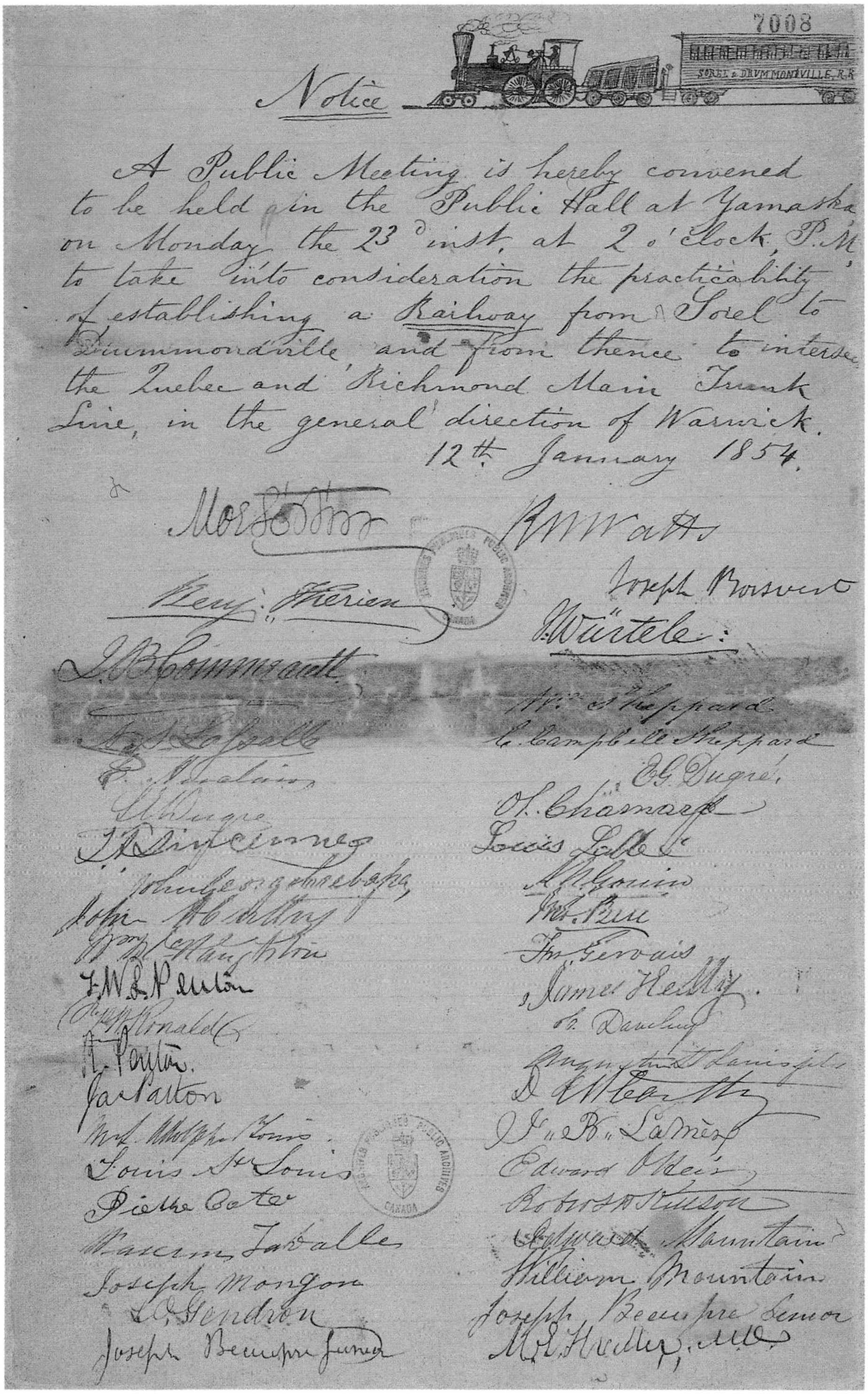
7008

SOREL & DRUMMONDVILLE R.R.

Notice

A Public Meeting is hereby convened to be held in the Public Hall at Yamaska on Monday the 23d inst. at 2 o'clock P.M. to take into consideration the practicability of establishing a Railway from Sorel to Drummondville and from thence to intersect the Quebec and Richmond Main Trunk Line, in the general direction of Warwick.

12th January 1854.

Joseph Boisvert

C. Campbell Sheppard

Jas Patton

William Mountain

Joseph Beaupre Senior

Joseph Beaupre Junior

34.3 cm x 21.6 cm

National Archives of Canada,
Manuscript Division,
MG 8, F 89, Vol. 15, pp. 7008-7009.

"The Great International Railway Suspension Bridge Over the Niagara River Connecting the United States and Canada"

This engraving, made by De Lay Glover, is based on a painting by Ferdinand Reichardt, who himself based his work on a daguerreotype image of the suspension bridge over the Niagara River. Daguerreotypes were the first form of widely-available and widely-used photographs. Reichardt was born in Denmark in 1819, and trained there as an artist. He came to New York in the early 1850s and earned a reputation as a painter of note, especially for his masterful depictions of falling water in such paintings as "Montmorency Falls" and his many views of Niagara Falls and the Gorge.

This engraving, fully in the spirit of positivism, celebrates man's mastery over nature. The geometric majesty of John Roebling's bridge, the regularity of spacing of struts, the half-ellipses of the main support cables — all this and more induces wonderment at how the structure defies gravity, and refuses to fall. Under the bridge, though, Nature's power manifests itself in the Gorge's walls which rise ruggedly upwards, in the river's waters which rage and roil, and in the clouds of mist that soar into the sky. The guy wires that drop downwards to stabilize the bridge look pathetically weak and sadly out of place. Perhaps it is less the idea of man's mastery over nature, which the engraving projects, but more the notion that man has learned, like a spider with abilities particular to him, to weave his own web in nature out of newer materials.

The building of this bridge was a marvellous feat of engineering. As the legends at bottom right and left indicate, the open span between the two towers was 800 feet. The bridge was suspended 245 feet above the river. The four main cables, each 10 inches in diameter, consist of 3,640 strands of #9 wire, braided for strength. And the bridge is two-tiered, to allow for non-railway traffic on the lower level. The bridge took four years to build, opening in 1854 shortly after the Hamilton-Windsor branch of the Great Western Railway (GWR) was completed. Soon thereafter, Toronto was linked into the GWR system and the market beyond the bridge. The structure itself was jointly managed by the New York Central and the GWR.

The Great Western was one of the very few Canadian railways that was ever financially solvent, largely because of its access to the United States heartland through the International Bridge and through the Windsor-Detroit corridor. The bridge opened in the first year of the Reciprocity Treaty, and the Great Western profited immensely, winning a large portion of the American midwest winter trade as every year winter closed down waterways. Railway expansion and bridge engineering were changing the tempo of economic life.

After Ferdinand Reichardt. 1859.

52 cm x 81.6 cm

National Archives of Canada,
Documentary Art and Photography Division,
C-104966.

"Ontario, Simcoe and Huron Union Railroad. Afterwards Northern Railway of Canada. 'Toronto No. 2'. Built by James Good May 1853. First Locomotive Built in Toronto"

James Good, a machinist and manufacturer, emigrated from Ireland in 1832, settling in York (Toronto). He acquired the Union Furnace Company, a large foundry. Hence he was well-placed to bid on contracts for locomotives when railway building began in earnest in the United Province of Canada.

Running north out of Toronto, the Ontario, Simcoe and Huron Union (OS&H) Railroad intended to link the three lakes after which it was named. The railway was Toronto's outreach into its northern hinterland, especially to the rich timber reserves north of the city. Also, it followed the age-old "Toronto Passage," the geographically most convenient overland route between Toronto and the Upper Great Lakes, which had been used by Indians long before Europeans came. The inaugural trip on this line occurred in May 1853; the train was drawn by the locomotive 'Toronto No. 2,' built in the Toronto Locomotive Works owned by James Good. This run, from Toronto to Machell's Corners (later Aurora), initiated the first regular train service in Canada West (in the same year that the important Montreal-Portland link was completed).

The 'Toronto No. 2,' depicted in this photograph, was the first locomotive built in the colonies (perhaps in all of Britain's colonies). The locomotive is in the "American" style. The earliest Canadian railways, laid down by British engineers, had originally employed British locomotives. These, however, soon proved themselves unequal to the task of heavy hauling over difficult terrain and under taxing climatic conditions. A simpler and heavier model more suited to North American needs had evolved in the United States throughout the 1840s. Good based his 'Toronto,' and the other eight locomotives which he built for the OS&H Railroad between 1853 and 1855, on this American model.

Behind the historic locomotive depicted in this photograph was Good's foundry, indicative of the stimulus that railway building imparted to colonial manufacturing. Good's foundry, the Grand Trunk Railway shops in Montreal (St. Charles) and other locomotive works that developed at this time in Hamilton and elsewhere are indicators of a quickening pulse of colonial economic development, and a diversification into new economic activity outside the production of staples which presaged entry into the industrial era.

Anonymous. 1860s.

ONTARIO SIMCOE AND HURON UNION RAILROAD
Afterwards
NORTHERN RAILWAY OF CANADA
"TORONTO" No 2
Built by James Good May 1853
First Locomotive built in Toronto
PA 138688

20.8 cm x 35.6 cm

National Archives of Canada,
Documentary Art and Photography Division,
PA-138688.

"View of Victoria Bridge under Construction"
"From Below North Abutment, 1st November 1859"
"Bridge in Progress from Point St. Charles"

These photographs of the Victoria Bridge were taken by William Notman, a Scots merchant who left his homeland following business failures, and settled in Montreal in 1856. After ventures into business, he turned to photography. With a background in fine art, he became a renowned portrait photographer, acquiring for his studio international fame. Notman and his staff were also contracted by the Canadian Pacific Railway, the Geological Survey of Canada and the Grand Trunk Railway (GTR) to photograph exploratory surveying and engineering activity. These photographs of the GTR's Victoria Bridge in various stages of construction were such contract photographs.

The two stereographic prints of the bridge are among the early Canadian stereos. Stereography developed in the 1850s and remained very popular right through to World War I. In its own right it was a revolutionary development in visual communication. When two slightly offset photographic images were viewed through a stereoscopic viewer, they leaped into a three-dimensional image. Viewers could, in their own home, experience the marvels of the world as if almost there. And the Victoria Bridge was indeed a marvel.

The Grand Trunk Railway was a relatively straight-forward engineering accomplishment, except for this bridge. In its time, the bridge was a monumental achievement. It took five years to complete, and employed 3,000 workers, including Cauhnawaga Indians, at the height of its construction. Unlike the suspension bridge over the Niagara Gorge, this structure was a squared tube of wrought iron, of girders and plates riveted together. The design gave the bridge spans strength, and protected the rails from snow and ice.

The bridge rested on two terminal abutments, one on each bank of the St. Lawrence, and on 24 piers of solid masonry. The piers were built of stones from 5 to 20 tons in weight, designed to withstand both the strong current of the St. Lawrence and the pressure of ice shoves during freeze and melt. Of the 25 spans of the bridge, 24 are approximately 240 feet in length each (the central span is larger, to allow for safer navigation). More than 2,700,000 cubic feet of masonry were used in its construction, while 1,500,000 rivets bound the iron plates and girders into squared tubes. Over 2,000 metres in length, the bridge in its time was the longest in the world.

The fact that the bridge was financed and engineered from Britain did not detract from the colonials' great sense of achievement once the bridge was completed, and officially opened by the Prince of Wales on his successful Royal Tour of 1860. The construction of the bridge was of colossal significance to colonial communications, and to Montreal's primacy in the carrying trade. From the southwestern end of Canada West and the American heartland beyond, to Montreal, and out of Montreal into the Eastern Townships and the United States, trains ran unhindered. They linked Canada East and Canada West, tied in with American markets at eastern and western termini, and were poised to connect with the Maritimes.

William Notman. 1859.

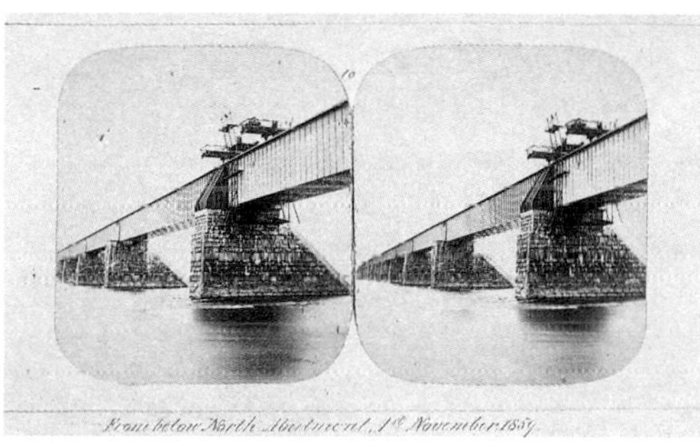

21 cm x 27.1 cm
7.3 cm x 12.8 cm
7.5 cm x 18.5 cm

National Archives of Canada,
Documentary Art and Photography Division,
[Large photo] PA-181435,
[Below North Abutment] PA-181445,
[From Pt. St. Charles] PA-181446.

"Island of Montreal and Isle de Jesus and Part of the Line of Communications with Carillon. Specification of Bridges"

As the American Civil War broke out in 1861, Britain rushed reinforcements to the colonies. British officers, hastily trained in the rudiments of surveying, initiated a military survey of strategic stretches of the colonial borders with the United States. In this context William Warren, an ensign with the 4th Battalion, 60th Rifles, produced this map, at a time when the victorious North was ill-disposed towards Britain and her colonies, and when the American-based Fenian Brotherhood was making its presence felt along the border with the United States.

Interesting as a record of colonial response to a possible military threat, this map has much greater historical value beyond the original purpose of its creation. For example, it provides information on cultivated land and on soil types, on bush lots and quarries, on creeks and streams. The land contours allow the viewer to almost sense the surface relief of the islands on which Montreal stands. One can understand why military men would be interested in such information. For us today, however, it is not so much the military value of this knowledge which elicits interest, but simply the overall commentary on the physical environs of Montreal.

The map imparts to the viewer a sense of Montreal as a crucial strategic, as well as communications, centre. The St. Lawrence canal system had been expanded, and the channel to Quebec City deepened; hence Montreal was a principal seaport. It was the eastern terminus of the Grand Trunk Railway; but it was also the hub of a railway system with other railways branching out into its hinterland. The great Victoria Bridge took the Grand Trunk across the St. Lawrence, into the Eastern Townships and to the United States. Roads, railways, canals and waterways all converged on Montreal and exited from it, reflecting the very rapid developments in transportation and communications in this time.

Communication was still difficult. Many of the roads described on the map were unsurfaced, dirt roads. The number of bridges linking islands and mainland was small and, as the legend indicates, most were not substantial. Reflecting the technology of the day, they were wooden bridges standing on piers of stone encased in wooden cribs. When using them might be dangerous, ferries would come in as an alternative; and overall, many ferry crossings, both inconvenient and at times dangerous, were in constant service.

William Warren. 1865.

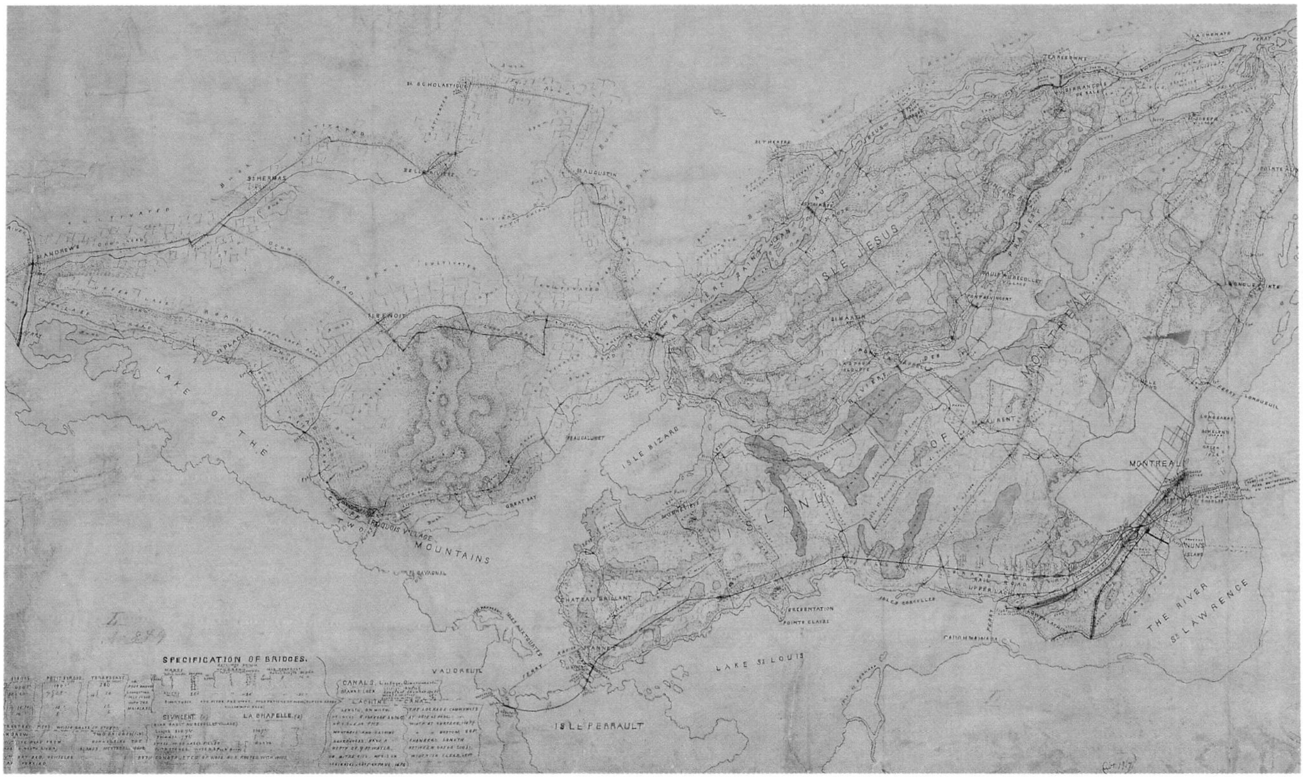

63.5 cm x 114 cm

National Archives of Canada,
Cartographic and Audio-Visual Archives Division,
NMC-16667.

Grand Trunk Railway Train Snowed Up at Chaudière. March 1869

Thomas Coltrin Keefer was a prominent civil engineer of the period. His engineering activity involved railway work, and also hydraulic engineering as he, over his career, managed successively the urban waterworks of Montreal, then Hamilton and, finally, Ottawa. In 1849 he published a very popular and influential work, *The Philosophy of Railroads*, in which he wrote that, in winter,

> ...an embargo which no human power can remove is laid on all our ports. Around our deserted wharves and warehouses are huddled the naked spars — the blasted forest of trade — from which the sails have fallen like the leaves of autumn.... The animation of business is suspended, the life blood of commerce is curdled and stagnant in the St. Lawrence — the great aorta of the North.... [B]lockaded and imprisoned by Ice and Apathy we have at least ample time for reflection — and if there be any comfort in Philosophy may we not profitably consider the PHILOSOPHY OF RAILROADS.

The pamphlet made a great impression and contributed amply to the pervasive railway mania of the time. This photograph captures Keefer's challenge to winter. When the waterways froze solid, commerce and traffic truly could move by rail.

In this photograph there are four locomotives coupled in sequence to power the snow plow. One can see how deep the snow lies (probably eight to ten feet) by comparing the snow bank to the telegraph poles in the background. Perhaps this was not the norm, but the result of an extraordinary snow fall. At all events, the tracks had to be cleared. Along the top of the snow bank is strung out the shovelling brigade, for the nature of plowing was laborious. At times shovelling crews went ahead of the locomotives, carving out and heaving away the gross accumulation of snow. Only once this was done could the plow thrust itself against the remaining snow and ice and, pushing it as far as possible — at times not very far, as high snow banks, almost tunnel-like, closed in along both sides of the track and allowed little lateral removal of snow — the shovelling brigade would again commence its back-breaking labour. Transportation was maintained; but winter did not surrender easily, and nature exacted a heavy toll in human labour to keep the arteries of commerce open.

Anonymous. 1869.

24.5 cm x 33.7 cm

National Archives of Canada,
Documentary Art and Photography Division,
PA-149764.

"ICR Grade at Smith's Brook, N.B." *and also* "Miramichi Bridges, North West Branch, Dredge Pumps in Operation in Foundation of Pier X, Newcastle, N.B., 16 May, 1873"

These two photographs record aspects of work on the Intercolonial Railway, which commenced only in 1867, following Confederation. A railway linking the Maritimes with the Province of Canada had been rumoured as early as the 1840s. To this end surveys were effected and deputations sent to Britain to solicit Imperial loan guarantees. When this failed, Nova Scotia and New Brunswick attempted local lines, but could finance only short stretches. In 1863, discussions between Canada and the Maritimes led to a decision on surveying out and financing the proposed railway. However, political sectionalism and paralysis in Canada stymied the project, enraging Maritimers who saw in this action a great betrayal.

Finally, however, the imperative of defence of the British colonies against the American North, which had just defeated the Confederate states, and against the Fenians, a radical Irish brotherhood dedicated to winning independence for its homeland from Britain, convinced the British colonies to get on with the building of the Intercolonial Railway. Sir Sandford Fleming surveyed out the route, choosing the less economical but strategically more defensible Chaleur Bay-Matapedia Valley-St. Lawrence route. Made a condition of Confederation, work on the Intercolonial commenced in 1867.

As these photographs indicate, work on the Intercolonial required considerably more labour and engineering skill than had been expended on earlier railways, which more or less traversed flat land or rolling valleys. The Notman photograph, taken by a photographer in Notman's employ, depicts the "cut and fill" method of laying out railway lines to avoid steep grades in the rougher countryside of New Brunswick. Engineers would survey out routes where cutting and filling could sequentially complement each other; what was cut to reduce grade was thus most economically moved the shortest distance possible to serve as fill. It was also important to get the slopes of cuts and fills so stable that neither rockfall nor washout would threaten the line. Given the nature of the tools and equipment available, and the fact that locomotive power was restricted to men and animals, the grade depicted here was no small achievement.

The photograph of bridge construction addresses another area of engineering achievement in the building of the Intercolonial. Chronic underfunding to this time had forced Canadian railway engineers to use wood in the construction of their bridges. They had adapted quickly to this limitation; in fact, they had earned a world reputation for their timber trestles. However, Sir Sandford Fleming, feeling that the Intercolonial was close to economical water transport, which would cheapen the transport of iron bridge components to bridge sites, and intending to take advantage of changing technology, broke with this practice. He sought to build the Intercolonial's bridges using "wrought iron bridge spans." The political row that this caused reached right to the British government which, as guarantor of the financing of the Intercolonial, had the final say; and the British Privy Council came out in support of Fleming.

In addition to their "wrought iron spans," Fleming's bridges also stood on piers of masonry, not on the usual rock-in-wooden-crib piers. In this photograph taken by an anonymous photographer, the donkey and steam engines may very well have pumped water out of pier caissons so that workers could prepare both pier foundations and the piers themselves. Thus the bridges on the Miramichi marked a significant engineering departure in bridge construction.

Attributed to Notman Studios. 1871.

Anonymous. 1873.

MIRAMICHI BRIDGES.

NORTH WEST BRANCH.

DREDGE PUMPS IN OPERATION IN FOUNDATION OF PIER X.

16TH MAY, 1873.

National Archives of Canada,
Documentary Art and Photography Division,
[Embankment] C-17696,
[Bridge] PA-22033.

22.6 cm x 19.5 cm
13.9 cm x 18.7 cm

"Town Line Road Bridge. Station 220 East. Grand Trunk Railway. Toronto and Sarnia Section. Guelph Division"

This document is a working drawing of its day, akin to the modern blueprint, as evidenced by the free-hand notations inscribed on it, probably by engineers working on the construction of this bridge. Colour-coding of the materials renders the drawing prettier, but there is a functional significance to it as well.

The design is a bridge typical of its day, constructed of materials readily available in Canada, i.e. wood and stone, with relatively little iron. In the Canadian context, this approach was both adaptable and economical. In fact, even as material availability and economy affected the character of British and European railways, which could both afford and had available much more iron, the same factors influenced bridge-building in Canada. Hence the dominance of wooden bridges over the countless streams, creeks, rivers and ravines of the British colonies in North America.

It is interesting to note the careful selection of wood for functions, based on wood's natural properties. The bridge surface was planked with oak, a hard wood which weathered well. The rest might have been spruce, renowned for longevity in wet conditions, or pine. Even as engineers utilized readily available material, they also designed with a view to locally available labour skills. The bridge roadbed is supported by trusses very suggestive of barn trusses; and often the same people who trussed barns were employed in erecting bridge structures.

The truss-work of this bridge calls for iron. Quite likely this bridge was to replace an original built wholly of wood for reasons of economy when the line was first laid down in the early 1850s, and which by the 1870s had either become structurally unsound or even burned down. A record of the early railway age, this drawing not only tells much about the development of communications, but also tells it through an aesthetically attractive document.

Grand Trunk Railway. ca 1872.

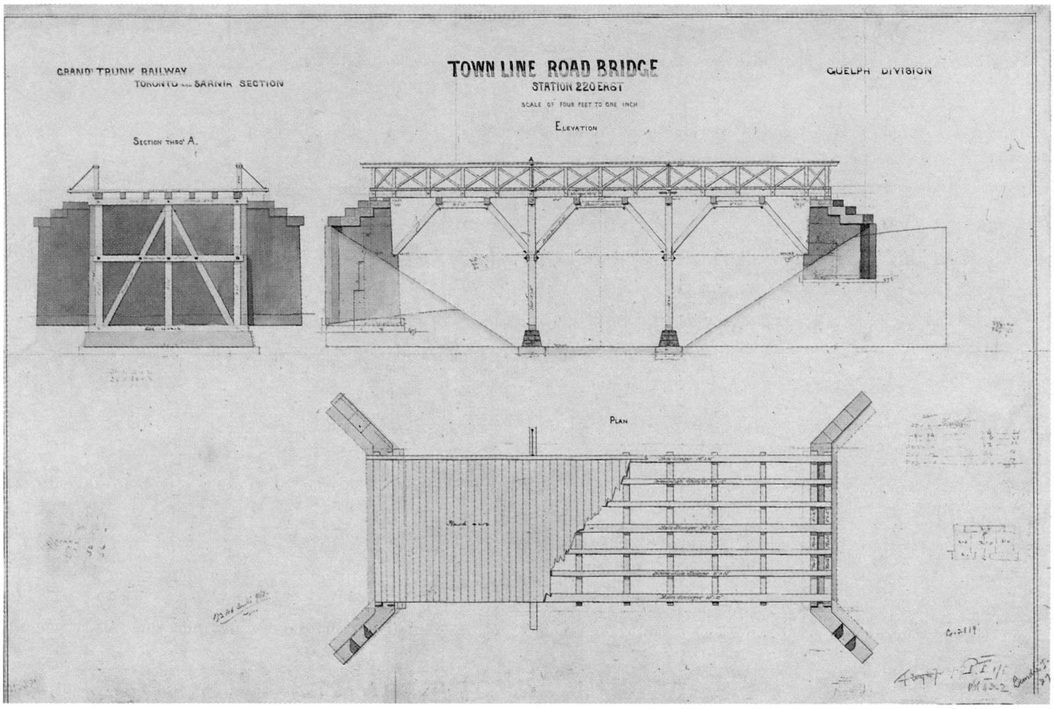

63.5 cm x 94.8 cm

National Archives of Canada,
Cartographic and Audio-Visual Archives Division,
NMC-121236.

"GWR. Harrisburg and Brantford Branch Brantford Passenger House"

As railways spread out, the ubiquitous railway station began to dot the iron lines of commerce and communication. The advent of the railways led to new service arrangements for travellers. For example, the old hostels and inns, spaced a day's coach ride apart, began to die away, replaced in major towns by railway stations for passengers.

This passenger house contract plan, showing side and front elevations as well as floor plan, represents a typical railway station of the time. It is long and narrow (84 feet long by 24 feet wide), its length strung parallel to the railway track. The large, overhanging eave provided protection against snow and rain, and shade against a hot summer sun. The relatively mild winters of southwestern Ontario allowed large windows admitting as much natural light as possible. Out of sanitary considerations, water closets were set off in a separate outbuilding; but engineers, perhaps out of thoughtfulness for passenger "emergencies," or out of Victorian gentlemen's concern for the "fairer sex," allowed for a water closet in the main building. *De rigueur* in Victorian Canada, ladies and gentlemen were provided with separate waiting rooms.

Much as with bridges, Canadian engineers used readily available materials for railway stations. This plan describes a wooden structure, both in frame and in cladding and shingling. Recognizing the properties of their materials, the engineers called for a cedar base under the platform, where moisture-resistant materials were needed.

Railway stations of such a design appeared in the towns and large villages of the pre-1867 British North American colonies and in Canada of the post-Confederation era. Though wholly utilitarian, there is something very pleasing, even elegant, in the simple lines and in the geometric harmony of this archetypal structure.

Great Western Railway. 1871.

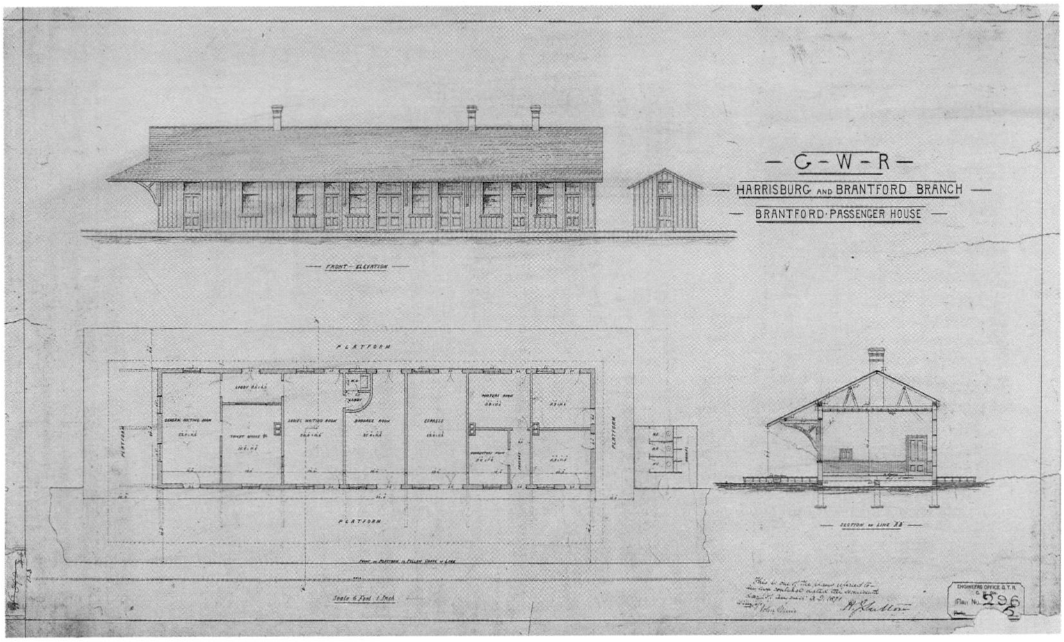

51.4 cm x 86.5 cm

National Archives of Canada,
Cartographic and Audio-Visual Archives Division,
NMC-51584.

III

Life in British North America / Canada

The aboriginal population of British North America experienced serious dislocation and suffering in this era. In certain regions, Indians legally ceded title to their lands; in other areas, they were simply displaced with no compensation. Additionally, new ways introduced by white immigrants harmed their lifestyles, while diseases introduced by white settlers, against which aboriginal people had no immunity, decimated many tribes. Many present-day native Canadian grievances stem from this period.

Colonial society experienced cultural and economic growth. Educational facilities — schools and universities — grew and improved. Newspapers multiplied, various meeting halls opened, often with their own libraries, where lectures were read. Both French- and English-language authors contributed to the cultural development of the future Canada, particularly as they sought to understand and explain the past and to create a new vision of the future.

Immigration, though on a far smaller scale than to the United States, continued, and new regions, such as the Eastern Townships and the Ottawa River valley, were more widely opened for settlement. Agriculture and logging, as before, provided staple products for export abroad, while the Maritimes gloried in the high noon of shipbuilding and the carrying trade. The petroleum industry, a harbinger of the future, made its appearance. Trade with the rest of the world, not only with the United States, increased. Though generally a time of extreme economic vicissitudes, this era was also characterized by significant economic development.

"Petition of the Subject Algonquins and Nipissing of the Lake-of-Two-Mountains to His Excellency the Governor-General"

In this petition to the Governor-in-Chief, 24 Indian family heads of the reserve at Lac des Deux Montagnes appealed to Lord Elgin for aid. By way of introduction, they recounted that they had accepted Christianity, had allied themselves with Europeans against invaders and, since the British conquest, had remained loyal to the British Crown. After forced wandering about the Isle de Jesus, they had been established at Two Mountains, and had resided there for 150 years under the protection of the Seminary of St. Sulpice. They had lived peacefully and obeyed all laws. But now, neither government authorities nor neighbouring inhabitants showed any signs of either Christian or civilized conduct toward them.

Their lands at Two Mountains and along the Ottawa River, the Indian petitioners pointed out, were being seized and occupied; hence their livelihood, the hunt, was being destroyed. Because they were inexperienced in the ways of whites, they were subjects of fraud. The demarcation of new townships along the north shore of the Ottawa River threatened their ownership of lands and compromised their livelihood. While in Upper Canada Indian lands were alienated through legal purchases, the petitioners continued, in Lower Canada the Indians were subjected to depredation, and the Church gave them no protection. By this petition, they called for legal confirmation of ownership of their lands in the Seigneurie du Lac, and asked Lord Elgin, through laws and "liberal, Christian civilization," to take the "savage" tribes of Lower Canada under his protection.

The Lac des Deux Montagnes and Kahnawake reserves near Montreal had been designated, during the French era, as Indian lands for Algonquin and Iroquois. The boundaries of their reserve land, however, had constantly been shifted away from the expanding urban limits of Montreal. Missionaries had sought to keep the Indians removed from the corrupting influences of the city. White settlers had encroached upon their land. As reserve soil had become exhausted, the Indians had had no option but to move away in search of productive land. By the early nineteenth century, as Indian lands and livelihood came under pressure, and thanks to the connivance of Montreal merchants, illicit trade in contraband goods across the Canada-United States border was already established in the reserve lands as a means of survival.

The document reflects the difficulty of adjustment to the new ways imposed upon aboriginal inhabitants by white society.

F. Papino et al. 1851.

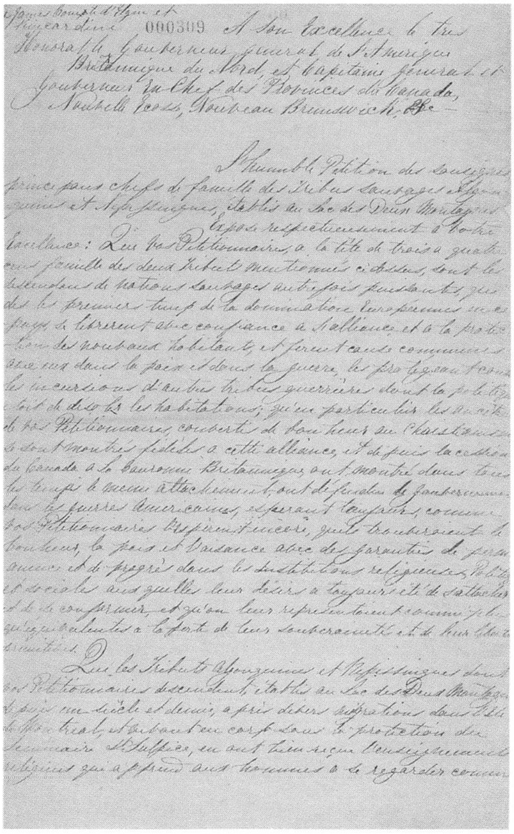

000309

A Son Excellence le très Honorable Gouverneur général de l'Amérique Britannique du Nord, et Capitaine général et Gouverneur en Chef des Provinces du Canada, Nouvelle Écosse, Nouveau Brunswick, &c. —

L'humble Pétition des sauvages principaux chefs de famille des Tribus sauvages Algonquines et Nipissingues, établis au Lac des Deux Montagnes

Expose respectueusement à Votre Excellence: Que vos Pétitionnaires, à la tête de trois à quatre cents familles des deux Tribus mentionnées ci-dessus, sont les descendants de nations sauvages autrefois puissantes, qui dès le premier temps de la domination européenne en ce pays, se livrèrent avec confiance à l'alliance et à la protection des nouveaux habitants, …

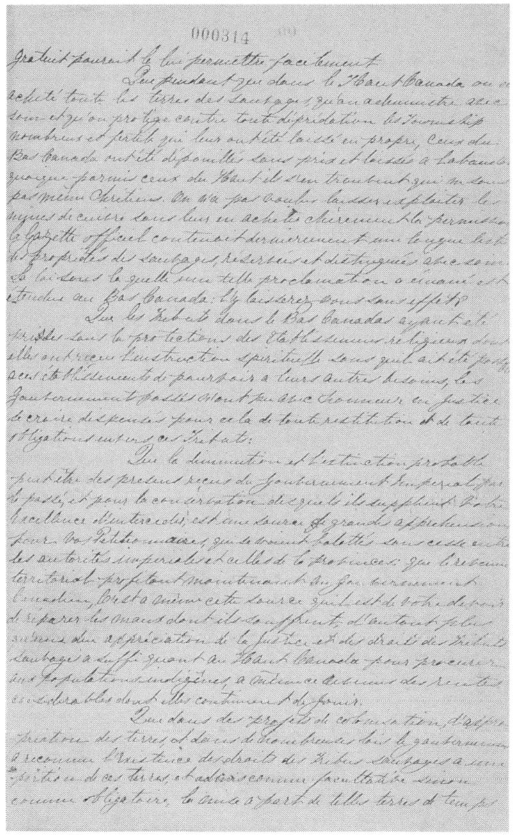

000314

34.1 cm x 21.2 cm

National Archives of Canada,
Manuscript Division,
MG 24, B 1, Vol. 26, pp. 309, 314.

III

"Camp of Nesahee Indians and Hudson's Bay Company's Post at NW River, Hamilton Inlet, Labrador, Newfoundland, August 29, 1860"

Conway Mordaunt Shipley, born in Britain in 1824, joined the Royal Navy in 1837. In the naval service, he travelled the world until 1855, when he resigned for reasons of health. In 1859-1860 he journeyed to Greenland and Canada; on this trip, he produced the watercolour shown here.

The Montagnais-Nascapi inhabited what would be northern and eastern Quebec and Labrador. In the nineteenth century the designation "Nascapi" was loosely applied to northern "unchristianized" Indians. In their own language, a dialect of Algonquin, the Nascapi called themselves "the barren land people," from the nature of the terrain they inhabited. They were a migratory people, living in easily transportable shelters of bark or animal skins, and travelling light in search of food and seasonal game. Organized in family groups, their possessions were few, and they manufactured their own implements.

Until the 1830s they relied on Cree intermediaries in trading with the Hudson's Bay Company. Around that time, they cut out the Cree middlemen, coming directly to Company posts, such as Fort Chimo and the North West River Post, to trade their fur pelts. Subsequently, the Nascapi fell victim to diseases against which their bodies had no immunity. Influenced by new ways, they deviated from their usual migrations in pursuit of the caribou; hunger and starvation followed.

Shipley's watercolour depicts a small Nascapi camp, with shelters built of bark or skins, outside the modest North West River post set in a rather harsh locale. The brownish tinge of the watercolour evokes a sense of misty gloom on a dismal day when rain clouds seem to touch the very earth. The effect is accidental, the result of over-exposure of the work in bright light which caused colours to fade, creating a unique sombre ambiance.

Conway Mordaunt Shipley. 1860.

32

23 cm x 35 cm

National Archives of Canada,
Documentary Art and Photography Division,
C-138100.
Purchased with a grant from the Minister of
Communications under the terms of the
Cultural Property Export and Import Act.

"Eskimos, Little Whale River"
"White Porpoise, Eskimaux and Kayak and Seal Skin"

George Simpson McTavish was born in Canada in 1834. He joined the Hudson's Bay Company in 1849, was assigned to the Southern Department in 1859 and, by 1875, was an Inspecting Chief Factor. He was for a time stationed in the "eastern Main." These photographs were taken there, along the eastern shore of Hudson Bay, near the delta of the Little Whale River. Perhaps, like many Company men, he had an anthropological interest, hence these photographs of Inuit.

The group photo probably depicts a family group, perhaps several families, in a small band. Social structure was loose among the Inuit. Family units were grouped into regional bands, which in turn constituted tribes of perhaps 500 to 1,000 individuals. The nature of the terrain which the Inuit inhabited did not generally allow for large concentrations, and as a rule they only congregated into larger groups for the winter seal hunt. In summer, the Inuit would break into smaller family units, and go in search of food. They would hunt game, especially the caribou, or fish the cold streams and rivers flowing into the Bay. Also gatherers, they would seek out berries and birds' eggs.

The Inuit diet and economy were based largely on the sea-mammal hunt. The photograph of the successful hunter, who has brought in a porpoise, depicts the effective traditional technology of a people who had adapted to a most trying climate and terrain. Bone, antler or horn and wood were fashioned into a harpoon. Mammal bladders were often used as floats to mark the spot of a kill, though the float shown here is made of sealskin. The kayak was created from bone or wood used for a frame, animal skins for sheathing, and animal or mammal oils for waterproofing. In the making of their implements, the Inuit used sinew or intestine for binding and securing.

Among our earliest photographs of the Inuit, these images constitute a significant visual record of one of Canada's most resourceful aboriginal groups.

George Simpson McTavish. ca 1865.

9 cm x 14.6 cm
10 cm x 15.2 cm

National Archives of Canada,
Documentary Art and Photography Division,
[Eskimo Group] C-75905,
[Eskimo Hunter] C-22942.

"An Ojibway Squaw with Papoose"
"'Wigwam' an Ojibway Half-Breed"

While attached to the Hind Expeditions (1857-1858), Humphrey Lloyd Hime took a series of photographs, two of which are shown here, documenting both the landscape and inhabitants of the Assiniboine and Saskatchewan districts.

Hime's photographs of Wigwam and the Ojibway "squaw," taken in Red River in the fall of 1858, have a very obvious historical value. While shot outdoors, a sense of the studio permeates these images; the photographic process of the time made this unavoidable. Wigwam sits on a buffalo robe, with his back to another robe. His clothing, both in material and cut, is more-or-less European; but his beaver cap and his leggings mark him as a man of the Indians. Both in his dress and in his physiognomy one can see the Indian and European mix. The buffalo hunt gave the Metis their chief sustenance, and one of their chief articles of trade with the Hudson's Bay Company — pemmican.

The Ojibway woman may also have been Metis, for in her clothing she shows more European influence than Indian. Like Wigwam, she sits against the background of a buffalo robe, perhaps no symbol more apt or respected by the Metis and Plains Indians. The papoose, like any young child anywhere would have done, moved his head during the time required to expose the photographic plate, hence the blurred face. Wigwam and the Ojibway woman might have been man and wife.

There is much documentary commentary in these photographs on Metis and the Ojibway woodland Indians. They are among the earliest surviving images that we have of inhabitants of Rupert's Land. They were used to illustrate the Hind Expedition's report, and reproduced in popular illustrated newspapers of the day.

Humphrey Lloyd Hime. 1858.

19 cm x 14.2 cm
16.8 cm x 13.8 cm

National Archives of Canada,
Documentary Art and Photography Division,
[Ojibway Squaw] C-728,
["Wigwam"] C-16447.

Explorations along the Saskatchewan River

Father Jean L'Heureux was an intriguing figure in Canadian frontier history. Born in L'Acadie (Quebec), in 1831, he died in Alberta in 1919. He studied for the priesthood at the Académie de St. Hyacinthe. Expelled from that institution, he went west in the 1850s and, a self-styled rogue missionary, wandered the west. For a while, in Montana, he passed himself off as a Jesuit missionary, and later worked with the Oblate fathers in Alberta. Always in communication with the Indians of the west, especially the Blackfeet, he came to know them well; blending Christianity with Indian shamanism, he became a shaman-priest of the Blackfeet, calling himself "Three Persons," i.e. the Trinity. Because of his substantial knowledge of Indian lore, he was later employed as a translator by the Indian Department.

This manuscript reflects the type of information that L'Heureux occasionally sent to Ottawa. The manuscript provides fascinating information about the North Saskatchewan and Battle River region. L'Heureux describes the geographical features of the land (rivers, valleys, hills and so on), and provides their Indian names. He writes of the flora and the fauna, and of other notable phenomena, such as sulphur springs. He assesses the quality of land for agricultural purposes, and describes mineral deposits. An amateur ethnographer and anthropologist, L'Heureux tells of "old tumuli" where Indians find various flint objects of great antiquity. He comments on dietary and religious practices of the Blackfeet; and he details for us their tribal organization and numbers. Perhaps the most remarkable of all his observations deals with "the vertebra of a powerful animal" which he had seen near the river of "the Solitary Tree," in all probability a reference to dinosaur bones. To the Indians, these were the bones of the "grandfather of the bison," and their location was the home of the "spirit of the earth."

The eccentric L'Heureux and his observations do not quite fit the tradition of the learned Jesuits and their *Relations*; but there is a parallel here. It is difficult to know what influence his writings might have had in Ottawa. However, L'Heureux and others like him, the not-so-great explorers, also contributed to the opening of the interior, and to the knowledge that Canadians were acquiring about the immense tracts of the continental heartland which, in 1870, came into the Dominion. Just as importantly, he recorded, for the benefit of later generations, nomenclature in the Algonquin language of the Blackfeet, Indian values and perceptions of life, Indian practices, lore and religion, thus helping to preserve some of the legacy of the Plains Indians.

Father Jean L'Heureux. 1871.

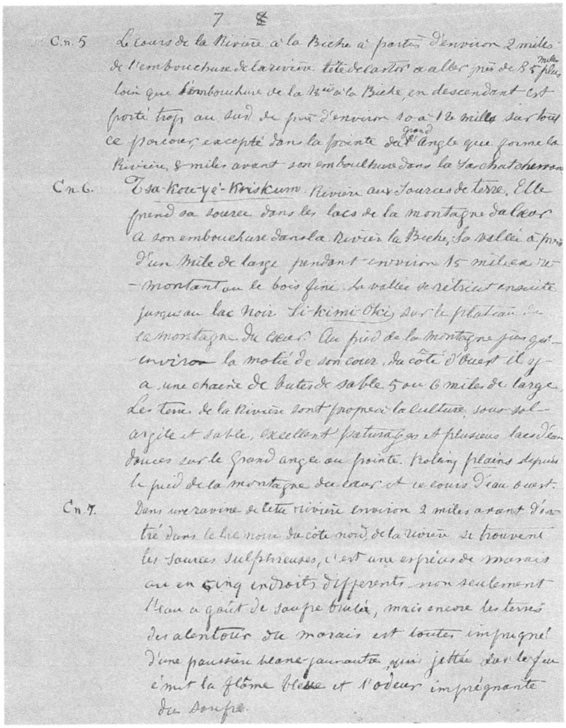

7 8

C.n. 5 Le cours de la Rivière à la Biche à partir d'environ 2 milles de l'embouchure de la rivière tête de castor à aller près de 85 milles plus loin que l'embouchure de la Rivière à la Biche, en descendant est porté trop au sud de près d'environ 10 à 12 milles sur tout ce parcour, excepté dans la pointe du grand angle que forme la Rivière, 8 miles avant son embouchure dans la Saschatchewan.

C.n. 6. Tsa-Kou-yé-Kriskum. Rivière aux Sources de terre. Elle prend sa source dans les lacs de la montagne du cœur à son embouchure dans la Rivière la Biche, sa vallée à près d'un Mile de large pendant environ 15 milles en remontant ou le bois fini. La vallée se rétrécit ensuite jusqu'au lac Noir Si-kimi-Oki, sur le plateau de la montagne du cœur. Au pied de la montagne jusqu'environ la motié de son cour, du côté d'Ouest il y a une chaine de butes de sable 5 ou 6 miles de large. Les terre de la Rivière sont propre à la culture, sous-sol argile et sable, excellent pâturages et plusieurs lacs d'eau douces sur le grand angle ou pointe. Roling plains depuis le pied de la montagne du cœur et le cours d'eau ouest.

C.n. 7. Dans une ravine de cette rivière environ 2 miles avant d'entré dans le lac noire du côté nord de la rivière se trouvent les sources sulphreuses, c'est une espèce de marais ou en cinq endroits differents non seulement l'eau a goût de soufre brulé, mais encore les terres des alentour du marais est toutes impregné d'une poussière blanc-jaunautre qui jettée sur le feu émet la flâme blue et l'odeur impregnante du soufre.

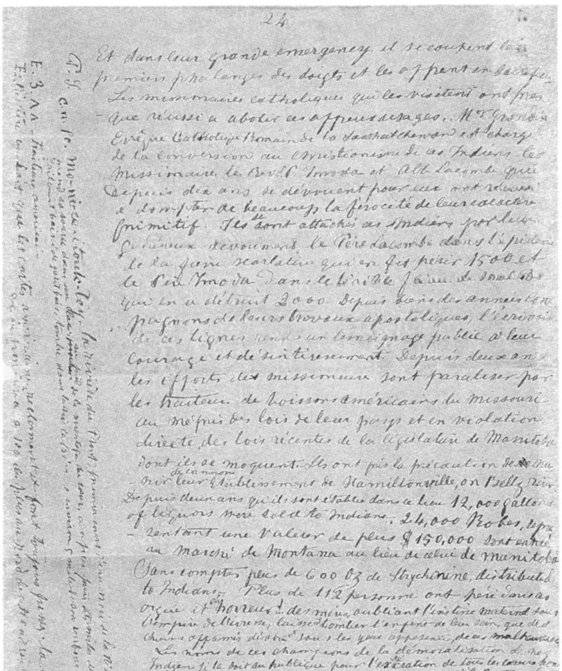

24

Et dans leur grande emergency il se coupent les premiers phalanges des doigts et les offrent en sacrifice. Les missionnaires catholiques qui les visitent ont pas que réussi a abolir ces affreux usages. Mgr Grandin Evêque Catholique Romain de la Saschatchewan est chargé de la conversion au Christianisme de ces Indiens les missionnaire le Revd C. Imoda et Alb Lacombe qui depuis dix ans se dévouent pour eux ont réussi à dompter de beaucoup la férocité de leur caractère primitif. Ils se sont attachés ces Indiens par leur généreux dévouement le Père Lacombe dans l'épidémie de la fièvre scarlatine qui en fit périr 1500 et le Père Imoda dans le terrible [illegible] de 1869-70 qui en a détruit 2000. Depuis bien des années compagnons de leurs travaux apostoliques, l'écrivain de ces lignes rend un témoignage public à leur courage et de[illegible]. Depuis deux ans les efforts des missionnaire sont paralisés par les traiteurs de boissons américains du Missouri au mépris des lois de leur pays et en violation directe des lois récentes de la législature de Manitoba dont ils se moquent. Ils ont pris la précaution de fortifier de canon leur Etablissement de Hamiltonville, ou Belly River. Depuis deux ans qu'ils sont établis dans ce lieu 12,000 gallons of liquors were sold to Indians. 24,000 Robes, représentant une valeur de plus $150,000 sont entré au marché de Montana au lieu de celui de Manitoba sans compter plus de 600 Oz de Strychnine, distributed to Indians. Plus de 112 personne ont péri dans ces orgie et on a vu horreur! des mères, oubliant l'instinct maternel sous l'empire de l'ivresse, laisser tomber l'enfant de leur sein, que des chiens affamés dévorèrent sous les yeux apprêsanti de ces malheureuses. Les noms de ces champions de la démoralisation de nos Indiens je le doit au publique pour l'exécration de tous les cœurs honnêtes. Les firmes de Baker and Co Benton A.T. & C. Benton [illegible] Healy and Hamilton from Helena [illegible] par la multitude de leurs agents [illegible]

25.5 cm x 20 cm

National Archives of Canada,
Manuscript Division,
MG 29, C 33, pp. 1, 24.

Observations on Plains Indians

Commissioned a lieutenant in the Royal Engineers in 1862, Valentine T. Rowe served on the North American Boundary Commission in 1873-1874, as it laid out the 49th parallel separating Canada and the United States. While on this assignment, he made notes of his experiences there, and later, from them, wrote these intriguing observations about the Indians of the Great Plains.

Rowe writes of the great Dacotah tribe, misnamed the Sioux. Before white settlers even came into contact with them, they had a jaundiced and unkind view of the Dacotah. That was, as Rowe points out, most unfair; the opinions of whites were shaped by the Ojibway, a forest people and sworn enemies of the Plains Indians, who did their best to malign them. Rowe's observations are an intentional corrective to this distortion.

In Rowe's view, "kindness, honesty and truthfulness" are the hallmarks of the Dacotah. In truth, the Plains Indians were driven to desperation by the destruction of the buffalo, by trespassers on their lands and by the traders who traversed the prairies dealing in worthless trinkets and peddling deadly whiskey. The white man, Rowe argues, introduced "deceit, drunkenness and death" to the Dacotah of the western plains.

There is much veracity in Rowe's commentary. As whites increasingly appeared in the Northwest, native people experienced heightened suffering. In 1865, for example, the Mackenzie and Yukon Valley Indians were decimated by scarlet fever, carried in by a Hudson's Bay Company's employee. In 1869 a frightful smallpox epidemic, brought up from the upper Missouri valley by American traders, killed thousands of Blackfeet, Assiniboine, Cree, Blood and Piegan Indians, and hit the Metis as well. As whites decimated the buffalo herds, Indians began to war amongst themselves for a declining food source; in 1870, Cree and Assiniboine met in battle with Piegan and Blood Indians, with the loss of over 500 Indian lives. In 1873 American whiskey runners and "wolfers," who poisoned wolves with strychnine for bounty money, slaughtered 20 Assiniboine near Fort Lethbridge, on the eastern edge of "whoop-up" country, for allegedly stealing one of their pack animals.

Rowe's observations on the Dacotah are worthy of attention. He writes of their lore, customs and habits, religion, inter-personal relations, and so on. But perhaps nothing touches the reader as poignantly, and captures as effectively the Dacotah's sense of self, honour and history, as the speech of Two Dogs, which Rowe reported verbatim, and which is displayed here.

Lieutenant Valentine T. Rowe. 1873-1874.

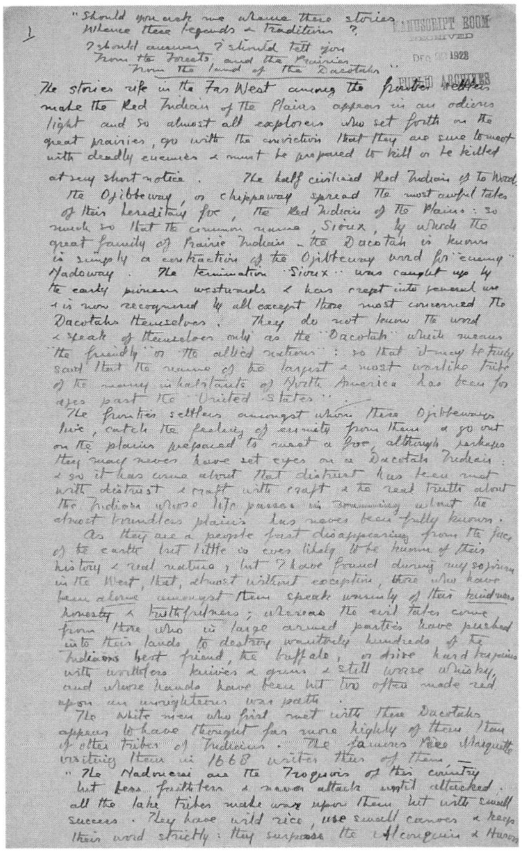

1

"Should you ask me whence these stories
Whence these legends & traditions ?
I should answer I should tell you
From the Forests and the Prairies
From the land of the Dacotahs"

The stories rife in the Far West among the frontier settlers make the Red Indian of the Plains appear in an odious light and so almost all explorers who set forth on the great prairies, go with the conviction that they are sure to meet with deadly enemies & must be prepared to kill or be killed at any short notice. The half civilised Red Indian of the Woods the Ojibbeway, or Chippaway spread the most awful tales of their hereditary foe, the Red Indian of the Plains: so much so that the common name, Sioux, by which the great family of Prairie Indians – the Dacotah is known is simply a contraction of the Ojibbeway word for "enemy" Nadoway. The termination "Sioux" was caught up by the early pioneers westwards & has crept into general use & is now recognised by all except those most concerned the Dacotahs themselves. They do not know the word & speak of themselves only as the "Dacotah" which means "the friendly" or "the allied nations": so that it may be truly said that the name of the largest & most warlike tribe of the many inhabitants of North America has been for ages past the "United States".

The frontier settlers amongst whom these Ojibbeways live, catch the feeling of enmity from them & go out on the plains prepared to meet a foe, although perhaps they may never have set eyes on a Dacotah Indian: & so it has come about that distrust has been met with distrust & craft with craft & the real truth about the Indians whose life passes in roaming about the almost boundless plains has never been fully known.

As they are a people fast disappearing from the face of the earth but little is ever likely to be known of their history & real nature, but I have found during my sojourn in the West, that, almost without exception, those who have been alone amongst them speak warmly of their kindness honesty & truthfulness; whereas the evil tales come from those who in large armed parties have pushed into their lands to destroy wantonly hundreds of the Indians best friend, the buffalo, or drive hard bargains with worthless knives & guns & still worse whisky, and whose hands have been but too often made red upon an unrighteous war path.

The White men who first met with these Dacotahs appear to have thought far more highly of them than of other tribes of Indians. The famous Père Marquette visiting them in 1668 writes thus of them, –

"The Nadouessi are the Iroquois of this country but less faithless & never attack until attacked. all the lake tribes make war upon them but with small success. They have wild rice, use small canoes & keep their word strictly: they surpass the Algonquin & Huron

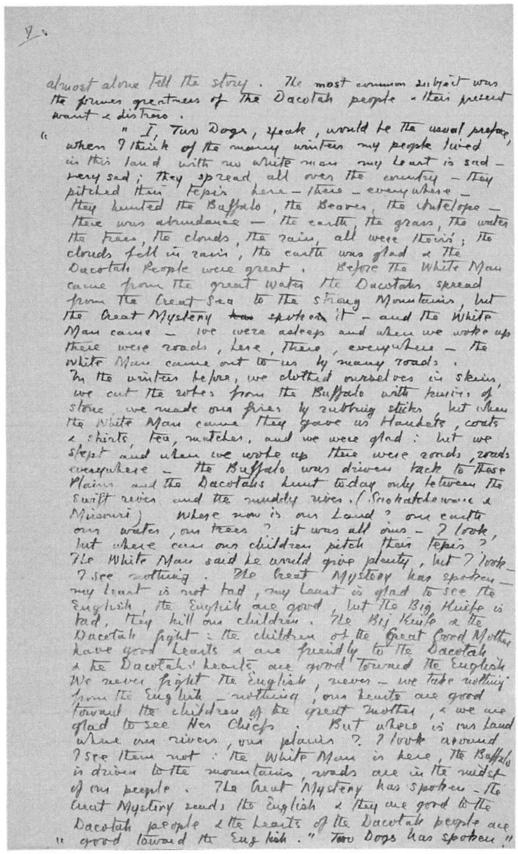

7.

almost alone tell the story. The most common subject was the former greatness of the Dacotah people & their present want & distress.

"I, Two Dogs, speak, would be the usual preface, when I think of the many winters my people lived in this land with no white man my heart is sad – very sad; they spread all over the country – they pitched their tepis here – there – everywhere – they hunted the Buffalo, the Beaver, the Antelope – there was abundance – the earth, the grass, the water the trees, the clouds, the rain, all were theirs; the clouds fell in rain, the earth was glad & the Dacotah People were great. Before the White Man came from the great water the Dacotahs spread from the Great Sea to the Strong Mountains, but the Great Mystery ~~has~~ spoken it – and the White Man came – we were asleep and when we woke up there were roads, here, there, everywhere – the White Man came out to us by many roads.

In the winters before, we clothed ourselves in skins, we cut the robes from the Buffalo with knives of stone, we made our fires by rubbing sticks, but when the White Man came they gave us blankets, coats & shirts, tea, matches, and we were glad: but we slept and when we woke up there were roads, roads everywhere – the Buffalo was driven back to these Plains and the Dacotahs hunt today only between the swift river and the muddy river. (Saskatchewan & Missouri) Where now is our Land? our earth our water, our trees? it was all ours – I look, but where can our children pitch their tepis? The White Man said he would give plenty, but I look – I see nothing. The Great Mystery has spoken – my heart is not bad, my heart is glad to see the English, the English are good, but the Big Knife is bad, they kill our children. The Big Knife & the Dacotah fight: the children of the Great Good Mother have good hearts & are friendly to the Dacotah & the Dacotahs' hearts are good toward the English. We never fight the English, never – we take nothing from the English – nothing, our hearts are good toward the children of the great mother, & we are glad to see Her Chiefs. But where is our land where our rivers, our plains? I look around I see them not: the White Man is here, the Buffalo is driven to the mountains, roads are in the midst of our people. The Great Mystery has spoken – the Great Mystery sends the English & they are good to the Dacotah people & the hearts of the Dacotah people are good toward the English." Two Dogs has spoken."

34.6 cm x 21 cm

National Archives of Canada,
Manuscript Division,
MG 29, C 24, pp. 1, 7.

"Indian Encampment on the Thompson"

Benjamin Baltzly was born in Ohio in 1835. After serving in the Union forces during the American Civil War, he migrated to Montreal. He took this photograph when, as official photographer, he accompanied the Canadian Pacific Railway-Geological Survey of Canada Expedition to British Columbia in 1871. Baltzly was employed at that time by William Notman, who paid all Baltzly's expenses; in return for this, Notman received all of Baltzly's negatives, and Notman's studio was still selling images from this expedition twenty years later.

The Indians encamped in this photograph are probably Salishan speakers, perhaps members of the Shuswap or Thompson (now Atlakyapamulc) tribes. They are Plateau Indians of the southern interior of British Columbia. Organized in egalitarian village communities, they lived by hunting, fishing and gathering, cyclically migrating to where food could be located. In the winter months, they dwelt in their semi-subterranean "pit houses"; with the coming of spring they would leave the pithouses, and move in search of sustenance.

The migratory nature of their existence was captured by Baltzly in this photo. Several tents and a lean-to are their main shelter. In the background, on a platform raised to keep them away from prowling animals, are their possessions and, possibly, food supply. There is evidence of contact with Europeans in the clothing of the Indians, in the tents they use, and in the fact that they have pitched camp at what seems to be a small settlement, perhaps Bonaparte, perched on the edge of a road winding towards it from the hills. Some distance back along the road can be seen covered wagons, making their way towards the settlement and encampment.

The lands of these Salish Indians were first subjected to surveys in the 1870s, and reserves were set aside. The Indians of the region, however, never accepted the land settlement. Their land claims dispute continues to this day.

Benjamin F. Baltzly. 1871.

14.6 cm x 24.5 cm

National Archives of Canada,
Documentary Art and Photography Division,
C-46347.

"Songish Village Opposite Victoria Island, B.C."

In the early 1850s the colony of British Columbia was virtually devoid of permanent European inhabitants. In the sister colony of Vancouver Island, only Victoria had a settled white population, and then only several hundred persons. At the same time, the two colonies were home to approximately 30,000 Indians, among them the West Coast Indians.

The West Coast Indians, while they existed by fishing, hunting and gathering, lived in a lush and fruitful land, hence the dwellings and villages they constructed in fixed locations. They were masters of elementary engineering, building substantial homes of post-and-beam construction, sheathed with split-cedar planks. Skilled weavers, they fashioned clothing out of cedar bark fibres, as well as ceremonial blankets out of either cedar bark fibre or various admixtures of bark and dog or mountain-goat hairs. Their dug-out canoes, stable, balanced and artistically decorated, could challenge the rollers of the Pacific Ocean.

The generosity of the land allowed them to acquire wealth, and they exercised control of property, governed by strict custom, as evidenced in the potlatch. Their communities were complex in structure, both internally within villages and externally in the relationships amongst clans. Their conduct was guided by strict conventions, with appropriate rites prescribed for the momentous events of life, such as birth, death, puberty and marriage.

Edward Parker Bedwell, active in 1851-1862, manages to capture something of this in his watercolour. Bedwell was a military artist trained in a tradition long-established in the British military. While in active service, he visited the west coast. Among his many landscapes is this work, titled "Songish Village...." The Indian homes that he painted are relatively large and stable structures; and on the still waters of the bay one can see lesser versions of the famed dugout canoes. This village, described as "opposite Victoria," may well have been one of the villages affected by the land treaties which James Douglas, Chief Factor of the Hudson's Bay Company, negotiated with local Indians on Vancouver Island in the vicinity of Fort Victoria. Since the Hudson's Bay Company received licences to manage the fur trade of the west coast on condition that it settle the colonies, Douglas wished to gain clear title to lands to be offered to settlers. Hence the treaties that he signed with the Sooke, Songhee and Klallam tribes on Vancouver Island. For 371 blankets and one cap, the Indians surrendered rights to much of their land. A small portion of ancestral land was granted to them in ownership, and they retained the right to fish and hunt on alienated lands as long as these remained unoccupied. Very few other treaties were ever signed in British Columbia.

The life of the West Coast Indians took a sharp turn for the worse when gold was discovered on the Fraser River in 1856. The large influx of outsiders — Americans, Europeans and Chinese — brought diseases against which the natives had no immunity. Drawn to Victoria and other settled points by trade, and into immediate contact with the foreigners, Indians caught infectious diseases. By 1862, disease swathed mercilessly throughout the West Coast tribes, killing thousands of Indians. For the native people of the west coast, the gentle and satisfying life suggested by Bedwell's watercolour was no more.

Edward Parker Bedwell. ante 1863.

25.2 cm x 35.2 cm

National Archives of Canada,
Documentary Art and Photography Division,
C-114507.
Purchased with a grant from the Minister of
Communications under the terms of the
Cultural Property Export and Import Act.

Report on the Mission of the *Capricieuse*

Paul-Henri de Belvèze, born in France in 1801, studied at the renowned École Polytechnique, after which he joined the French Royal Marines in 1823. He had a number of important tasks entrusted to him, one of which was to resuscitate both cultural and trade relations between France and the Province of Canada. Changes on the international scene allowed such a development. Britain had, by the late 1840s, shifted to a policy of Free Trade, the logic of which allowed her colonies to trade with any market they chose. Also, France and England had drawn closer together in the Anglo-French Alliance of 1854 aimed at the Russian Empire. It is not surprising then, that Britain had no qualms about a French mission to Canada in 1855, at a time when both she and her ally France were engaged in the Crimean War.

In command of the *Capricieuse,* de Belvèze put in at Quebec City on 14 July 1855 to a rousing welcome. The *Capricieuse,* after all, was the first French naval vessel to fly the French flag on the St. Lawrence since 1760. De Belvèze travelled by steamer and train to Montreal, Ottawa and Toronto, and then back to Quebec City, which he departed on 25 August. On the basis of these visits and discussions with prominent people, he prepared an account of his mission, of which the National Archives has a contemporary copy.

The report is a most interesting assessment of the economic, cultural and military situation at that time in the Province of Canada. The mission achieved its objective; in 1859 a French consulate was opened in Quebec City, and, thanks to reciprocal tariff reductions, trade improved between the Province of Canada and France.

As important, however, was the significance that some French-Canadians ascribed to the mission of the *Capricieuse.* The mother once again had remembered and found time for a forgotten daughter, who had remained faithful all the while that she had been ignored. De Belvèze dedicated a chapter of the report displayed here to the French language, the struggle to survive anglicization and the imperative of establishing a representative of France in Canada to secure the existence of the "French Nationality."

Captain Paul-Henri de Belvèze. 1856.

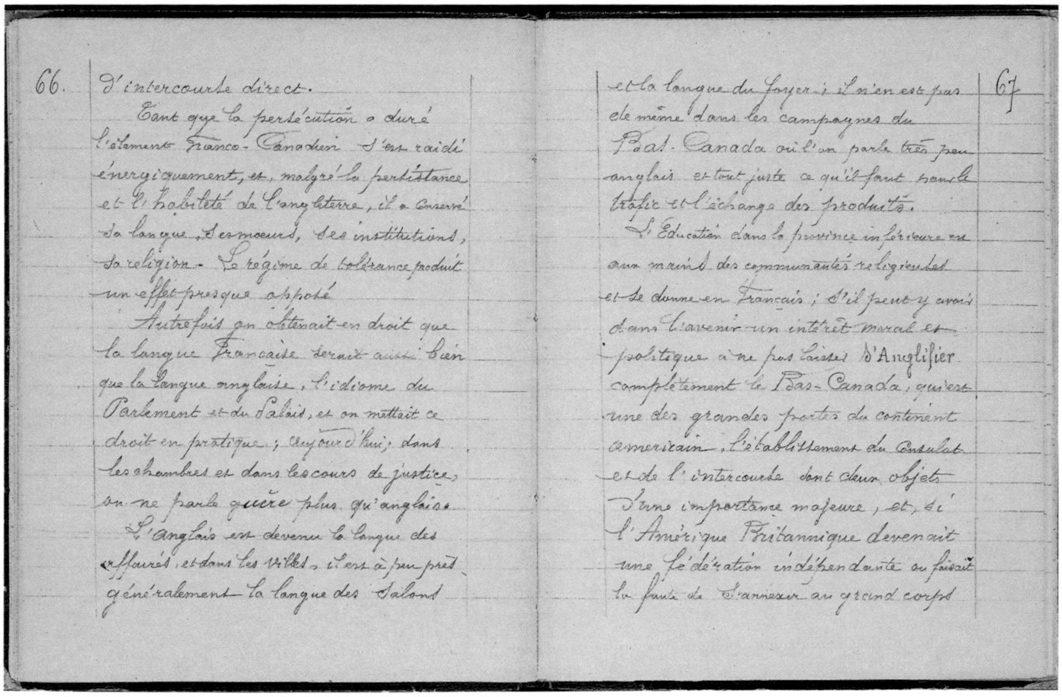

66. D'intercourse direct.
Tant que la persécution a duré l'élément Franco-Canadien s'est raidi énergiquement, et, malgré la persistance et l'habileté de l'angleterre, il a conservé sa langue, ses moeurs, ses institutions, sa religion. Le régime de tolérance produit un effet presque opposé.
Autrefois on obtenait en droit que la langue Française serait aussi bien que la langue anglaise, l'idiome du Parlement et du Palais, et on mettait ce droit en pratique; aujourd'hui, dans les chambres et dans les cours de justice, on ne parle guère plus qu'anglais.
L'anglais est devenu la langue des affaires, et dans les villes, il est à peu prest généralement la langue des Salons

et la langue du foyer; il n'en est pas de même dans les campagnes du Bas-Canada où l'on parle très peu anglais et tout juste ce qu'il faut pour le trafic et l'échange des produits. 67
L'Education dans la province inférieure est aux mains des communautés religieuses et se donne en Français; s'il peut y avoir dans l'avenir un intérêt moral et politique à ne pas laisser d'Anglifier complètement le Bas-Canada, qui est une des grandes portes du continent americain, l'établissement du Consulat et de l'intercourse sont deux objets d'une importance majeure, et, si l'Amérique Britannique devenait une fédération indépendante ou faisait la faute de s'annexer au grand corps

23 cm x 17.9 cm

National Archives of Canada,
Manuscript Division,
MG 24, F 42, pp. 66-67.

"To Commander de Belvèze in Canada"

The visit of the *Capricieuse* so touched A. Chalifoux, a French-Canadian tailor of Montreal, that he, despite his modest means, commissioned the photographer Thomas Coffin Doane to prepare a special commemorative daguerrotype in honour of the event. Chalifoux intended to present it to the Empress Eugénie of France, through Captain de Belvèze, as a symbol of the close and lasting bond between French Canada and France.

The daguerreotype recorded fundamental symbols of the French Canadian past. The image consists of four children at the "Fêtes nationales de Montréal," who represent "all the religious and patriotic memories of the French Canadians." The first is dressed as St. Jean Baptiste, the patron saint of French Canada. The second child represents Jacques Cartier, the sixteenth-century discoverer of New France, who also brought the Holy Scriptures with him. The third figure stands for the Indian chief of the village of Hochelaga who befriended the first French arrivals. And, lastly, there is a young French Canadian in French military dress. Holding the colours of France, he symbolically bridges the past represented by the other three figures, and takes the image into 1855.

The significance of this daguerreotype lies not only in its evidentiary aspect, i.e. the information it transmits to us about times past, but also in the medium itself. Daguerreotype was the first practicable photographic process, formulated by Louis Jacques Mandé Daguerre in France. There was no negative stage in the process, which directly produced a positive image. But the end product was so delicate that, for survivability, it was placed under glass, and then mounted in a silk- or velvet-lined case. This daguerreotype is made by one of Canada's best and best-known daguerreotypists, hence its extraordinary quality.

Thomas Coffin Doane. 1855.

8.9 cm x 12.2 cm

National Archives of Canada,
Documentary Art and Photography Division,
PA-139246.

Haps and Hazards in North America

Travel accounts were a favourite literary genre of the time; hundreds of accounts were published, recording the travels, travails and impressions of explorers, tourists, missionaries, military men, artists, surveyors, administrators and their spouses. Walter Sinclair, a surveyor and railway construction engineer, came to the New World to try his luck at railways. In these memoirs, he recounts a trip of three years duration (sometime between 1853 -1858) which took him from Liverpool to Canada via New York, and back again to England.

Sinclair's manuscript account is written in a direct style but with some grace and a lot of humour. The book has two watercolours, as well as quaint chapter illuminations. In a bit of self-deprecatory whimsy, on the title page Sinclair has inscribed that his account is "Intended for Private Circulation and Public Education" (a bit of an oxymoron), and "Published by the Society for the Issue of Private Trash."

The memoir is a wonderful recollection of life and mores in colonial Canada. Sinclair describes work on the railways, and various shenanigans of unscrupulous railway contractors. He recalls city life in Toronto, Montreal and Quebec City, and captures the hustle and bustle of colonial towns trying to break out of mud streets and timber houses. He comments on the life of the ordinary people: on the culinary and drinking habits of labourers and habitants; on the dwellings they inhabit; on the great guard dogs kept in every Quebec City yard; on the severity of North American winters, and the great pot-bellied stoves kept flaming red against the numbing frosts.

As a railway man, he reports knowledgeably on many aspects of transportation. He writes about colonial roads and streets, many of which turned into mud flats in spring and fall, and about Montreal's wooden sidewalks, which kept a person free of mud but posed the threat of injury when boards underfoot would give way. He recalls crossing the St. Lawrence on "ice bridges" which formed in late fall, a practice of the period that was both usual and dangerous.

Sinclair's recollections of everyday society, of the values and attitudes, manners and customs of the people, of communication developments and how they touched humans directly, capture the flavour of colonial life, making his manuscript an important historical source.

Walter Sinclair. 1862.

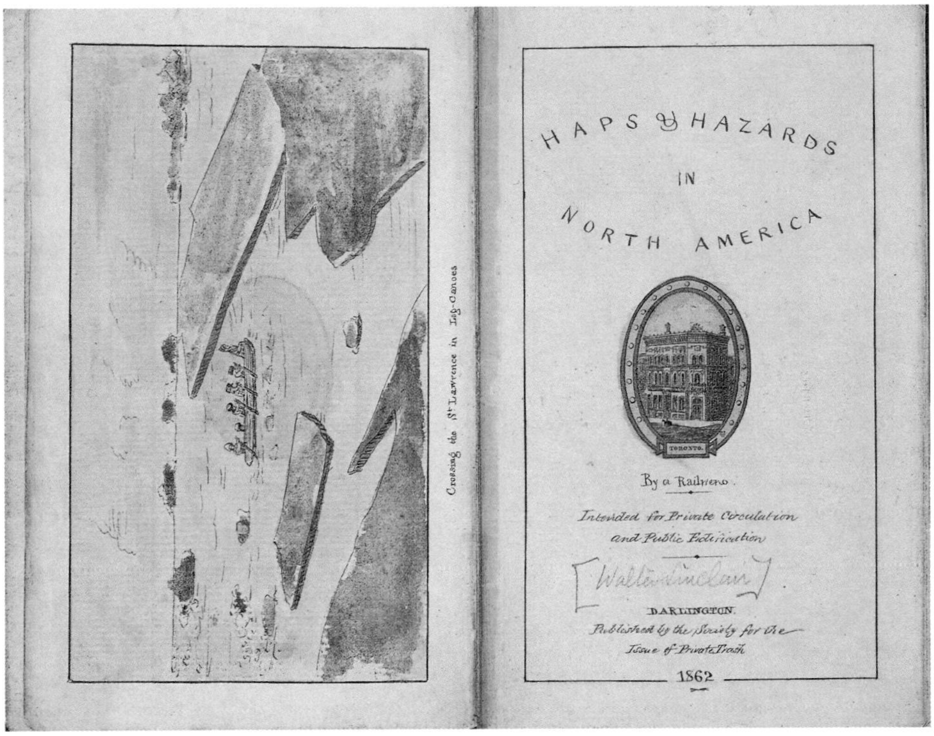
Crossing the St Lawrence in Ice-Canoes
HAPS & HAZARDS
IN
NORTH AMERICA
TORONTO
By a Railroader
Intended for Private Circulation
and Public Edification
[Walter Sinclair]
DARLINGTON
Published by the Society for the
Issue of Private Trash
1862

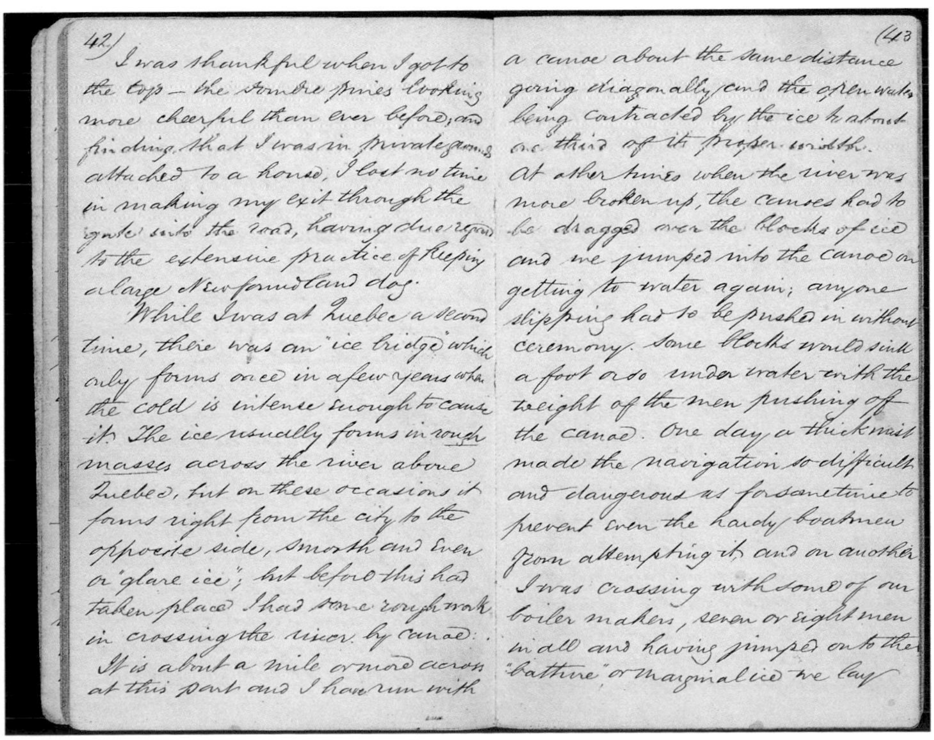

42/ I was thankful when I got to the top – the sombre pines looking more cheerful than ever before; and finding that I was in private grounds attached to a house, I lost no time in making my exit through the gate into the road, having due regard to the extensive practice of keeping a large Newfoundland dog.

While I was at Quebec a second time, there was an "ice bridge" which only forms once in a few years when the cold is intense enough to cause it. The ice usually forms in rough masses across the river above Quebec, but on these occasions it forms right from the city to the opposite side, smooth and even or "glare ice"; but before this had taken place I had some rough work in crossing the river by canoe: It is about a mile or more across at this part and I have run with

(43 a canoe about the same distance going diagonally, and the open water being contracted by the ice to about one third of its proper width. At other times when the river was more broken up, the canoes had to be dragged over the blocks of ice and we jumped into the canoe on getting to water again; anyone slipping had to be pushed in without ceremony. Some blocks would sink a foot or so under water with the weight of the men pushing off the canoe. One day a thick mist made the navigation so difficult and dangerous as for sometime to prevent even the hardy boatmen from attempting it, and on another I was crossing with some of our boiler makers, seven or eight men in all and having jumped onto the "batture", or marginal ice we lay

18.8 cm x 11.5 cm

National Archives of Canada,
Manuscript Division,
Title Page and Illustration,
MG 24, H 34, pp. 42-43.

Poem on Womanhood and Motherly Love

Rosanna Leprohon, née Mullins, was born in Montreal in 1829, and died there in 1879. Of Irish Catholic ancestry, she was educated at the Convent of the Congrégation Notre Dame, where she developed her talent for writing. Her first poems appeared in *The Literary Garland* when she was only seventeen. In 1852 she married Jean-Lucien Leprohon, a Montreal doctor of French-Canadian ancestry. Her married and family life thus straddled two cultures, which influenced the subject matter and treatment of themes in her literary career.

In the 1860s Leprohon wrote her most significant novels: *The Manor House of de Villerai; a Tale of Canada under the French Domination,* serialized in *The Family Herald* in 1859-1860; *Antoinette de Mirecourt; or Secret Marrying and Secret Sorrowing. A Canadian Tale,* published in 1864; and *Armand Durand; or, a Promise Fulfilled,* published in 1868. The novels realistically reflect French Canadian life before, during and after the conquest; and they address the psychological problems of adjustment to new ways and the development of new relationships between English and French. They were written with understanding and sensitivity, which explains why they were almost immediately translated into French, becoming significant contributions to both French and English literature in Canada.

While Leprohon was not a feminist beyond her time, she did believe that women had more than a reproductive-housekeeping function in life. She valued education for women; and she held that marriage, rather than meaning submission for women, was a partnership, with each partner responsible for a necessary sphere of family life. The short poem displayed here reflects Leprohon's religiously-based education in a convent school and her views on a woman's role in life. The woman is the strength of the family, the home her empire. Ruling that home with love would overcome all obstacles. In an earlier time, the woman's moral strength — expressed through love in the kingdom of the home which she managed — was, in Leprohon's view, a vital requirement to deal successfully with life's harsher demands. The woman, through moral suasion, ruled the household, even as Queen Victoria ruled her Empire. Intentional or not, the parallel is there.

Rosanna Eleanor Leprohon. 1867.

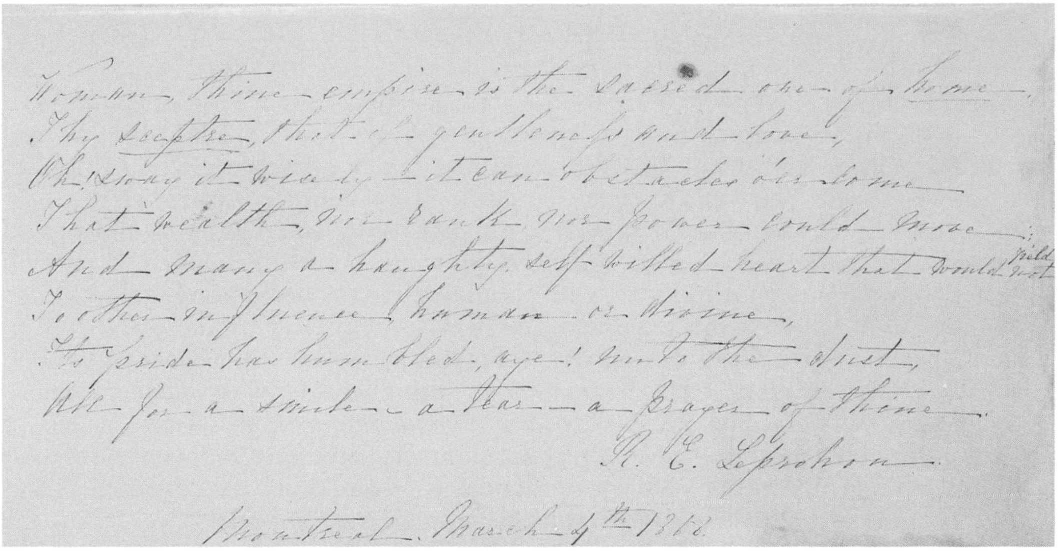
Woman, thine empire is the sacred one of home,
Thy sceptre, that of gentleness and love,
Oh! sway it wisely — it can obstacles o'ercome
That wealth, nor rank nor power could move;
And many a haughty self willed heart that would not yield
To other influence, human or divine,
Its pride has humbled, aye! unto the dust,
All for a smile — a tear — a prayer of thine.
R. E. Leprohon
Montreal. March 4th 1868.

16.6 cm x 29.2 cm

National Archives of Canada,
Manuscript Division,
MG 24, K 71.

Manuscript on Pioneering

Catharine Parr Traill (1802-1899), née Strickland, emigrated to Canada from Britain in 1831. She settled with her husband in the Peterborough area of Upper Canada, where he had received a military land grant. Traill belonged to a family of writers; even before her emigration to Canada, she was already an accomplished and published writer herself.

In 1836 she published *The Backwoods of Canada; Being Letters from the Wife of an Emigrant Officer; Illustrative of the Domestic Economy of British America.* The book reflected the pioneering experiences of people new to a demanding, though also rewarding, land. In 1854, she published *The Female Emigrant's Guide, and Hints on Canadian Housekeeping*; the following year it was re-published as *The Settler's Guide.* The *Guide* was immensely popular, judging from the fact that it went through some ten editions by 1860. Both the *Guide* and *The Backwoods of Canada* informed prospective settlers of life in the British colonies, gave advice on practical matters and counselled women on what to expect and how to cope with life where nature, the climate, economic development and social mores were so very different from what they were leaving behind.

Throughout her life, Traill maintained an interest in the settlement and development of Canada. In 1871, she sent two manuscripts, "suitable for publication as guides to immigrant settlers," to the Department of Agriculture, in the hope that they might be published in some paper as a guide. The document displayed here was likely a draft for one of those updated guides. The manuscript points out how, in a new and rough land, a person is forced to develop his head and hands, to become a jack-of-all-trades, to change, adapt, and turn to new means and ways — this is a matter of survival. Life is difficult in the new land; but in the new land, there is also human renewal and much gratification.

Catharine Parr Traill. ca 1871.

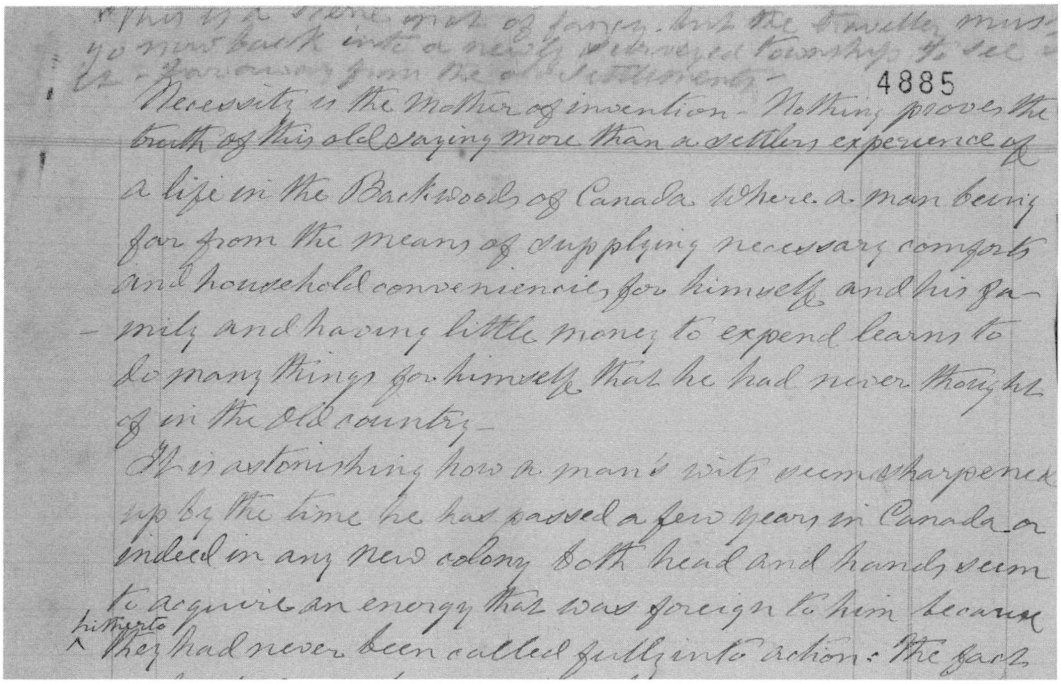
*This is a scene not of fancy. but the traveller must go now back into a newly surveyed township to see it — far away from the old settlements —

4885

Necessity is the Mother of invention — Nothing proves the truth of this old saying more than a settlers experience of a life in the Backwoods of Canada Where a man being far from the means of supplying necessary comforts and household conveniencies for himself and his family and having little money to expend learns to do many things for himself that he had never thought of in the Old country —

It is astonishing how a man's wits seem sharpened up by the time he has passed a few years in Canada or indeed in any new colony both head and hands seem to acquire an energy that was foreign to him because hitherto they had never been called fully into action — The fact

18.6 cm x 22 cm

National Archives of Canada,
Manuscript Division,
MG 29, D 81, Vol. 3, p. 4885.

III

Education of Blacks in New Brunswick

Individual blacks had appeared in the British colonies since the early days of trans-Atlantic settlement; however, they came in large numbers only after the American Revolution. The first influx accompanied the United Empire Loyalists. Over 3,000 came as free men, having won their liberty through allegiance to the Crown during the American Revolution. Several thousand more came as slaves of United Empire Loyalists, most of whom were freed within several generations. Blacks also fled American slavery during the War of 1812, and several thousand who found refuge behind British lines were mostly settled in Nova Scotia in the years 1813-1816. Until the mid-part of the nineteenth century, most blacks in the British North American colonies were concentrated in Nova Scotia and New Brunswick.

They faced many obstacles. Allowed small land grants on marginal soil, they could not develop self-sufficient agriculture. Forced to work as day labourers, many fell victim to exploitation and discrimination. Many colonials of European ancestry frankly encouraged blacks to migrate elsewhere.

In the black communities of the Maritimes, schooling was a serious concern. While Canada West and Nova Scotia had legally segregated public schools for blacks, and most blacks had access to either such a public school or a school funded by some charitable institution, New Brunswick did not at that time have a fully-structured public school system. Many schools were funded directly out of the treasury, receiving grants annually upon approval of their application for funding.

In this letter, J.W. Duval, teacher at the black school in Loch Lomond, appeals to Leonard Tilley (then Provincial Secretary) to secure the school's grant for the upcoming year. The black community is dedicated to improved schooling, proven by their successful drive to raise money to build a new school house. However, local whites, through the pretence of a proposed union, are trying to seize control of the school. Duval implores Tilley to aid the black community, especially by continuing to fund its school out of the public treasury.

Duval's letter is a reminder of the long black presence in the Maritimes, and touchingly expresses the constraints blacks endured because of discrimination.

J. W. Duval. 1859.

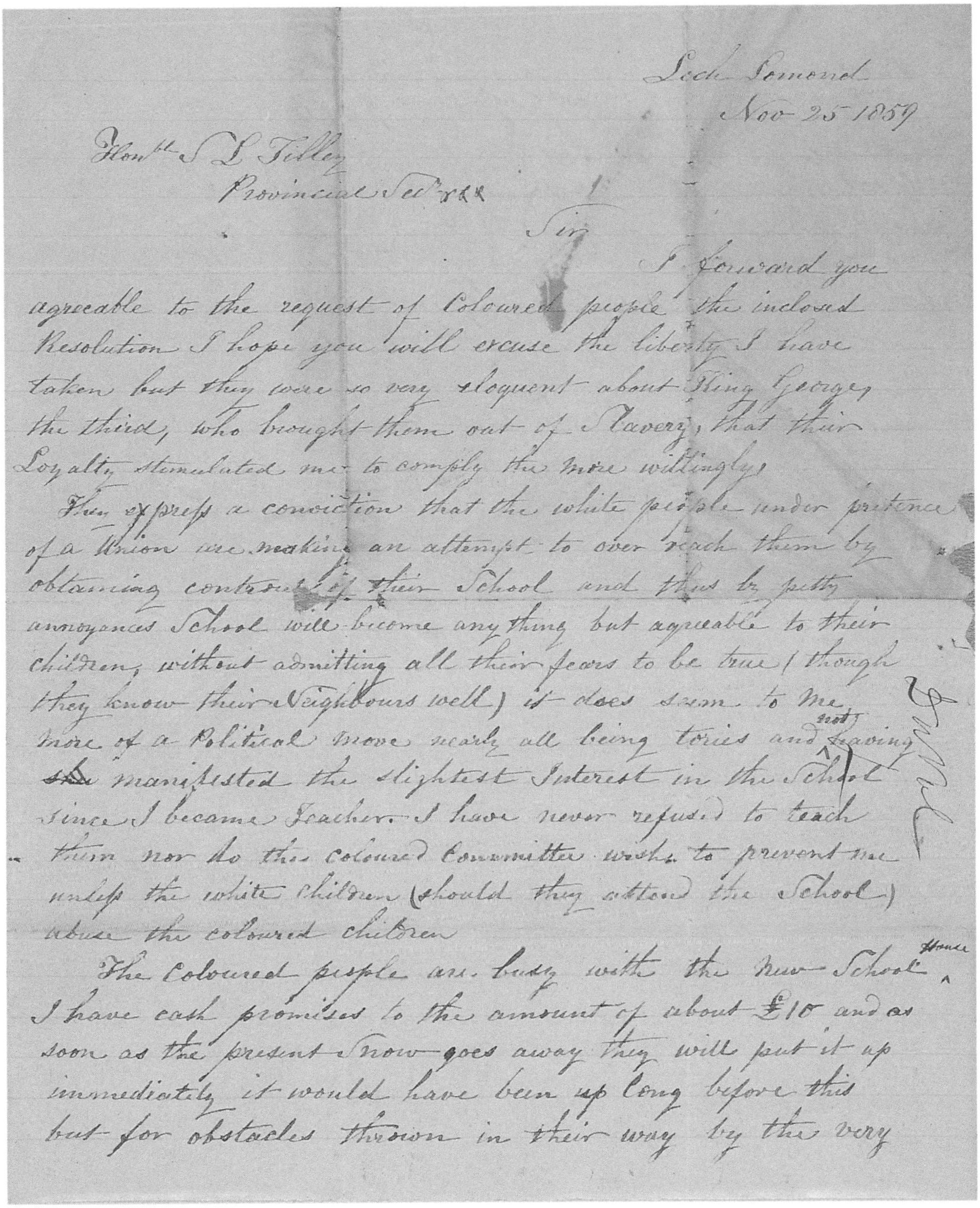
Loch Lomond
Nov 25 1859

Honble S L Tilley
Provincial Secy &c

Sir

I forward you agreeable to the request of Coloured people the inclosed Resolution I hope you will excuse the liberty I have taken but they were so very eloquent about King George the third, who brought them out of Slavery, that their Loyalty stimulated me to comply the more willingly

They express a conviction that the white people under pretence of a Union are making an attempt to over reach them by obtaining controul of their School and thus by petty annoyances School will become any thing but agreeable to their children, without admitting all their fears to be true (though they know their Neighbours well) it does seem to me more of a Political move nearly all being tories and not having manifested the slightest Interest in the School since I became Teacher. I have never refused to teach them nor do the coloured Committee wish to prevent me unless the white children (should they attend the School) abuse the coloured children

The Coloured people are busy with the new School House I have cash promises to the amount of about £10 and as soon as the present Snow goes away they will put it up immediately it would have been up long before this but for obstacles thrown in their way by the very

25.8 cm x 20.6 cm

National Archives of Canada,
Manuscript Division,
MG 27, I, D 15, Vol. 7.

Fugitive Slaves in Canada. Posters

William King was born in Ireland in 1812. After studying theology at the University of Glasgow, he migrated to Louisiana where, through marriage, he came to possess slaves. As a practicing Presbyterian minister, Reverend King could not countenance slavery. He freed his slaves and led them north into Canada to escape the draconian Fugitive Slave Laws of 1850 (Britain had abolished slavery throughout the Empire in 1833). Once in southwestern Canada, appeals to the Christian community and the government brought $18,000.00 and a land grant of 9,000 acres in Raleigh township, near Buxton. He and his former slaves founded a black settlement there, named Elgin in honour of their patron, Governor-in-Chief of Canada, Lord Elgin.

Throughout the 1850s, as the slavery issue wrenched apart the American union, it found a powerful resonance north of the border. Slavery then was a great moral issue — churchmen, social leaders and politicians inveighed against this "abomination." A vocal Anti-Slavery Society and George Brown's *Globe* waged an unrelenting campaign against it. The publication of Harriet Beecher Stowe's *Uncle Tom's Cabin* heightened the campaign. In the strongly anti-slavery environment of Upper Canada, Harriet Tubman, working from her St. Catharines base, managed the "Underground Railroad" for a decade, a chain of safe houses leading out of the United States into Canada which sheltered fugitive slaves as they made their way north to freedom.

Perhaps 30,000 slaves reached Canada along Tubman's "railroad," settling in the Windsor-to-Hamilton corridor. They founded other communities modelled after the Elgin settlement, especially in the Buxton-Chatham-Dresden area. None of these later communities, however, received free land grants, and thus many newly-arrived blacks became day labourers. Set off in their own communities, blacks developed a sense of unity; they also fell victim to an attenuated discrimination. Nonetheless, the 1850s were years of achievement for blacks in Canada. Henry Bibb, for example, in 1851 began to publish out of Windsor, *The Voice of the Fugitive*, the first black newspaper in Canada; and Mary Ann Shadd did much to advance the cause of black education in the populous and vibrant black communities of Upper Canada. At the close of the American Civil War, very large numbers of blacks, including Tubman, left Upper Canada for the United States. Many were drawn back by family ties; and many left after experiencing various hardships and disappointments in a new land.

The anti-slavery movement, much like the Temperance movement, had been a great moral crusade. The posters shown here reflect the black experience in Upper Canada in the 1850s, and give evidence of the role played in this crusade by churchmen, including Reverend King himself.

Reverend William King. 1859.

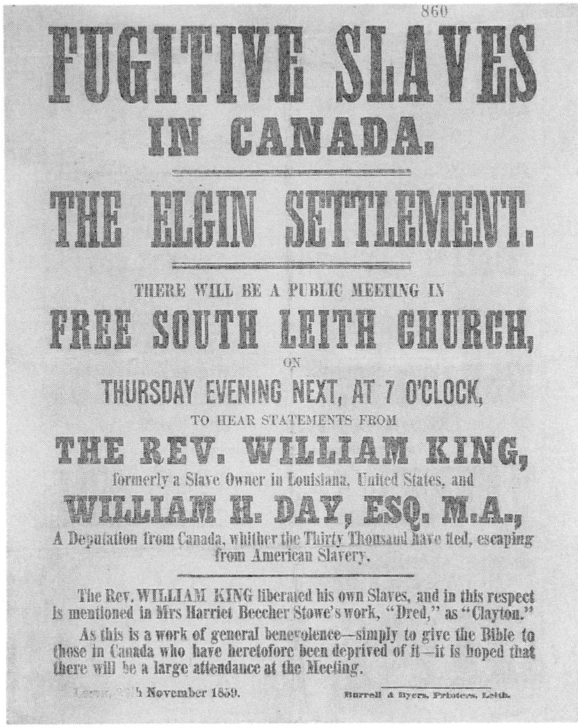

860

FUGITIVE SLAVES
IN CANADA.

THE ELGIN SETTLEMENT.

THERE WILL BE A PUBLIC MEETING IN
FREE SOUTH LEITH CHURCH,
ON
THURSDAY EVENING NEXT, AT 7 O'CLOCK,
TO HEAR STATEMENTS FROM
THE REV. WILLIAM KING,
formerly a Slave Owner in Louisiana, United States, and
WILLIAM H. DAY, ESQ. M.A.,
A Deputation from Canada, whither the Thirty Thousand have fled, escaping from American Slavery.

The Rev. WILLIAM KING liberated his own Slaves, and in this respect is mentioned in Mrs Harriet Beecher Stowe's work, "Dred," as "Clayton."

As this is a work of general benevolence—simply to give the Bible to those in Canada who have heretofore been deprived of it—it is hoped that there will be a large attendance at the Meeting.

[illegible] h November 1859. Burrell & Byers, Printers, Leith.

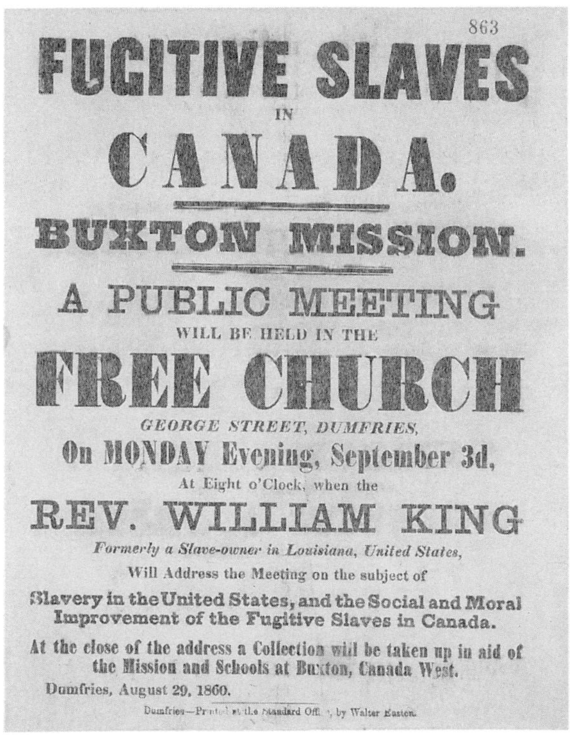

863

FUGITIVE SLAVES
IN
CANADA.

BUXTON MISSION.

A PUBLIC MEETING
WILL BE HELD IN THE
FREE CHURCH
GEORGE STREET, DUMFRIES,
On MONDAY Evening, September 3d,
At Eight o'Clock, when the
REV. WILLIAM KING
Formerly a Slave-owner in Louisiana, United States,
Will Address the Meeting on the subject of
Slavery in the United States, and the Social and Moral Improvement of the Fugitive Slaves in Canada.

At the close of the address a Collection will be taken up in aid of the Mission and Schools at Buxton, Canada West.

Dumfries, August 29, 1860.

Dumfries—Printed at the Standard Office, by Walter Easton.

31.6 cm x 25 cm
28.6 cm x 22.1 cm

National Archives of Canada,
Manuscript Division,
MG 24, J 14, p. 860, p. 863.

Universities: Incorporations and Significant Events

Higher education in the British North American colonies came into its own in the 1850s and 1860s, as the commemorative university medals shown here attest.

Of the universities commemorated by these medals, the University of New Brunswick had the most established roots. Founded in 1785 as the Provincial Academy of Arts and Sciences, after several reorganizations it became in 1859 the University of New Brunswick. McGill University traced its origin back to 1813, to a rich endowment bequeathed by the merchant James McGill to the cause of higher education. While McGill was chartered in 1821, the issue of tertiary education in Montreal was resolved only in 1852, when the Royal Institution for the Advancement of Learning, founded in 1801 in response to a popular demand for public education, finally amalgamated with McGill. The University of Toronto, (although chartered in 1827 as King's College), was founded in 1842, but took final form only in 1849-1850 after a furious debate over the role of the church in state-funded education. Founded in 1843 by Joseph Mountain, Anglican Archbishop of Quebec, Bishop's College won university status in 1853. Laval University opened in 1852, the first francophone university in North America, named after Monsignor François de Laval, who in 1663 had established the Seminaire de Québec.

Most colonial universities, at the time of their establishment, had been affiliated with religious denominations. This era, however, saw the decline of church affiliation for universities, particularly following the celebrated University of Toronto struggle. Bishop John Strachan, Anglican Bishop of Toronto, pressed the case for the established Anglican Church in education as in politics. He was opposed by A. Egerton Ryerson, a Methodist minister, an educator and, from 1844 to 1876, Superintendent of Education for Canada West and, later, Ontario. Ryerson advocated a Christian-based non-denominational common education; but he furiously opposed the notion that government should publicly fund a denominational (Anglican) University of Toronto. The result of this conflict produced a secularized University of Toronto, based on the principle of separation of church and state in all educational institutions funded out of the public purse. This development established the pattern for future provincial universities, although privately funded denominational universities did not disappear.

Secularization was not only politically advisable in a time when religious passions burned hot in public and social life; it was a sign that colonial universities were coming out of local parochialism, reflecting a broadening of horizons and a transition to modernity. In Quebec, however, the church-state link in higher education would hold strong for another century.

nd, 1860-1864.

4.5 cm (diameter) bronze
3.9 cm (diameter) white metal
4 cm (diameter) bronze
4 cm (diameter) bronze
4.5 cm (diameter) bronze

National Archives of Canada,
Documentary Art and Photography Division,
McGill University 1864 C-57452,
University of New Brunswick 1860 C-42905,
University of Toronto nd C-42865,
Laval University nd C-42871,
Bishop's University 1860 C-47262.

Indian Treaty No. 148 (Robinson-Lake Huron)

As colonial populations grew through natural increase and immigration, as more land was brought under the plow, it became more imperative to deal with the original occupants of the land, the native peoples. This was particularly the case in Upper Canada, where, by 1850, a great deal of the good, arable land south of the Pre-Cambrian Shield had been occupied. Also by 1850 a preliminary pattern of Indian land cessation had been established. The pattern was premised on the *Royal Proclamation of 1763*, which had recognized Indian ownership of land. Indian tribes could surrender ownership of land, but only to a duly-appointed representative of the Crown.

This Treaty reflects the above developments. Farmers of Canada West were moving northwest. Mining companies were also beginning their early activity in the Province of Canada, opening mineral deposits near Sault Ste. Marie. In 1849, in fact, Indian resentment against the operations of the Quebec Mining Company at Mica Bay on Lake Superior had lead to a dangerous situation, with the conflict earning the name of the "Michipicoten War."

William B. Robinson, a former Commissioner of Public Works, was commissioned to negotiate the transfer to the Crown of lands along the northern and eastern shores of Lake Huron from Sault Ste. Marie to Penetanguishene (from the shoreline inland to the Hudson's Bay Company's territory), including all islands in Lake Superior. Robinson concluded such a treaty. For a lump sum payment of £2,000, and an annuity of £600, sixteen chiefs of Ojibway bands ceded the lands affected to the Crown. The first clear definition of Indian reserves appeared with this Treaty, securing at least a portion of former lands for Indian bands. In what would also prove to be a common feature of future treaties, Indians were permitted to hunt and fish in ceded lands, except when these were sold or leased by the Crown. The Treaty established three Indian reserves. Equally important, it set a precedent for a number of other significant treaties (Robinson-Superior in 1850, Saugeen in 1854, and Manitoulin Island in 1862) which peacefully completed the transfer of non-Hudson's Bay Company land to the Province of Canada.

United Kingdom: Office of the Governor-in-Chief of Canada. 1850.

This Agreement made and entered into this Ninth day of September in the year of our Lord One thousand, eight hundred and fifty, at Sault Ste Marie in the Province of Canada, between the Honorable William Benjamin Robinson of the one part, on behalf of Her Majesty the Queen, and

71.1 cm x 48.2 cm

National Archives of Canada,
Government Archives Division,
RG 10, Vol. 1844.

III

"The Attention of Emigrants, Old Settlers, and Others is Invited By the Canada Company to their Huron Lands..."

The Canada Company was conceived as a colonization corporation by John Galt (1779-1839) of Scotland. Chartered in 1825, it was dissolved only in 1953. In 1826 it acquired 2,500,000 acres of land to settle, half of which were scattered throughout Canada, while the other half were consolidated in the Huron Tract, which this promotional advertisement describes. This company literature reflects an interesting experiment in organized settlement of Canada.

Even allowing for promotional hyperbole, this publication contains interesting historical data. For example, it touts the easy communications of the region, noting the existence of a "Plank Road" between Hamilton, London and Port Stanley, other good roads, developed harbours and ease of water communication, all of which would appeal to settlers. It demonstrates the "push-pull" phenomenon of immigration, observing that new settlers would often meet former old-country neighbours settled in Canada, and notes how ethnic groups tended to settle in their own communities. It recounts that there was already at that time a substantial number of Germans established in Canada. And it gives evidence of the rapidly increasing population in Canada West, pointing out that in its Huron Tract the population had increased fourfold in seven years, from 7,101 in 1842 to 26,000 in 1849.

The Company's achievements were spotty, its commitment to immigration and colonization questionable. The verdict is still out on how effective such colonization companies were; but, for better or worse, they did play a role in the development of Canada.

Canada Company. 1850.

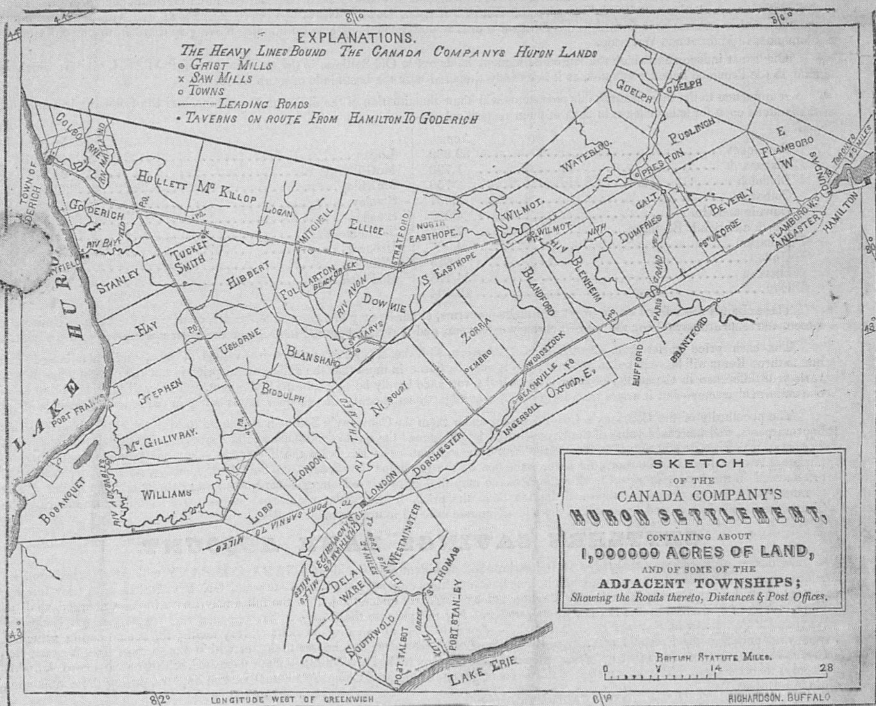

LANDS IN CANADA WEST (LATE UPPER CANADA).

THE ATTENTION OF

EMIGRANTS, OLD SETTLERS, AND OTHERS,

IS INVITED BY THE CANADA COMPANY TO THEIR

HURON LANDS,

CONSISTING OF A BLOCK OF

ONE MILLION ACRES OF LAND,

Extending Westward from the Gore and Wellington Districts to the Shores of Lake Huron, which bounds it for sixty miles.

The Land in the Canada Company's Huron Settlement is of the finest character, and of the description best adapted to the cultivation of Wheat. This Settlement possesses advantages which render it peculiarly eligible to every class of Settler: scarcely a bad Farm is to be found in it: it is well watered by living Streams, and the climate is most healthy. The principal Port is Goderich, the District Town, which has a population of about 1200—good Stores or Shops, Mechanics, a large Grist Mill, a Fulling and Carding Mill, an Iron Foundry, places of Religious Worship, resident Clergymen, and good Schools, where the higher branches of the Classics are taught, &c. &c. &c.

33.1 cm x 20.9 cm

National Archives of Canada,
Manuscript Division,
MG 24, I 46, Vol. 1.

III

"London, Canada West"

London, a significant regional centre in Canada, began to experience discernible changes from mid-century onwards. A large influx of settlers came to the London area in the 1830s. Following the failed rebellions of 1837 it became a garrison town, which spurred its growth. Improved communications through the 1840s and 1850s, best represented in the appearance of the Great Western Railway in 1854, further stimulated development. By 1855, incorporated as a city, London's future was assured. Railway construction in the area, continued settlement of its fertile hinterland and an incipient oil boom to the west of the city boded well for London, which by that time was a diocesan seat, and a budding centre of finance, brewing and light manufacturing.

This print by Endicott & Co. of New York shows London in transition. There is much of the pre-railway, pre-industrial era reflected here. Livestock grazes right up to the periphery of the city, and waters in the Thames River. Worked fields stretch away on all sides. In the foreground, people repose, or boat, or fish. Nature and agriculture, in bucolic serenity, press right up against the city.

However, the city and its tempo of life are changing. From the mid-lower left a train steams into London, on a highly banked up rail-bed; and the railway bridge, by comparison to the other bridges, is a massive construction engineered of iron girders. Just south of the railway tracks laid on the southern edge of town is a new growth area, where industrial or manufacturing concerns are opening up to take advantage of the railway. Throughout the city itself, smokestacks of factories or shops, at least ten of them, rear up. And as indicated in the legend, the city had its own gas works, the main purpose of which was to illuminate city streets.

Perhaps this scene should not to be taken literally. Edwin Whitefield may have packed it, "condensing" rural well-being with comfortable urban prosperity to make a point. Some of the smokestacks may have been added for effect. This admitted, however, fundamental change is coming upon the city. Improved communications (roads, and then the railways) and the rise of manufacturing concerns denote the entry of the city into a new era, into industrial manufacturing. London never lost the agrarian connection with its hinterland, and never became an industrial town of the first magnitude. But, as this print suggests, in an experience it shared with many Canadian towns in the mid-nineteenth century, London stepped out of an exclusively agrarian domination and into a new age.

After Edwin Whitefield. 1855.

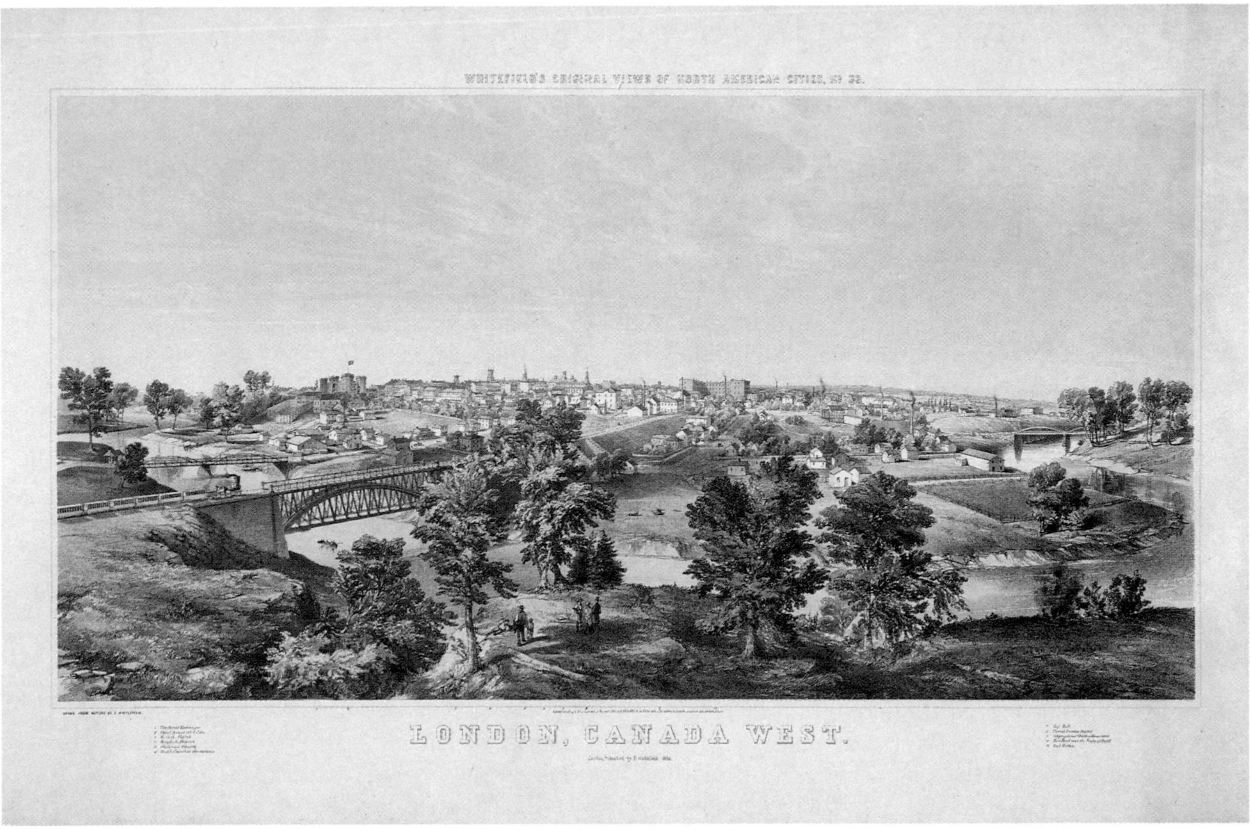

WHITEFIELD'S ORIGINAL VIEWS OF NORTH AMERICAN CITIES,
LONDON, CANADA WEST.

48.3 cm x 91.7 cm

National Archives of Canada,
Documentary Art and Photography Division,
C-612.

III

"Immigration Decrease and Remedies Suggested"

Until the mid-nineteenth century, the British colonies in North America were characterized by slow and erratic settlement. In 1847-1848 came the waves of "Famine Irish," fleeing famine in their homeland. The "Famine Irish" altered the former immigration pattern of largely English and Scottish migrants — including the Protestant Irish, most of whom were descended of Scots and English who had settled earlier in Northern Ireland — to the British colonies in North America.

Though coming from an area of the United Kingdom and speaking English, differences in religion, culture and outlook made the "Famine Irish" the first "foreign" migrants to come en masse to British North America, and they were treated as such. They were Roman Catholics in a largely Protestant society (save in Canada East); in an age when conformity was required to prove loyalty to the British Crown, the Irish were thus already suspect.

They successfully took up farming when they could purchase land, which was no longer freely granted in the colonies. They also worked as day labourers, digging canals, laying down railway lines, logging the forests and working the dockyards of major colonial ports. Some of this was seasonal work in the rough outback where men drank and brawled lustily as they worked. This only reinforced the prevailing perception held by established, Protestant colonial society that the Irish, suspect in religion and loyalty, were also migratory drunks and brawlers, and a cheap labour force to be used and abused.

Irish working-class neighbourhoods appeared in most colonial cities and towns. By 1871 the Irish were the dominant ethnic group in every urban centre in Canada save Montreal and Quebec City, and they constituted sizable wards in the major Maritime centres. They also settled in the countryside, particularly in regions recently cleared of timber, and often on marginal land. By the mid-nineteenth century, half a dozen counties in the Maritimes and most of the counties east of Toronto to the Ottawa River valley had strong Irish populations.

The arrival of the largely destitute "Famine Irish" led the colonies to legislate restrictive laws to exclude the infirm, ill and impoverished. This slowed immigration; and yet the colonies were very much in need of immigrants. The Irish, immigration restrictions, the ongoing need for settlers — these concerns are reflected in the document displayed here, prepared by Alexander Carlisle Buchanan.

Buchanan (1808-1868) was Chief Immigration Agent in the Province of Canada. His work was hampered by the colonial government's inefficiency and lack of co-ordination in immigration activity. Dedicated to his task, Buchanan strove to provide for and to protect immigrants. He argued for a forward recruiting policy in Europe, which was realized only in 1869, when the Dominion government finally opened a central immigration agency in London.

This document is a record of the response to questions put to Buchanan by a committee of the Legislature. He explains the dramatic fall-off of immigration, especially Irish, during the 1850s; he demonstrates the much greater attraction of the United States over the British colonies to immigrants (in fact, a majority of the "Famine Irish" resettled in the United States); and he enumerates the various measures a concerned government has undertaken to promote immigration to Canada, including agents abroad in foreign lands and promotional literature in foreign languages.

It is worth noting that these considerations — selection of immigration source, the powerful attraction of the United States, and governmental promotion of immigration — still affect Canadian immigration to this day. Moreover, Buchanan's promotional program foreshadowed the future policy of Sir Clifford Sifton in the 1890s, with the exception that Sifton would turn to central and eastern Europe, as well as traditional sources, for immigrants to Canada.

Alexander Carlisle Buchanan. 1860.

4.

Decrease of Immigration and Remedies suggested.

J. P. O'Hanley Esq. P. L. S. Ottawa 1860.

Ques. 15. What, in your opinion, has been the cause of the progressive decrease of emigration into Canada?—I shall confine my reply to Irish emigration, for it is to that only I have given attention; and because it is only with the causes of of their emigration that I am sufficiently acquainted to offer any evidence. During the y ears 1846, '47, '48, famine and destitution pressed so heavily on the Irish people, that emigration became with the peasantry or lower classes an absolute necessity. It is not surprising that people in their circumstances would seek the cheapest route across the Atlantic; and unladen vessels sailing to the Port of Quebec for cargoes of timber, offered them a cheaper passage than the regular American and Liverpool Packets. But as the cause of this exodus has been gradually removed, the effect has likewise in a corresponding ratio ceased. Those only emigrate now who have friends in this Hemisphere, or who are ambitious of seeking their fortune, or bettering their condition; besides a new field for emigration has been opened in Australia. The Irish in the United States also continue to draw their relatives in large numbers to themselves. I have recently read in an American paper, taken from the bank statistics of the State of New York, that in the year 1859 the Irish of that State sent to their friends in Ireland the almost incredible sum of £1,000,000 sterling, chiefly to assist their relatives in reaching the States. Of course all these sailed in vessels bound for American ports. The arrivals at New York last year were 2,000 in excess of 1858.

Ques. 16. What means, in your opinion, would be best calculated to increase a productive emigration into Canada?—I would suggest that an Agent or Agents be sent to the British Isles, with correct and reliable information relative to the advantages offered in th s country to intending emigrants, shewing the rate of wages in different localities, the price of land in partly settled districts, and in the unsettled tracts; the cost and kind of living; the certainty of procuring employment, whether mechanic or labourer; the various routes of travel and the respective fares; the state of the highways; the quality and productiveness of the soil; the principal cities; the distance from market; the proximity of church and school; and the certainty of making a comfortable livelihood. I would recommend above all things that these Agents should not delude the emigrant with hopes of peedy wealth, thereby creating false hopes and certain disappointment, than which, nothing can be more detrimental to the character of the country in the public mind at home. These Agents should be well provided with maps of the newly surveyed districts, and should act under carefully prepared instructions from the Government.

With respect to the latter part of the question: I think it very wrong to induce emigrants to settle on land in the "Bush" for the first year; for they are wholly unacquainted with the improvements of husbandry used here, and the system of farming in the forest; and before they should attempt it they should learn this. But after one year's probation, I cannot too strongly recommend that every inducement be held out to them, such as free grants, to commence farming. And I believe by adopting this system, that 2,000 settlers could annually be introduced into the unsettled parts of the Ottawa Valley.

A. C. Buchanan Chief Emigrant Agent 1860.

Ques. 104. What in your opinion are the chief causes of the decline of the European Emigration to this Province?—A principal cause is undoubtedly to be found in the present condition of the British and Irish laboring population. According to authorities that are entitled to confidence, the increased average rates of wages of agricultural and manufacturing operatives and almost all classes of labourers, taken in connection with the reduced cost of a large proportion of their necessaries of life, have made a difference in the resources of these classes which reaches 33 and even 40 per cent. Under such circumstances, it has followed that emigration from the mother country has diminished generally in a large degree: and there is little doubt that even had things remained in the same condition in regard to Canada separately considered, our immigration must have fallen off to a considerable extent. —The emigration from the United Kingdom to all parts amounted in the five years ending with 1854 to - - - - - - - - - 1,639,005

And in the five years ending with 1859 to - - - - - - 794,180

The emigration to Canada has fallen off in a much larger ratio than that from the United Kingdom to all parts, as will appear from the following statement:—

	1850 to 1854.	1855 to 1859.
Emigration from England	56,600	40,865
Emigration from Scotland	26,589	13,093
Emigration from Ireland	86,918	17,385
	170,107	71,343

From a consideration of this comparative statement, it appears plain that, independently of the reduction in the emigration from the United Kingdom, this Province has been suffering from some causes specially affecting the route to Quebec.

The Imperial Passengers Act of 1855 has materially added to the security as well as the comfort of the Emigrant on his passage; but inasmuch as its regulations are more stringent than those of the American Law, and particularly since they are very strictly enforced, the shipowner appears to consider the Quebec voyage less advantageous to him than that to New York, even when his prospects of a full Steerage are equal. In confirmation I beg to submit extracts from letters received from highly respectable shipowners in the United Kingdom.

32.6 cm x 18.8 cm

National Archives of Canada,
Manuscript Division,
RG 14, C 3, Vol. 4.

"View on Barnaby River, New Brunswick"
and also
"New Clearing — 'Ireland' — Grenville"

The first photograph, taken by an anonymous photographer employed by Sir Sandford Fleming on the Intercolonial Railway, shows railway men, probably a surveying crew, in the Barnaby River valley; the Barnaby River flows into the Miramichi from the south, just upstream of Newcastle. What is more interesting is how the photograph comments on established agriculture. The land is cleared of stone; probably the river valley had easier soil to work, relatively free of stone. In the background rich-looking fields undulate away gently, and other farms are visible in the distance. Around the wood-frame house constructed of sawn lumber in the mid-ground is a fine log fence. The whole scene depicts well-established agriculture in a fertile river valley.

Alexander Henderson's photograph, on the other hand, reflects agriculture in the rough. Henderson, born in Scotland in 1831, emigrated to Montreal in 1855. A man of means, photography for him was a hobby; and even when he took it up professionally, his economic independence allowed him to photograph as an artist, rather than have to photograph what his clients paid for. His images, including the photograph "New Clearing," are a rich legacy of this era; the photograph was originally published in his *Canadian Views and Studies*, an album produced for public sale in 1865.

"New Clearing" shows the establishment of agriculture in the Grenville area, on the north shore of the lower Ottawa River valley, in Canada East. The land is decidedly hilly, while the ground is carpeted with rocks and stones. Stumps still stand, and they, along with the rock and stone, imply the magnitude of the task before the settlers' farming can begin. The settlers have just raised their dwelling (note the fresh shingles and the roof boards still protruding over the gable end of the home, yet to be trimmed away). The cabin is of squared logs; the upper gable end, however, is of sawn lumber, indicating accessibility to a saw mill nearby. To the right of the cabin is the hooded portable developing tent in which this photograph's negative was developed. The technology of photography of that time required immediate processing, which is why photographers on the road packed exceedingly heavy loads of equipment and supplies with them.

The two photographs are a study in contrast in agriculture. On good soil or bad, established or just clearing, more than half of the population of the colonies lived by agriculture and, at the time of Confederation, more than 50 per cent of houses in Canada were of log construction.

Anonymous. ca 1870.

Alexander Henderson. ante 1865.

13.6 cm x 18.5 cm
11.5 cm x 19.3 cm

National Archives of Canada,
Documentary Art and Photography Division,
[Anonymous] PA-22119,
[Henderson] PA-181769.

III

Lower Canada and Upper Canada Agricultural Medals

Before 1850, local agricultural associations had come into existence in the colonies; in fact, a Society for Promoting Agriculture in Nova Scotia had been founded as early as 1791. However, it was only in mid-century, when agricultural life quickened and began to shed its early pioneer practices and values, that agrarian organizations began to play more significant roles in colonial life.

In the Province of Canada the Agricultural Association of Upper Canada and the Société d'agriculture du Bas Canada had been chartered in 1846 and 1847 respectively, to co-ordinate the activity of local societies. The provincial government also created the Board of Agriculture of Upper Canada in 1851 and the Chambre d'agriculture du Bas Canada in 1852 as quasi-governmental institutions to provide leadership in the development of agriculture. Such organizational activity was capped in 1852 with the creation of a Bureau of Agriculture with its own minister.

These developments were a reflection of fundamental changes in agriculture, which employed half of the population at that time. The above-named agencies, as well as the local associations under them, were authorized to operate model farms and acquire new model machinery, to purchase improved seed and animal stock, and to disseminate scientific farming knowledge among their membership through the publication of journals, discussion sessions and invitation of agronomists and various experts to address their memberships.

All such activity was geared to increasing farm productivity through the application of new knowledge. Agriculture was in the midst of a sea-change. Rationalized utilization of time and the use of best seed and improved livestock, as well as improved machinery, would maximize production and profits — so read the farm literature of the time, breathing the entrepreneurial spirit which made the agricultural revolution possible, and which agricultural associations wished to impart to farmers.

The medals displayed here were awarded to farmers at provincial agricultural fairs in recognition of achievement. But they also strove to promote agriculture and scientific farming by imparting to the agrarian calling a new dignity equal to the profession of arms, for farmers also served monarch and men. This is well reflected in the Chambre d'agriculture du Bas Canada medal, created by Armand A. Caqué, engraver to Napoleon III, who assembled pictorial representations of farm animals, activities and implements in a shield, topped by two cornucopias from which flow sheaves of wheat. Above the shield, in the centre, sits a somewhat emaciated beaver. The motto "Pratique avec Science" can be translated as "Apply knowledge," encapsulating in several words the spirit underlying the modernization of agriculture in the British colonies of North America.

nd, 1860, 1868.

National Archives of Canada,
Documentary Art and Photography Division,
[Lower Canada Agricultural Association] 1860 C-110009,
[Lower Canada Agricultural Association] 1868 C-110015,
[Upper Canada Agricultural Association] nd C-127904,
[Upper Canada Agricultural Association] nd C-138582.

4.2 cm (diameter) silver
4.2 cm (diameter) silver
4.6 cm (diameter) silver
4.6 cm (diameter) bronze

"Certain Improvements in the Method of Constructing Threshing Machines"

In the mid-nineteenth century, agriculture in the British colonies of North America underwent significant and increasingly rapid change. Until then, most agricultural implements — such as hoes, rakes, scythes, flails and even plows — were fashioned from wood, often home-made or crafted at a local smithy. Most agricultural activity was very labour-intensive. The agricultural revolution — based, among other factors, on new, mechanized modes of performing farm labour — led to much greater productivity. Agriculture could thus free up hands for expanding factories, and could certainly produce more than enough excess foodstuffs to feed growing urban centres and export large amounts of grain overseas.

Many things made the agricultural revolution possible: new and better seed, better breeding of farm animals, and, very importantly, the development of scientific husbandry and the dissemination of sound agricultural practices through agricultural societies and model farms. However, the appearance of new technology, itself based on the "iron revolution," was key to the fundamental changes that appeared in agriculture at this time. Whereas earlier the local smithy might have produced agricultural implements, now large manufacturers produced them in factories, concentrated at the western end of Lake Ontario. From here, through a burgeoning rail network, they had access to the rich American and Upper Canadian agricultural markets.

One such manufacturer was John Abell (1822-1903). He migrated to Canada in 1845, settling in Woodbridge. An inventive man, he turned his talents to mechanical improvement of agricultural implements. By 1862 he had a large operation, employing more than 100 men. Abell won a reputation for his threshing machines. Until mechanization, the grain harvested in fall was threshed on barn floors; the kernels were separated from the straw by treading with farm animals or beating with flails. A mechanical thresher greatly eased the operation. The threshing machine consisted of a cylinder with rasp bars that rotated against fixed bars. Grain fed through the thresher would be shaken and abraded; under the impact, seed would separate from straw. The document shown here is a patent application for one of Abell's many inventions; it describes proposed improvements in the construction of a threshing machine, and in the gearing mechanism for driving it.

Abell's Woodbridge works were destroyed by fire in 1874. Afterward he relocated to Toronto, where his factory prospered. His machinery won very many prizes over the years. This document attests to Abell's inventiveness, as well as to the fundamental changes occurring in Canadian life, and the coming of the agrarian revolution, without which later urban-centred and industrialized society would not have been possible.

John Abell. 1859.

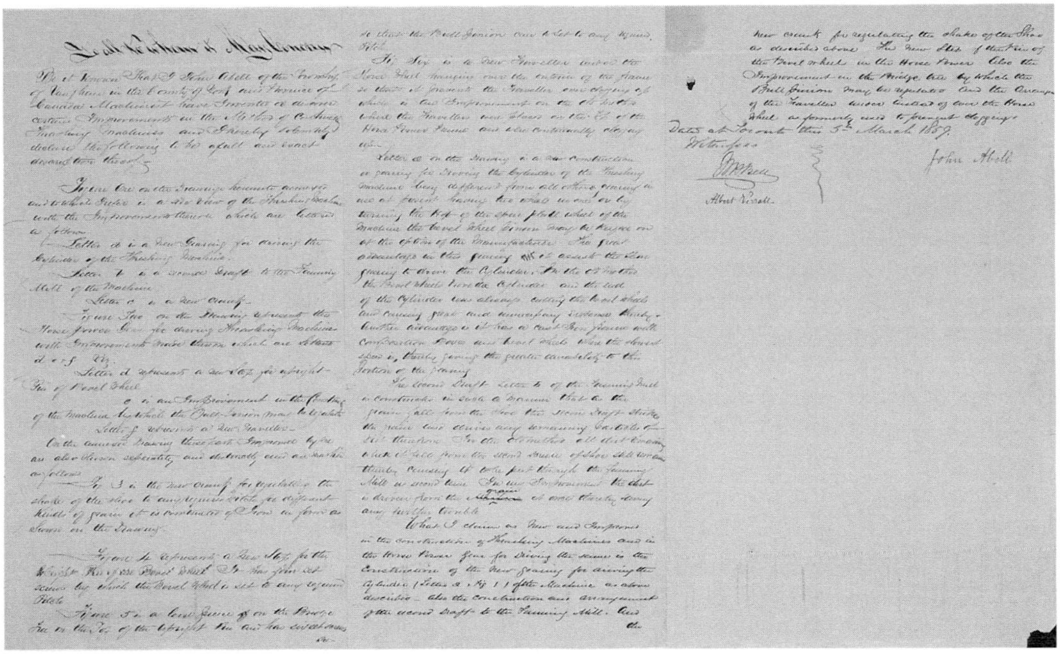

73.7 cm x 53.3 cm

National Archives of Canada,
Government Archives Division,
RG 125, Vol. 27, case 289.

"Charlevoix and Chicoutimi Counties — Roads. Malbaie and Grand Baie Roads"

This survey was prepared by G.F. Baillairgé at the request of the Department of Public Works of the Province of Canada. Baillairgé was to locate the best route for a road leading from Malbaie on the St. Lawrence to Grande Baie on the Saguenay, in country that was being opened up for colonization in a land-hungry Canada East. The Department had commenced a road into the region 15 years earlier; it now wished to determine if this route, with 45 miles of it in various stages of construction, should not be abandoned for a newer, easier route.

Once Baillairgé had completed his investigations, he prepared this map as an accompaniment to a report that he submitted to the Department in 1862. The document is much more than a map. The manuscript text on the right-hand side and annotations throughout the map portion actually recount a history of attempts to develop communications into the region, and assess the region for its economic viability. Baillairgé comments on the nature of terrain and topography, noting the location of tillable land. He reports on types of forests located along the roads, both existing and proposed. On the basis of such information, government made informed decisions on how best to open land for settlement and agriculture.

Baillairgé recommended a new route for the road, to be called the Chemin Cartier. In support of his proposal, he pointed out that the new road would be shorter than the one underway, would make settlement of planned new townships easier and would travel through potentially richer farmland. In his most telling point, he indicates that, through "natural selection" in this terrain, habitants are already using his proposed Chemin Cartier as a winter road, and are desirous of the government upgrading it to a "summer road" as well. (It should be recalled that winter travel, on sleighs over snow, was far easier than summer travel through mud, hard dry ruts or potholes). The Department, probably because of money already invested in the original route, did not accept Baillairgé's recommendations.

The map, colourful and filled with commentary and text on roads and road-building in the region, is historical evidence of the importance assigned by colonial government to land communication and in the form of colonization roads.

George Frédéric Baillairgé. 1862.

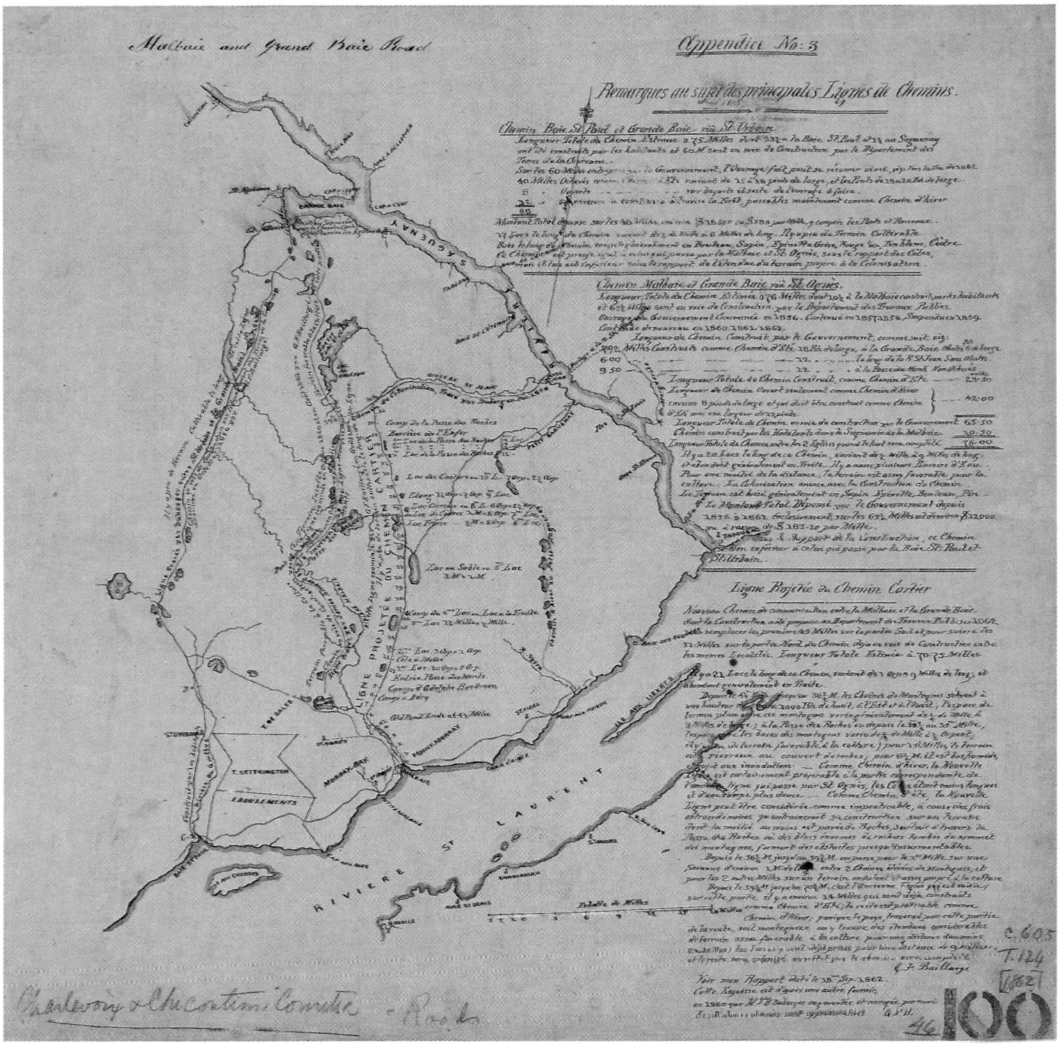

40 cm x 37 cm

National Archives of Canada,
Cartographic and Audio-Visual Archives Division,
NMC-1237.

"Field Notes of Township of Fisher, Etc."

Immigration and settlement were of primary importance to the British colonies. As A.C. Buchanan, Chief Emigrant Agent for Canada, declared in 1860, "a first and chief object of the Province of Canada must be the acquisition of colonists for the occupation and profitable settlement of her wild lands." Before settlement could actually occur the land had to be acquired from its aboriginal owners by treaty, and then laid out in concessions and lots by surveyors.

The surveyors of the British colonies performed arduous work, especially those who went into lands where few, if any, whites had been. Using a few simple instruments (the surveyor's chain 66 feet long, theodolite, magnetic compass, and levels and barometers for vertical measure), they laid out township boundaries, concession roads and farm lots. Surveyors sloshed through bogs, crossed rivers and creeks, and scratched their way through dense forests. They often worked in winter to avoid the frightful insects of the forest; but they paid a price for this relief, suffering the winter cold and snows. While the grander expeditions, like Palliser's and Hind's, acquired knowledge on a grand scale about the British colonies and the future Dominion, the ordinary survey men, who went into the unmarked bush, contributed no less to opening the land.

George Kirkpatrick was such a surveyor. Working out of Kingston, he was contracted by the province in 1865 to lay out a number of townships in the Batchewaung Bay area of the Algoma District, the most northwesterly point ceded by the Ojibway in the Robinson-Huron Treaty of 1850. The document displayed here is from Kirkpartrick's field survey notes of the township of Fisher, showing the concession road laid out between sections one and twelve of that township. One can see from the record that surveyors, in addition to laying out land boundaries, accumulated much useful detail on virgin lands and commented on types of forest. They also captured in drawings and maps, the nature of terrain and the relief of the land they worked. In addition, they prepared extensive manuscript notes on the flora and fauna, geography and geology of areas surveyed.

Whether in the form of manuscript notes or in the artistic geometry of survey drawings, Kirkpatrick's notes attest to the invaluable contributions of surveyors to mid-nineteenth century society in the colonies of British North America.

George Brownly Kirkpatrick. 1865.

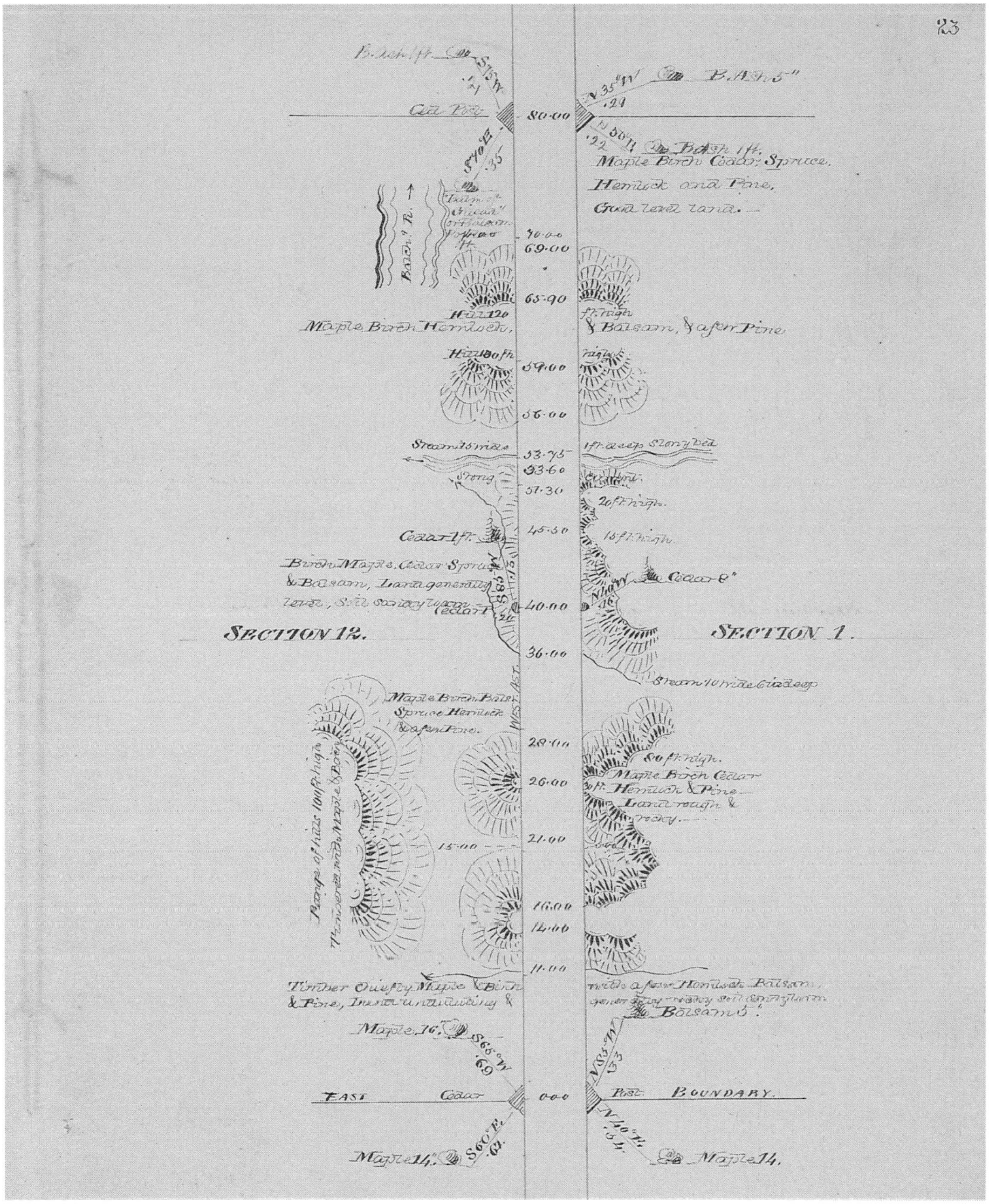

25.4 cm x 20 cm

National Archives of Canada,
Manuscript Division,
MG 9, D-8, No. 50, p. 23.

"Toronto, Canada West. From the Top of the Jail"

In the 1840s Toronto became a busy steamboat port; gaslighting and sewers made their appearance, an indication that the city was coming into its own as a significant urban centre. Toronto benefitted greatly from the railway boom of the 1850s; by the end of the decade, a web of railways radiated out to centres in New York State, to Montreal, to Georgian Bay and westward along the Hamilton-London-Windsor-Detroit corridor. Although its harbour was Toronto's original *raison d'être*, the railway network strengthened the city's hold over an increasingly large economic hinterland. Transportation, wholesaling of staples, banking, manufacturing and servicing railway needs were the cornerstones of Toronto's regional pre-eminence.

In this appealing handcoloured lithograph, printed by Endicott & Co. of New York, we have the image of a healthy, vibrant town. The focal point of the image is the harbour, wharves jutting out, with lake schooners and steamboats either moored or in motion. On the wharves, or stacked just behind them, is the quintessential staple of the day — lumber. Between the harbour and the town lies the Esplanade, down which traffic moves. In the 1850s, railways arrived at the waterfront, built on lands released from garrison reserves along the lakefront; thus began the transport zone which sundered the city proper from its harbour.

Behind the Esplanade are comfortable-looking homes built on streets laid out in a regular grid. Significant buildings, many of them still standing, are identified on the print. Churches of the major denominations dominate the skyline — St. James', St. Andrew's, St. Michael's, St. George's and others. The Lunatic Asylum, then recently built, seems lost in greenery far to the west of the city. In fact, just in from the harbourfront the whole city seems lost in trees, with no perceptible border in the distance between city and countryside.

But signs of change are already evident in the several smokestacks which, as they rise up among the church steeples in the very centre of Toronto, emit plumes of smoke. Industry is making its appearance, and within several decades, the greenery would be gone, replaced by shops and factories at the terminal ends of the transport zone which is still visible in this lithograph.

After Edwin Whitefield. 1854.

48.6 cm x 90.5 cm

National Archives of Canada,
Documentary Art and Photography Division,
C-46109.

III

Lumberman's Shanty Diary

During the era covered by this exhibition, timber dominated commercial activity. Logs and squared-timber rafts made their way down rivers great and small to sawmills for processing or to port cities for export. Railway lines opened new hinterlands for the exploitation of forest wealth. Lumber merchants grew rich, and influenced the course of politics. Europe was hungry for lumber; and the small lumber preference which Britain allowed until 1860 after the dismantling of the mercantile system secured for the British colonies a very significant lumber market. In addition, the Reciprocity Treaty of 1854 opened up the American market for the colonies. Millions of linear feet of logs and squared timber, and millions of board feet of sawn lumber and staves, left the colonies, and later Canada, for markets abroad. It was perhaps a fitting apotheosis that Ottawa, the lumber capital, standing on a river down which floated the forest wealth of the interior to the St. Lawrence ports, was also chosen as the political capital, first of the Province, and later of the Dominion of Canada.

Members of the Meech family were important players in the lumber trade in the Ottawa area. Charles George Meech, who maintained this "shanty" diary, was the son of the prominent lumber merchant, Asa Meech. Charles Meech was often away, working the rivers and forests north of the Ottawa River, and managing shanty operations. The shanties became fully operational in early winter, when loggers would fell trees and transport them over snow to river banks or to timber slides in preparation for the spring break-up. This diary records Meech's winter experiences in 1856-1857, in a shanty near St. Guillaume, Canada East.

Meech comments on the local customs, habits and life of lumbermen. He records the vagaries of weather, how it was often far too cold or stormy to work when winter ruled. He speaks of the monotony of enforced isolation in a shanty. He explains various operations in locating, felling, trimming, squaring and hauling of logs. The diary, though written in a cryptic, no-nonsense style by a man with rudimentary education, is a rich source of information concerning lumbering at its basic level. Life was rough-and-tumble in the forests and shanties. On page 156, Meech recounts a "recreational" event in the shanty, during which he got a belt around the necks of two loggers and dragged them about the structure.

The diary is a remarkable record which not only reflects its time, but also conveys to us the colourful experiences of a lumberman from a time past "when lumber was king."

Charles George Meech. 1856-1857.

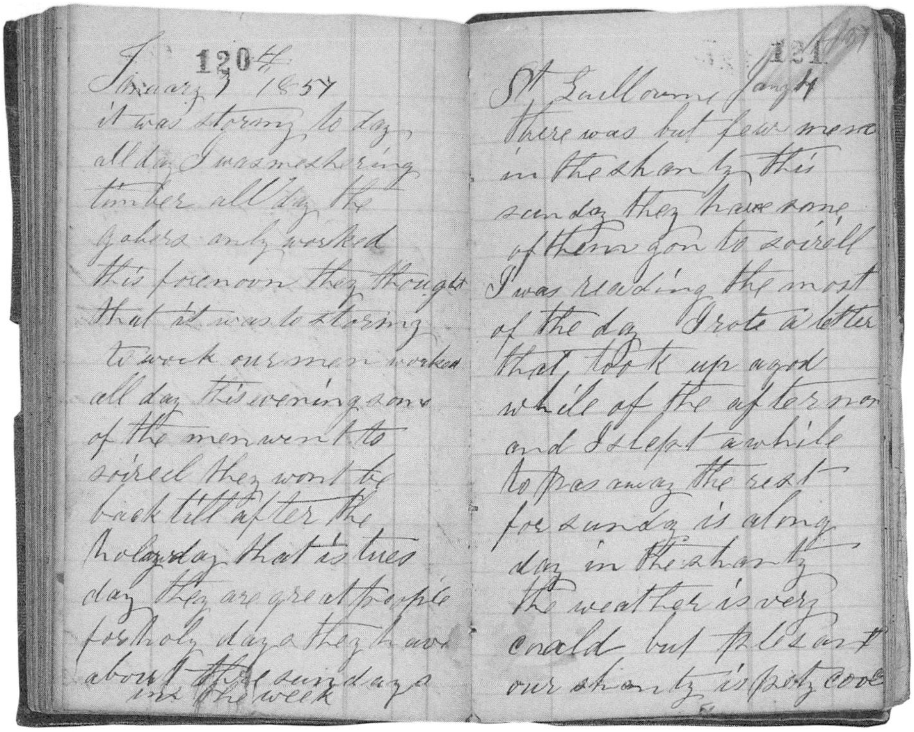

120

January 1 1857
it was storming to day
all day I was mesuring
timber all day the
gobers only worked
this forenoon they thought
that it was to storming
to work our man worked
all day this evening some
of the men went to
soireel they wont be
back till after the
holyday that is tues
day they are great people
for holy days they have
about three sundays a
in the week

121

St Guillaume Jany 4
there was but few men
in the shanty this
sunday they have some
of them gon to soirell
I was reading the most
of the day I rote a letter
that took up a good
while of the afternoon
and I slept awhile
to pas away the rest
for sunday is a long
day in the shanty
the weather is very
could but plesant
our shanty is prety cool

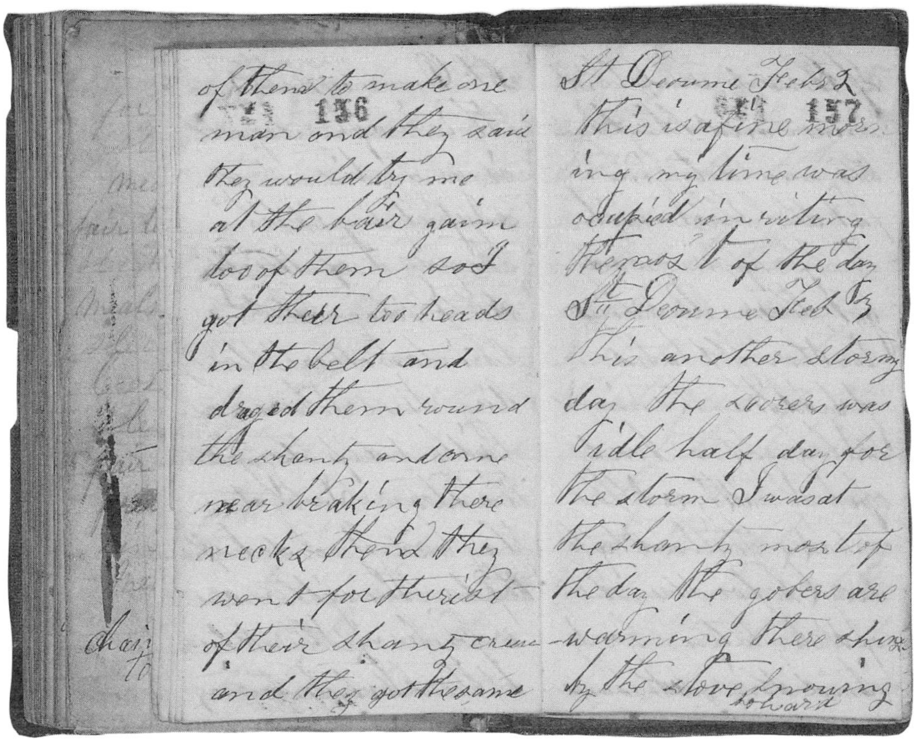

156

of them to make one
man and they said
they would try me
at the bair gaim
too of them so I
got their too heads
in the belt and
draged them round
the shanty and com
near breaking there
necks then they
went for the rest
of their shanty came
and they got the same

157

St Jerome Feb 2
This is a fine morn
ing my time was
ocupied in writing
the most of the day
St Jerome Feb 3
This another storming
day the scorers was
idle half day for
the storm I was at
the shanty most of
the day the gobers are
warming there shins
by the stove throwing
toward

13.3 cm x 7.8 cm
12.5 cm x 6.8 cm

National Archives of Canada,
Manuscript Division,
MG 24, D 103, pp. 120-121,
MG 24, D 103, pp. 156-157.

"Plan of Proposed Booms at Carillon. Surveyed at the Request of Henry Richard Symmes, Esq., for the Department of Public Works (Three Rivers)"

The running of logs down rivers was not a simple case of just throwing them into water and letting them float downstream. It called for hydraulic engineers to modulate log flows along rivers, and for men of extraordinary skill with practical river knowledge to manage the actual flow of rafts or loose logs. At all times, control of movement was imperative; hence, currents, whirlpools, eddies, rapids, shallows, seasonal rates of water flow — all these observations and more came under consideration as hydraulic engineers strove to expedite the movement of logs and rafts from source to either market or port of export.

While not as spectacular as timber slides, such booms as depicted in this plan were as significant, both in objective and in execution. The booms shown in this plan were built in 1857-1859 at Carillon Station, a strategic point on the Ottawa River approximately 30 miles before its debouch into the St. Lawrence. They were designed specifically to manage the flow of squared timber, sawn lumber and especially logs. The mid-river, wedge-like structure deflected floating timber toward the deeper water near the banks, where, behind massive retaining booms, the logs could be harnessed into rafts for the rest of the run down river. The booms were massive, each approximately one-half mile in length, with various gating mechanisms along their length to allow for manipulation of logs or rafts.

This drawing was prepared for Henry Richard Symmes, Superintending Engineer in 1858-1875, of the St. Maurice slides and booms, with a view to improving these works. It captures for us the significance of the staples trade in lumber, which justified the substantial costs of such booms all along major rivers. It reflects significant achievements by the engineers who built the booms and slides. And it does so in an image which is graphically pleasing, characterized by an effective simplicity of line.

Joseph F. Gaudet. 1867.

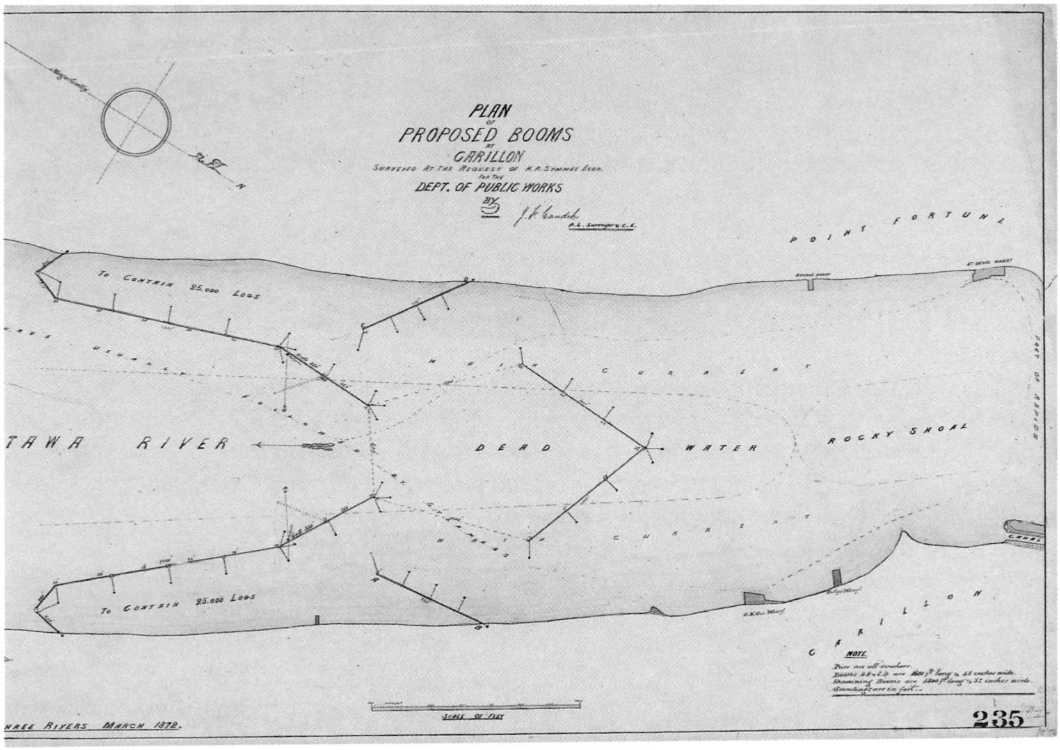

61 cm x 95 cm

National Archives of Canada,
Cartographic and Audio-Visual Archives Division,
NMC-96391.

"Oil Wells at Bothwell, Ontario"

This watercolour records the early years of a new industry in Lambton and Kent counties of southern Ontario, which were rich in petroleum reserves. The Lambton-Kent area become home to an incipient petro-chemical industry; as early as 1864, 27 small refineries were already at work in Petrolia alone. Bothwell was located in this petroleum-pioneering region.

Petroleum, strictly speaking, was not "discovered" at this time. Such was the natural concentration of petroleum in this region that it occasionally surfaced in tar pools and was known to local inhabitants. What stimulated petroleum development was the creation of a market for petroleum products, and technology to refine it.

In the creation of a market, Abraham Gesner, a geologist, inventor and chemist born in Nova Scotia in 1797, played a remarkable role. His geological work for the government of New Brunswick led him to successfully experiment with the distillation of "coal tar" from solid hydrocarbons. He gave the end product the name of "kerosene," lamp oil, which very rapidly displaced all other lighting oils on the market. With a market now for kerosene, as well as for various lubricants, all distilled from petroleum, the petroleum resources of southern Ontario were ready to be "discovered."

This watercolour informs us about the petroleum industry in its infancy. The building with the smokestack houses a steam engine for pumping the crude, while the tower shields the drill rig. There is a pump line from tower to storage tanks fashioned of wood. These reservoirs were tapped by spigot, to release oil into barrels for shipping. Intentionally or not, the artist used a brown wash to execute this watercolour, representing the image through colours which remind one of oil.

Shipping oil was a difficult proposition then, whether by horse cart or train wagon; the crude often leaked through wooden barrels, contaminating everything in its vicinity. With further development of the petroleum industry came pollution. Before gas engines made them desirable, the more volatile, light cuts of oil were often discarded in favour of the heavier oils, out of which kerosene and lubricants were distilled. Some rivers in the region became so fouled that they actually caught fire.

The petroleum industry was another harbinger of the dawning of a new era in the British North American colonies.

Unknown Artist 87. ante 1873.

20.9 cm (diameter)

National Archives of Canada,
Documentary Art and Photography Division,
C-36679.

"Canada and New Brunswick Courts — International Exhibition"

The Great Exhibition of 1851, housed in the Crystal Palace in London, England, initiated a series of expositions staged periodically in the English capital. Such international trade fairs became a phenomenon of the second half of the nineteenth century, reflecting the headiness of the European age of positivism when, it was held, people through scientific knowledge, could achieve unlimited aims. The fairs boasted the achievements of science and industry, and promoted unencumbered trade. It was thus perfectly logical that such fairs in the modern industrializing world should have been first conceived and lavishly staged in Britain, the first nation into industrialization, the most fervent advocate of free trade, and the world centre of trade and commerce. To the British, and to British colonials who participated, such fairs were also a celebration of the achievements of the British Empire, and an advertisement of the Empire's future, blessed as it was with every natural product and manufactured good conceivable.

The British North American colonies participated in the International Exhibition of 1862-1864. This photograph captures what the colonies of Canada, New Brunswick and (barely visible) Vancouver Island promoted at this exhibition. We see here some of the usual staple or natural products of the colonies, such as timber and pelts; stuffed birds and deer provide a rustic ambience.

However, it is interesting to note that the colonies offered much more than natural products. The New Brunswick pavillion displays faucets, hammers, leather harnesess and saddles, furniture, carriages, timber saws, ships' helms and agricultural machinery, all of which indicate that the colonies, while not yet industrialized, were certainly manufacturing diverse goods, and competing for markets abroad. This was the point the colonies wished to make, to demonstrate that they were industrializing in emulation of the mother country.

London Stereoscopic and
Photographic Company.

1862.

21.7 cm x 28.2 cm

National Archives of Canada,
Documentary Art and Photography Division,
PA-126886.

III

On the Improvement of Trade Relations Between France and Canada

This letter of introduction was penned by the Baron Gauldrée-Boilleau, the French Consul stationed in Quebec City from 1859 on; the consulate was opened as a result of the mission of Captain de Belvèze of the *Capricieuse* in 1855. It introduces Alexander Tilloch Galt, Minister of Finance of the Province of Canada, to the Comte de Lesseps, and asks that the Comte assist Galt in his desire to meet with the French Minister of Trade.

Alexander Tilloch Galt (1817-1893) was born in England, and emigrated to Montreal in 1835, working for the British American Land Company (founded by his father) as it opened land for settlement in the Eastern Townships. He became president of the St. Lawrence and Atlantic Railway, well aware that the development of rail transport and the Townships went hand-in-hand.

Like many railway promoters, Galt entered politics, to be better positioned to acquire subsidies and loan and bond guarantees, from both provincial and Imperial coffers. Because of his business connection through the St. Lawrence and Atlantic Railway with New England, he was one of the original "annexationists" of 1849. A most able manager, Galt joined the Cartier-Macdonald ministry of 1858 as Finance Minister, on condition that the ministry support his resolution for a federal union of all British North American colonies.

In his capacity as Finance Minister of the Province of Canada, Galt wished to strengthen the province's economic situation through expanded trade in new markets; hence this mission to Paris, to find another trading partner for the province. As the letter suggests, Galt was well known to the French consul. He was most responsible for a recent reduction of provincial tariffs which hindered trade; and he was most interested in developing direct commercial relations with France. The letter's contents are an intriguing indication of a certain coming of age of the Province of Canada which, though still a colony, was beginning to look for markets overseas.

Baron Charles-Henri-Phillipe Gauldrée-Boilleau. 1860.

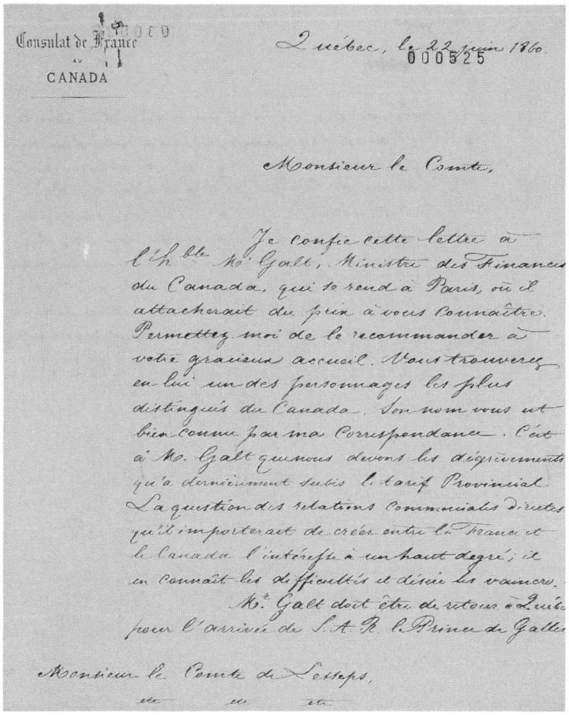
Consulat de France
au
CANADA

000525

Québec, le 22 juin 1860.

Monsieur le Comte,

Je confie cette lettre à
l'hon^ble^ Mr Galt, Ministre des Finances
du Canada, qui se rend à Paris, où il
attacherait du prix à vous connaître.
Permettez-moi de le recommander à
votre gracieux accueil. Vous trouverez
en lui un des personnages les plus
distingués du Canada. Son nom vous est
bien connu par ma Correspondance. C'est
à Mr Galt que nous devons les dégrèvements
qu'a dernièrement subis le tarif Provincial.
La question des relations Commerciales directes
qu'il importerait de créer entre la France et
le Canada l'intéresse à un haut degré; il
en connaît les difficultés et désire les vaincre.
Mr Galt doit être de retour à Québec
pour l'arrivée de S. A. R. le Prince de Galles

Monsieur le Comte de Lesseps,
etc. etc. etc.

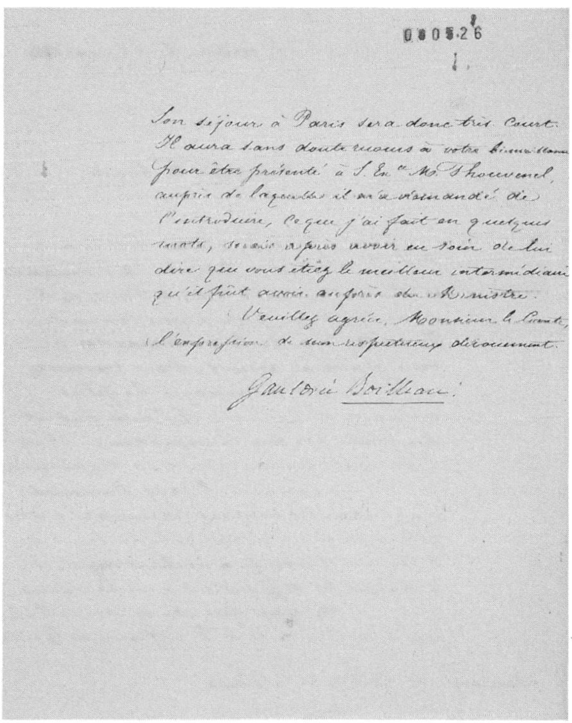
000526

Son séjour à Paris sera donc très court.
Il aura sans doute recours à votre bienveillance
pour être présenté à S. Ex^ce^ Mr Thouvenel,
auprès de laquelle il m'a demandé de
l'introduire, ce que j'ai fait en quelques
mots, mais après avoir eu soin de lui
dire que vous étiez le meilleur intermédiaire
qu'il pût avoir auprès du Ministre.
Veuillez agréer, Monsieur le Comte,
l'expression de mon respectueux dévouement.

Gauldrée Boilleau.

26.4 cm x 21.3 cm

National Archives of Canada,
Manuscript Division,
MG 27, I, D 8, Vol. 2, pp. 525-526.

"Grand Feu de Québec"

This triptych is attributed to Élise-L'Heureux de Livernois, the wife of Jules-Isaï. A photographer in her own right from 1856 on, she was active in the work of the Livernois studio; when Jules-Isaï died in 1865, she continued his photography business. The field work in the preparation of this triptych might have been performed by another photographer of note, Louis Fontaine *dit* Bienvenu, whom Madame de Livernois hired six months after the death of her husband.

This triptych records the remains of Quebec City's Lower Town after the great fire of 1866. It is a spectacular piece, demonstrating in the starkest manner possible the absolute destruction that this fire visited upon the Lower Town. Quebec City suburbs had known fires before (St. Roch and St. John Baptiste, both in 1845), and would know many more before the century was up. But other towns burned as well. For example, fires swept wards of Halifax in 1857 and 1859; in 1866, four blocks in the centre of Charlottetown were destroyed; and in 1868 Barkerville, the capital of the Cariboo gold region, was almost wholly incinerated.

Fires were a scourge of urban life of that time. In response to them, urban administrators developed or expanded fire codes which regulated the types of building materials, roofing materials and spacing of dwellings. They provided for water works to deliver water. They also acquired fire-fighting equipment and organized fire-fighting companies. Since fires often destroyed older neighbourhoods, new building on fire-destroyed sites could be better controlled by improved regulations.

However, because many city dwellings continued to be constructed of wood, because of the need to keep stoves flaming hot in cold northern winters, because of human oversight, great fires would yet devastate many towns and villages in British North America.

Attributed to Élise-L'Heureux de Livernois. 1866.

25.9 cm x 33.8 cm
26.4 cm x 33.2 cm
26.2 cm x 32.8 cm

National Archives of Canada,
Documentary Art and Photography Division,
[Westerly part of triptych] C-457,
[Central part of triptych] C-4733,
[Easterly part of triptych] PA-148774.

III

"View of St. John, Portland and Carleton, New Brunswick. — Photographed from Fort House by Bowron and Cox"

Founded on a spot where several merchants commenced a trade with Indians in the 1760s, Saint John received a powerful stimulus to growth with the coming of the United Empire Loyalists in 1783. It became the dominant urban centre in New Brunswick (administratively separated from Nova Scotia in 1784).

Saint John developed as a port noted for the timber trade, receiving the great booms of timber coming down the Saint John River for re-shipment abroad. Sawmills were set up to process timber into sawn lumber. Shipyards sprang up in profusion, building vessels which often carried the timber to markets in Britain and the West Indies, and were then themselves sold along with their cargo. The town grew rapidly in the years 1820-1840, especially with the coming of the "Famine Irish." This influx put so great a strain upon the town's inhabitants that fierce riots in 1849 between Protestants and Roman Catholics resulted in deaths.

By the mid-nineteenth century, Saint John epitomized the economy of "wood, wind and sail." As this panorama suggests, the port was the nerve-centre of the town, nurturing it as long as trade flowed through. Some years before this panoramic view was taken, however, the remaining British preference for colonial timber was ended, hurting New Brunswick much more than the Province of Canada, which was centrally situated to take advantage of Reciprocity with the United States. Steam and iron were beginning gradually to displace wooden vessels, with ominous implications for the town.

Saint John's glory days were not yet done; the market for wooden ships would linger for several decades more. The merchants of Saint John also counted on Confederation and the Intercolonial Railway to secure Saint John's future, to win the interior trade from the Montreal-Portland railway route. But the world market for the city's products — lumber and ships — was shrinking. Saint John never did win out as the terminal port for goods from central Canada. Its merchants, despite attempting to diversify into manufacturing, could not easily compete with central Canadian or American business, especially after the completed Intercolonial (1876) brought in cheaper goods from central Canada. In the 1860s the town began to lose dynamism, its population to stagnate; and in the 1870s "the exodus" to the "Boston states" began, a phenomenon paralleling the French-Canadian outmigration, both of which would last into the twentieth century.

Attributed to Bowron and Cox. 1864.

27.5 cm x 182.7 cm

National Archives of Canada,
Documentary Art and Photography Division,
C-6121.

"Ship in Dry-Dock, Quebec City" *and also* "Shipbuilding in Field Near Dorchester, N.B."

These two photographs reflect a premier Canadian industry of the nineteenth century. Shipbuilding extended back into the French era. With an extensive coastline, a long tradition of shipping and fishing, rich forests descending virtually down to the banks of great rivers or the seashore, the British colonies in North America were well situated to develop this industry. By the early nineteenth century, Quebec city, the Bay of Fundy, the coves of Prince Edward Island, the Miramichi Estuary with shipyards strung out 20 kilometres up each bank from its debouch into the sea — these were great centres of shipbuilding. The second half of the nineteenth century constituted the glory years of full riggers and barques, a time of colour, adventure and profit.

Samuel McLaughlin's photograph shows a three-masted vessel in dry-dock. It is probably a merchantman, judging by its deep draught and broad beam which gave it a large cargo capacity. The "gunports" seem just painted on. This was often done to frighten off pirates, still a threat at that time, particularly in the Indies trade. The vessel may be undergoing a re-caulk or re-coppering, perhaps with Muntz metal (a tin-copper alloy then commonly used for such purposes). A new rudder may be going on the vessel as well, given the shears that are visible just to the rear of the vessel's stern.

In Henderson's "Shipbuilding" we see a vessel in frame, a scene representative of thousands of such undertakings throughout the coves and river mouths of the Maritime colonies. In the foreground is the mill, yard and pond. Timber, the raw material, was floated down to the pond from the forest, visible in the background, by way of the river just back of the mill. Drawn up as needed, the timber was sawn in the mill, in front of which lies a large heap of sawdust and chips. The absence of a stack suggests that the mill was powered by water. To the right of the mill is the ships's hull, its ribbing having taken shape on stocks and scaffolding; it is now ready to be planked. It is a fairly large merchant vessel, possibly a barque; judging by the human figures next to it, the vessel may be approximately 45 feet from keel to top of ribs.

As documents of the past, these two photographs reflect the talents of colonial shipbuilders of the majestic age of sail, when ships built in the British North American colonies came to ply every ocean and every sea.

Samuel McLaughlin. ca 1858.

Alexander Henderson. ca 1870.

15.9 cm x 20.1 cm
15.5 cm x 20.4 cm

National Archives of Canada,
Documentary Art and Photography Division,
[McLaughlin] C-8042,
[Henderson] C-17565.

III

Steele's Brick-Making Machine. Montreal

This attractive drawing, executed in Montreal in 1866, was probably prepared for a patent application. It reflects well the progress of technology.

Until technological development mechanized the process of brick-making in the closing decades of the nineteenth century, bricks continued to be made in a slow and time-consuming process. Once prepared, the clay mix was packed by hand into hand-moulds, and the bricks baked in kilns.

The push-pull dynamic of need and technological development touched the process of brick-making. A growing population, developing urban centres and growing affluence sustained a demand for more brick. Affluence could underwrite a more expensive dwelling made of brick rather than of wooden planks or clapboard. And brick provided more surety against fires, an all-too-common occurrence in that time.

This drawing, showing various views and elevations of a proposed brick-forming machine, reflects an early attempt at mechanizing the process. The drawing is important as an indication of technological development, of the search for mechanized ways to perform what traditionally was done by manual labour. It is also a testament to the artistic skills of the draftsman who produced it.

Anonymous. 1866.

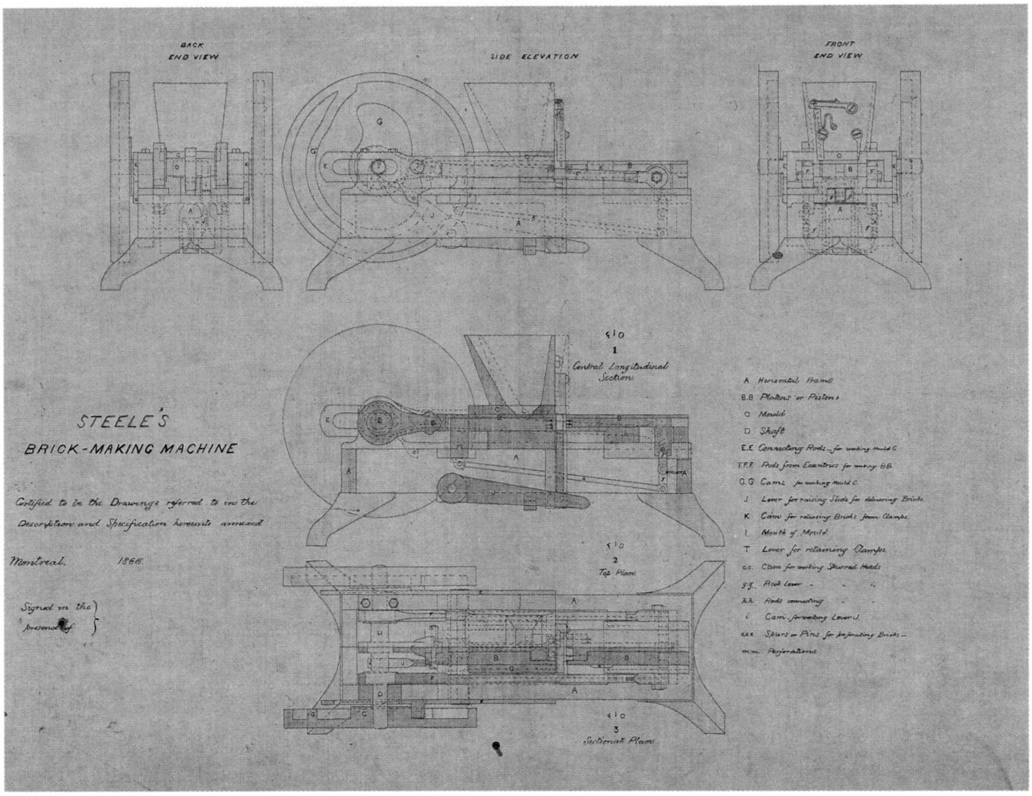

51.5 cm x 67 cm

National Archives of Canada,
Cartographic and Audio-Visual Archives Division,
NMC-132508.

"Du Loup Gold Company's Hotel. Linière, Canada East"

While gold rushes are generally associated with the west coast, from the Fraser River valley to the Klondike, they also occurred in other parts of British North America. In the pre-Confederation period gold rushes drew adventurers to Nova Scotia, the Northwest (in the North Saskatchewan River area) and to the Eastern Townships.

This poster advertises the Du Loup Gold Company's hotel in the Linière region of the Beauce, 75 miles south of Quebec City, located on the banks of the Rivière du Loup. The Linière region generally was part of the Chaudière Gold District, which was very actively worked in the 1860s and 1870s. The company's poster advises that the company has leased 2,000 acres of gold-bearing land, and that it will sub-lease parts of this land to prospectors. Numerous tributaries provide water for sluice-works. The poster also sets out various routes to get to the Du Loup gold fields, providing evidence of the continuing expansion of the railway network throughout the Eastern Townships south of the St. Lawrence River and into the New England states. Judging by the transportation information provided in the poster, the company hoped to attract miners from the United States.

Prospecting and working gold fields brought profit only to a very few. But there was money to be made by individuals and companies who knew how to benefit from gold rushes which brought great numbers of gold-seekers into a region and stoked the local economy. The Du Loup Gold Company obviously intended to make its fortune by indirect and less spectacular, but more reliable, means, such as providing hotel services. By sub-leasing its claim, the company wisely shared the financial risks involved in searching for gold.

Attractively hand-coloured, this poster is a fine example of promotional literature which reflects the significance of gold rushes of the period, the dynamism of the Eastern Townships of Quebec and early American investment in Canada (which would increasingly displace British capital in the following years).

Du Loup Gold Company. ca 1870.

46 cm x 39.7 cm

National Archives of Canada,
Cartographic and Audio-Visual Archives Division,
NMC-1059.

"Tremaine's Map Of The Counties of Lincoln and Welland, Canada West. Compiled and Drawn from Actual Surveys by the Publishers Geo. R. & G.M. Tremaine, St. Lawrence Building, Toronto, 1862"

This map of Lincoln and Welland counties is indicative of a unique cartographic phenomenon of the mid-nineteenth century which spilled over into the British colonies from the United States — the county map. American county mapmakers used official surveys where available in their work; where necessary, they either surveyed or compiled required topographical information with odometer and compass. Once a map was complete, showing the survey grid, concession roads and lots, the mapmakers acquired the names of property owners from tax rolls and inscribed them on the maps. Several American mapmakers who came to work in the British colonies produced 58 county maps in all, ranging from Nova Scotia to Canada West. Thirty-two of these maps represented counties in Canada West. Of these, George C. Tremaine (1805-ca 1875) and his two nephews, George R. (d. 1901) and Gaius M. Tremaine, produced 15, including the Lincoln and Welland counties map, which is displayed here.

Drawn to a scale of 1:39,000, the map is large, which allows for great detail. Hence the map shows not only lots and landowners' names, but also the location of their houses. Symbols indicate public buildings, such as post offices, churches and schools, as well as the various mills scattered throughout the two counties. The map shows communications routes and urban centres such as St. Catharines, Thorold, Fort Erie, Niagara (-on-the-Lake) and so on; the urban centres are shown in accurate and detailed spatial relationship to the rest of the map.

The map is graced by a number of vignettes of notable landmarks, public buildings and homes of the wealthy. The latter paid for the honour of a graphic representation of their establishment; in fact, such vignettes were advertisements promoting businesses or services. Professionals and craftsmen who could not afford a vignette paid for a notation of their services; grouped by town or village, their names were listed in open spaces near the map's edges. The commercial purpose of this map becomes fully evident when one realizes that it also noted which lots in the two counties were for sale.

Such county maps, compiled at private expense, could be prepared only for populous and economically well-developed counties, where the mapmaker could hope to recoup his costs. The Tremaines and others produced county maps for commercial reasons. However, in doing so, they left behind maps that have become historical records shedding light on land ownership, on genealogy, and on agrarian, urban and social history.

George R. and Gaius M. Tremaine. 1862.

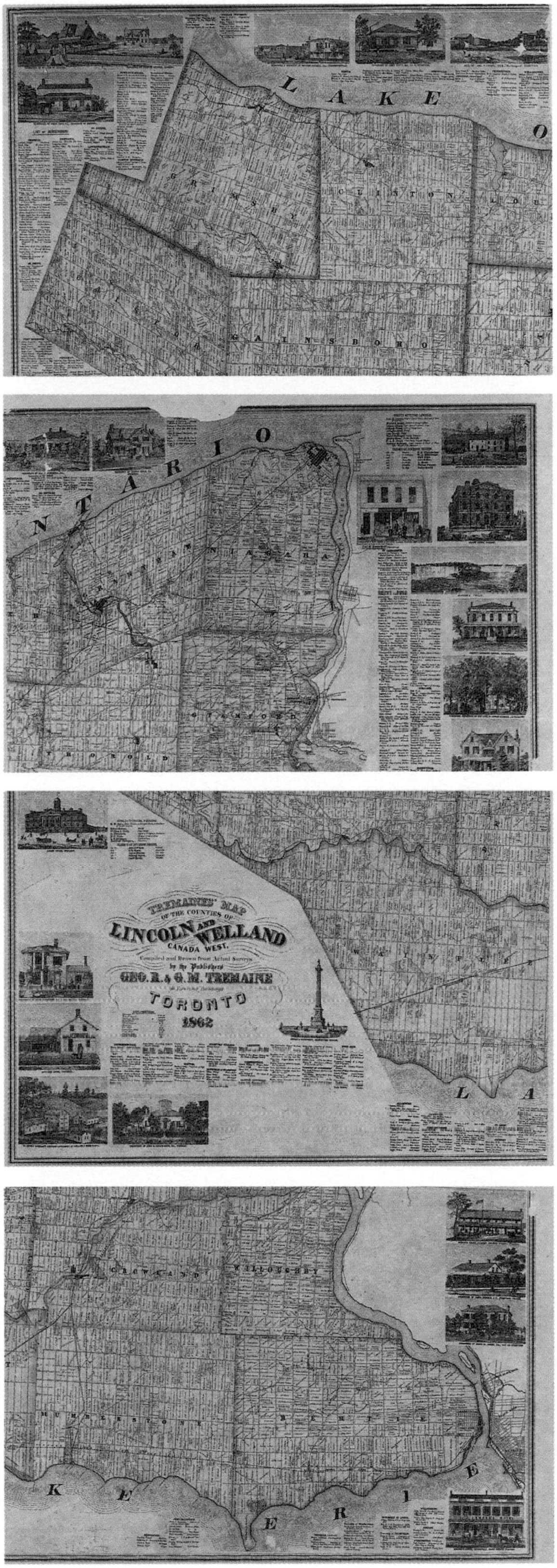

4 panels, each measuring 68 cm x 94 cm

National Archives of Canada,
Cartographic and Audio-Visual Archives Division,
NMC-19014.

Political Life, Confederation and the Northwest

The Province of Canada, the most populous and economically developed region of British North America fronting on the great expanse of Rupert's Land, was the dominant colonial player in the political manoeuvring that led to Confederation. Its political system, based on sectional co-operation between an English Canada West and a predominantly French Canada East, was unstable; its long border with the United States rendered it strategically vulnerable; and it stood to lose most if Rupert's Land and the North-Western Territory were lost to American expansion. A *modus vivendi* between the two sections, worked out through practice, made colonial government possible — but just possible.

In the search for a new order to secure political stability, economic development, the continental interior and improved defence against the very real threat of invasion by the United States and actual incursions by the Fenian Brotherhood, the province's political leadership gradually turned to the idea of Confederation of the British North American colonies. Supported by Britain, the idea carried the day. On 1 July 1867 the new Dominion of Canada came into existence, incomplete but a Confederation nonetheless.

The Dominion government moved to incorporate Rupert's Land and the territory beyond. Its apparent heavy-handedness provoked a rebellion of the Metis in the Red River Settlement. Negotiations resulted in the admission into Confederation of a small area of Rupert's Land, under the name of Manitoba, while the rest of the territory became Crown land of the Dominion government. Indian treaties, the Dominion survey, and promotion of settlement through a *Homestead Act* characterized the Dominion government's activity in the newly-acquired territory.

1851 Census

Until Confederation, there was little regularity in census-taking in the colonies. The 1848 *Statistical Act of Canada* established the principle of decennial censuses, starting in 1851. Jurisdiction over census and statistics would be accorded to the future federal authority by the *British North America Act*, a significant function because House of Commons representation and provincial subsidies were based on population. From 1871 on, regular decennial census have been held in Canada.

The results of the census of 1851, displayed here, offer very interesting data about the Province of Canada. Demographic data reveal population totals by county and population by origin. Economic data provide information on agricultural production and crop type by county, on saw and grist mills, and on other types of mills, factories and undertakings, with note made of capitalization of ventures and extent of labour force. Other significant social criteria, (religious affiliation, for example), are reflected in the census results. It is a very important source of historical information on social and economic history in mid-nineteenth-century Canada.

The 1851 census statistics revealed that Upper Canada was developing at a much more rapid pace than Lower Canada, and that, for the first time since the Union of 1841, the population of Upper Canada had surpassed that of Lower Canada. The original *Act of Union* had given both sections of the province equal representation in the Legislative Assembly. Canada West, then with a significantly smaller population than Canada East, had thus been re-assured that its interests would be protected. However, political and cultural tension had strained relations between the two sections, and many in Canada West, now that it was more populous, began to demand representation in the assembly based on population. From 1853 onwards, George Brown and the Grits would champion the cause of "representation by population," one of the chief causes of parliamentary paralysis and breakdown in Canada by 1864.

This census of 1851 not only recorded history; in the use to which it was put by some contemporaries, it helped to make history. Some in Canada West grew heady with the census findings and saw in them confirmation of their ungenerous perception of French Canada East. In their view, Canada West was economically vibrant while Canada East was stagnant. This, they held, had its root in racial and social factors, proving that Anglo-Saxon Protestants were superior to corrupted French Papists. In their perception, Canada East was a dead weight, paralyzing growth and development. Deductions of such a nature, not surprisingly, only increased sectional tensions between the two Canadas.

Province of Canada. 1852.

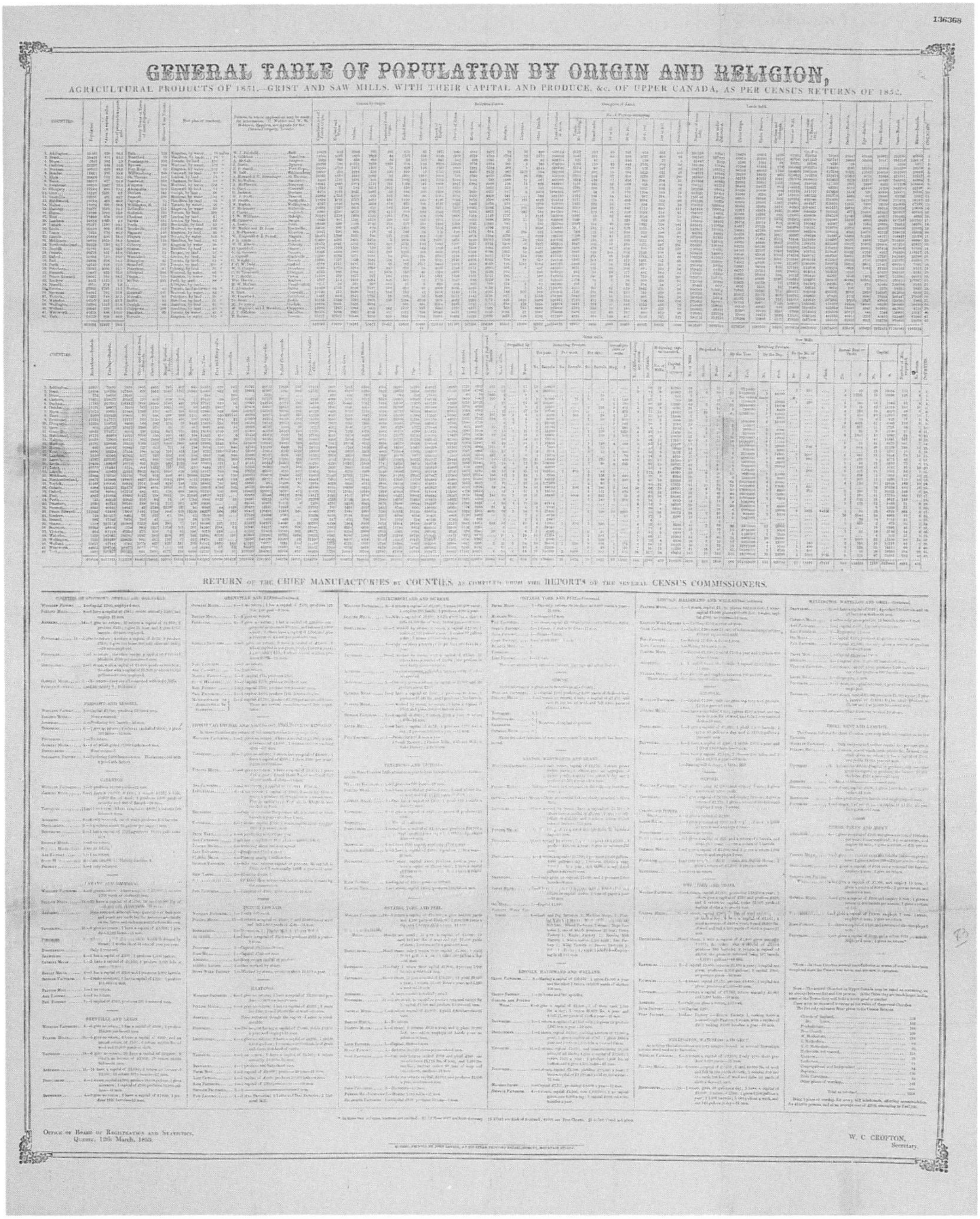

84.2 cm x 67.9 cm

National Archives of Canada,
Manuscript Division,
MG 26, A, Vol. 298, p. 136368.

IV

Letter to Joseph Howe on French-English Understanding

This letter was written to Joseph Howe by François-Xavier Garneau, the most renowned of Quebec's historians and writers of the nineteenth century. Born in Quebec City in 1809, he chose the notarial profession in 1825. Garneau clerked for Archibald Campbell for five years, where he benefitted from a splendid library. He undertook some travel to the United States and Britain and France. In the late 1830s he began his three-volume *Histoire du Canada*, a sweeping synthesis of French Canadian history. Its leitmotif was the struggle of French Canadians to survive all adversity and enemies, first the Indians, then the Anglo-Americans, and finally the English-Canadian oligarchs. Published in 1845-1848, Garneau's elegantly-written *Histoire* excited French-Canadians (although the Catholic Church did not warm to Garneau's proto-Rougiste sentiment that religion should remain outside the political realm, a position he later modified). Garneau became the national historian of Quebec, giving French Canadians a sense of self, achievement and pride.

After attending a function in Quebec City in 1851, at which Joseph Howe spoke in favour of a railway linking Halifax with Quebec City, Garneau afterwards addressed this letter to Howe. He expresses his appreciation of Howe's kind words about French-Canadians. Reciprocating Howe's kindness (perhaps said tongue-in-cheek), Garneau is forwarding to Howe a copy of his *Histoire*, so that Howe might come "to better understand [Garneau's] compatriots." Noting that Scots, French, Irish and English have been thrown together in a "vast and beautiful land," Garneau warns that if old hatreds are sustained, "life will be intolerable in Canada." Regarding Howe's observations elsewhere about the "static" nature of French-Canadian life, Garneau informs Howe that there are weighty political reasons to account for this. Garneau closes with approbation of Howe's activity, which could lead to "colonies permanently united, happy, strong and rich."

The letter reflects significant problems of the time — the lack of understanding between the French and English elements, and Old-World tensions amongst the newcomers which they brought with themselves to the New World. The letter points to future confederation; but only awareness and tolerance, it implies, can lead to a happy future.

François-Xavier Garneau. 1851.

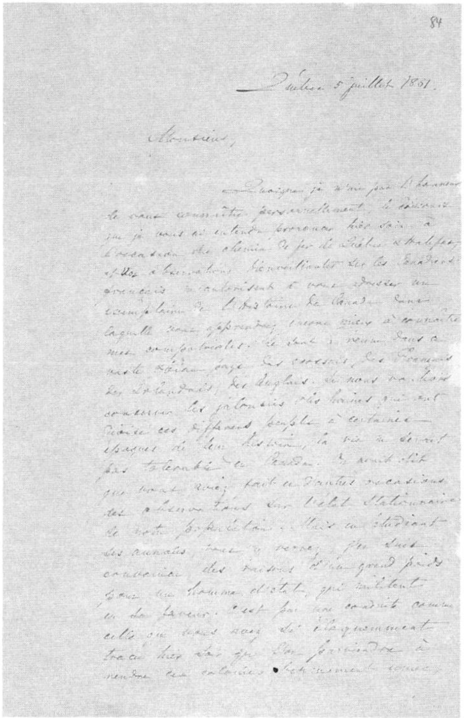

84

Québec 5 juillet 1851.

Monsieur,

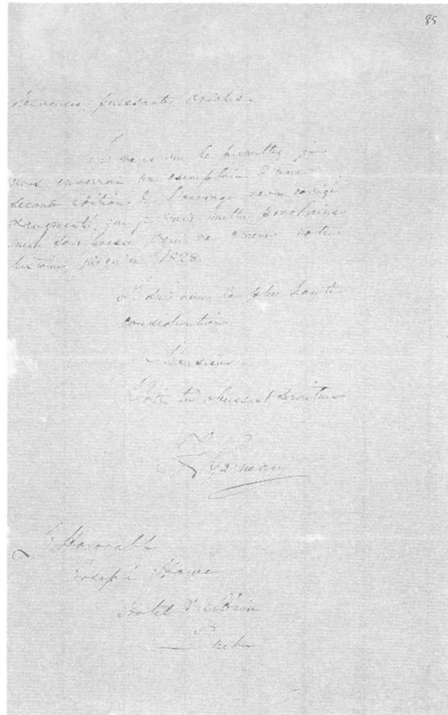

85

32.1 cm x 20.3 cm

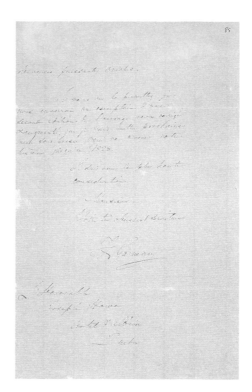

National Archives of Canada,
Manuscript Division,
MG 24, B 29, Vol. 51, pp. 84-85.

"A New Convention to Consider the Abolition of Seigneurial Tenure"

This document addresses a significant issue, which troubled the political and economic life of the Province of Canada — the seigneurial system of land tenure in Canada East.

The seigneurial system had shaped the physical pattern of Quebec's landholding, its property laws, its social mores and its administrative structure. Rooted in the history of New France, the seigneurial system included most of the land along both banks of the St. Lawrence, from Quebec City to Montreal, as well as the Richelieu and Chaudière valleys. Habitants held their land as leaseholders, paying established rents to legal holders of the seigneuries. Modernizers, particularly members of the Institut canadien, led the movement to terminate the system and secure the habitants/*censitaires* in full ownership of the lands they held.

Canada West also had a historical anachronism whose time was past, the clergy reserves. The clergy reserves had been created by the *Constitutional Act of 1791*, at a time when church and state were still tightly welded. It had set aside one-seventh of the public lands of Upper and Lower Canada for the maintenance of the Protestant clergy. In Canada West, the reserves were originally intended to fund only the Church of England. Other Protestant denominations vociferously began to demand their proportional share of income from these lands, and the volatile debate spilled over into politics. To put an end to the increasingly anachronistic church-state connection, and to remove from the political scene an issue that was particularly divisive in a time of proud sectarianism, the movement for abolition of the reserves gathered force.

In 1859, the McNab-Morin ministry (Sir Alan McNab, leader of the Upper Canada Liberal Conservatives, and Augustin-Norbert Morin, leader of the remaining Lower Canada Reformers), in a political trade-off that won support from both sections of the United Province of Canada, abolished both seigneurial tenure and the clergy reserves. Two political institutions of the past were successfully removed from the hothouse of Canadian political life. The document displayed here marks a stage in the complex process of liquidating the seigneurial system, which for several centuries had shaped the life of one of Canada's founding peoples.

Institut canadien. ca 1852.

NOUVELLE CONVENTION POUR L'ABOLITION

DE LA

Tenure Seigneuriale.

Les résolutions qui suivent sont adressées, pour recevoir leur exécution, aux personnes influentes des différentes paroisses, qui conséquemment doivent partager les vues de l'assemblée qui les a adoptées.

Il n'est pas nécessaire d'ajouter que l'on compte sur leur concours cordial et empressé, pour une cause destinée à promouvoir les intérêts généraux du Bas-Canada.

Elles s'empresseront donc de voir à l'élection de délégués et à l'organisation de comités dans chaque paroisse, conformément aux résolutions, afin de hâter l'abolition d'une tenure qui a été un si grand obstacle au développement des ressources du pays et à la prospérité de ses habitans.

Conformément à la convocation, publiée dans les journaux à l'instance de quelques membres de la législature, une assemblée publique des personnes des différentes parties du pays a eu lieu à Montréal le 12 du courant, à onze heures du matin, dans la salle de l'Institut-Canadien, afin d'organiser une nouvelle convention pour l'abolition de la tenure seigneuriale dans le Bas-Canada.

M. L. Lacoste, M. P. P., a été appelé à la présidence, et M. D. Latte, prié d'agir comme secrétaire.

Etaient présens:—MM. Lacoste, Boucherville; Jobin, Berthier; Mongenais, Vaudreuil; Poulin, Rouville Ste. Marie; Valois, comté de Montréal; DeWitt, ancien membre; Doutre; Delesderniers, Vaudreuil; Blanchet; J. B. Sorrette, St. Jean Baptiste; E. Mercier; A. Dugas, St. Jacques; J. O. Bureau, St. Rémy; L. Archambault, maire du comté de Leinster; Ls. Voligny, St. Thomas, Maxime Fernét, St. Thomas; André Beaupré, St. Paul; L. H. Derome, St. Paul; Chs. Guilbault, fils, Ste. Mélanie; Narcisse Michaud, Ste. Mélanie; P. E. Dostaler, Berthier; Ed. Scallon, L'Industrie; Christophe Capistran, Ste. Elizabeth; Méd. St. Amour, St. Paul; André St. Amour, St. Paul; A. Dufresne, St. Athanase; L. Noiseux, St. Jean Baptiste; E. Vien; J. Allard, Lachine; P. C. Valois, Pointe-Claire; Dr. Tavernier, C. J. N. De Montigny, J. E. Ferté, J. J. Bibaud, C. H. Lamontagne et plusieurs autres.

Sur proposition de Jacob DeWitt, écr., secondé par M Jobin, M. P. P., il est résolu à l'unanimité:

Que le projet de réforme et d'abolition de la tenure seigneuriale, proposé par le procureur général du Bas-Canada, avait fait concevoir l'espoir que le sujet étant posé constitutionnellement devant le pays, les deux branches de la législature le traiteraient avec cette maturité de réflexion que méritait son importance, et rendraient définitivement ce projet également acceptable au censitaire et au seigneur;—que le projet en question tel que modifié lors de son adoption dans l'assemblée législative, consacrait des iniquités vis-à-vis des censitaires,—mais que dans le désir de régler enfin cette question, les membres de la législature favorables à l'abolition, avaient cru devoir l'accepter;—que le conseil législatif, fidèle au passé qui rend son abolition impérieuse et immédiate, s'étant placé comme le représentant des seigneurs et ayant traité d'une manière outrageusement légère, un sujet d'où dépend la prospérité et la condition individuelle de presque tous les habitans du Bas-Canada, a par là dégagé les censitaires et leurs représentans en chambre, de l'espèce de compromis auquel ils avaient souscrit à regret; et qu'en conséquence les deux parties reprennent leur position indépendante, et n'auront plus que la stricte justice pour principe de réforme et d'abolition.

Sur proposition de P. E. Dostaler, écr., Berthier, secondé par E. Scallon, écr., il est résolu à l'unanimité:

Que vu la position faite aux censitaires par les procédés de la dernière session du parlement, une nouvelle convention soit organisée, avec pouvoir de préparer un projet de réforme et d'abolition auquel adhéreront strictement et sans composition tous les censitaires et leurs représentans en chambre;—lequel projet devra d'abord définir les droits respectifs des seigneurs et des censitaires et poser les bases d'une commutation et d'une abolition définitive.

Sur proposition de J. N. Poulin, M. P. P., secondé par L. Archambault, écr., il est adopté à l'unanimité:

Que cette convention se compose de trois branches, dont l'une pour le district de Montréal, une pour le distrit de Québec, et la troisième pour le district des Trois-Rivières,—les trois branches devant se réunir sur la réquisition de celle de Montréal, pour nommer un comité central.

Sur proposition de P. F. C. Delesderniers, écr., secondé par A. Dugas, écr., il est résolu à l'unanimité:

Que les membres du parlement sont *ex officio* membres de la branche de leur district; que les censitaires de chaque paroisse soient invités à s'organiser en comités et que le représentant de chaque comté, et à son défaut d'agir, le maire de chaque comté et les conseillers municipaux soient spécialement chargés d'organiser leur comté en comités de paroisse, qui devront envoyer chacun deux députés à la branche du district;—chaque branche pourra s'adjoindre telles personnes qu'elle croira pouvoir être utiles au but que cette assemblée a en vue.

Sur proposition de A. Dufresne, écr., secondé par J. O. Bureau, écr., il est résolu à l'unanimité:

Que chaque branche soit organisée pour s'assembler le premier jeudi du mois de septembre prochain, aux fins de nommer ce jour là ceux qui devront composer le comité central.

Sur proposition de J. B. Mongenais, écr., secondé par J. Doutre, écr., il est résolu à l'unanimité:

Que Louis Lacoste, écr., représentant du comté de Chambly, soit chargé de fixer l'heure et le lieu de la réunion des députés de la branche de Montréal, le premier jeudi de septembre prochain;—que F. X. Lemieux, écr., représentant du comté de Dorchester, soit chargé de fixer le lieu et l'heure de la réunion des députés de la chambre du district de Québec pour la même époque, et que P. B. Dumoulin, écr., représentant du comté d'Yamaska, soit chargé de la même chose pour la branche du district des Trois-Rivières.

Sur proposition du Dr. Valois, M. P. P., secondé par L. A. Derome, écr., il est résolu à l'unanimté:

Que tous les censitaires et chaque comité de paroisse et chaque branche, soient priés d'organiser des souscriptions pour défrayer les dépenses nécessaires pour donner de l'efficacité aux procédés et aux travaux du comité central.

Sur proposition de J. O. Bureau, écr., secondé par P. Blanchet, écr., il est résolu à l'unanimité:

Que les procédés de cette assemblée soient publiés dans les journaux de cette ville, avec prière à tous les journaux du Bas-Canada de les reproduire.

L. Lacoste, président.
D. Latte secrétaire.

[Imprimerie De Montigny & Cie., 79½, Rue St-Paul, Montréal.]

28.3 cm x 16.3 cm

National Archives of Canada,
Manuscript Division,
MG 24, B 170.

"Reciprocity Treaty Between The United States of America and Her Britannic Majesty"

Traders, merchants and staples producers throughout the British North American colonies were shocked into a new reality when Britain dismantled mercantilism. Not only had they lost a secure market for their own goods; they also lost the benefits that had accrued to them by processing and trans-shipping American goods, which, to avoid duties, could enter the Imperial market only out of British territory and on British vessels. One response to the new situation was the annexationist movement of Montreal; but supported by few, condemned by Britain as "treasonous" and largely ignored in the United States, it fizzled out. The quandry remained, however — whither now?

Whatever course the colonies would take, most English speaking colonials were still committed to Britain, to the Imperial connection, to British ways of governance and traditions, which they counterposed against "levelling Yankee republicanism." Economic survival, however, dictated closer ties with the large and dynamic market of an expanding United States; this could replace the guaranteed staples market lost in Britain. The idea was not new; free trade, or "reciprocity," had been advocated earlier in the colonies. But it took on a new urgency then, especially as the world slipped into a severe depression in the early 1850s.

Lord Elgin saw reciprocity as the colonies' salvation, and lobbied the Colonial Office to press the matter with the Americans. The latter, themselves bountifully supplied with staples, saw little gain in reciprocity. However, Americans wished access to the coastal fisheries of the Maritimes; disputes in 1852 raised fears of naval conflict. Navigation of the St. Lawrence — wholly under British control — was also of interest to the Americans. Negotiations, handled by Elgin with remarkable finesse, resulted in the Reciprocity Treaty shown here.

The Treaty established free reciprocal trade in virtually all staple and primary products. For the right of free American navigation of the St. Lawrence and colonial canals, British subjects were allowed free navigation of Lake Michigan. In return for American access to Maritime coastal fisheries, fishermen of the British North American colonies received access to American coastal fisheries north of the 36th parallel. The Treaty also created a Fisheries Commission to resolve fisheries disputes.

To what degree the Reciprocity Treaty aided economic recovery is a matter of debate. There are indications that recovery was on the way before the Treaty; the railway boom, the Crimean War (1854-1856) and, later, the American Civil War (1861-1864) all stimulated economic activity and provided markets. However, this Treaty remains a signal event, an indication of a new direction for the British colonies in the three-cornered relationship between Britain, her colonies in North America and the United States.

United Kingdom. 1854.

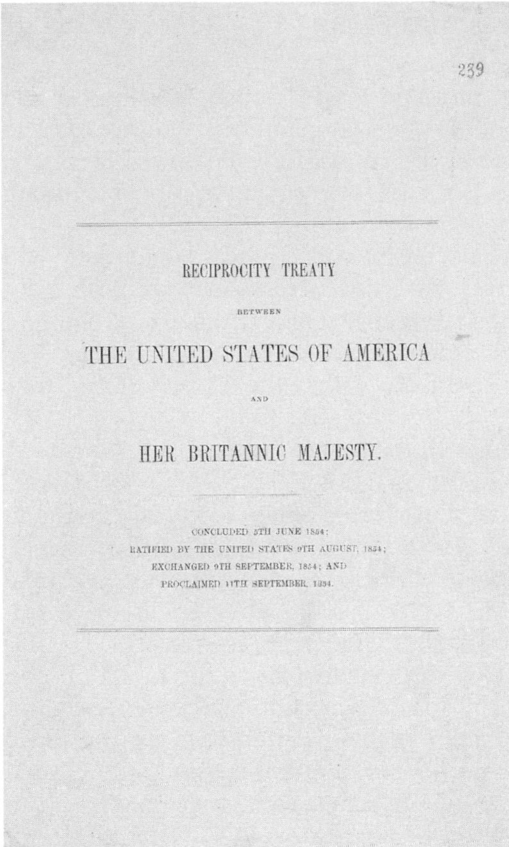

239

RECIPROCITY TREATY

BETWEEN

THE UNITED STATES OF AMERICA

AND

HER BRITANNIC MAJESTY.

CONCLUDED 5TH JUNE 1854;
RATIFIED BY THE UNITED STATES 9TH AUGUST, 1854;
EXCHANGED 9TH SEPTEMBER, 1854; AND
PROCLAIMED 11TH SEPTEMBER, 1854.

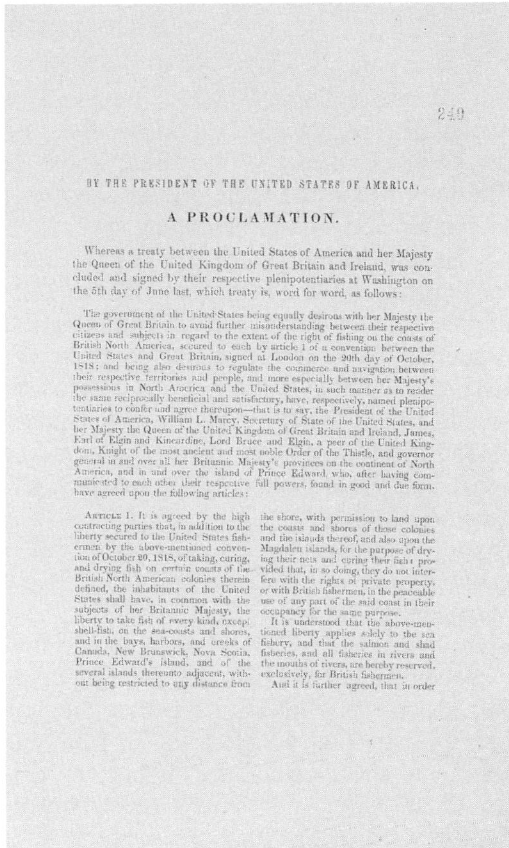

240

BY THE PRESIDENT OF THE UNITED STATES OF AMERICA.

A PROCLAMATION.

Whereas a treaty between the United States of America and her Majesty the Queen of the United Kingdom of Great Britain and Ireland, was concluded and signed by their respective plenipotentiaries at Washington on the 5th day of June last, which treaty is, word for word, as follows:

The government of the United States being equally desirous with her Majesty the Queen of Great Britain to avoid further misunderstanding between their respective citizens and subjects in regard to the extent of the right of fishing on the coasts of British North America, secured to each by article 1 of a convention between the United States and Great Britain, signed at London on the 20th day of October, 1818; and being also desirous to regulate the commerce and navigation between their respective territories and people, and more especially between her Majesty's possessions in North America and the United States, in such manner as to render the same reciprocally beneficial and satisfactory, have, respectively, named plenipotentiaries to confer and agree thereupon—that is to say, the President of the United States of America, William L. Marcy, Secretary of State of the United States, and her Majesty the Queen of the United Kingdom of Great Britain and Ireland, James, Earl of Elgin and Kincardine, Lord Bruce and Elgin, a peer of the United Kingdom, Knight of the most ancient and most noble Order of the Thistle, and governor general in and over all her Britannic Majesty's provinces on the continent of North America, and in and over the island of Prince Edward, who, after having communicated to each other their respective full powers, found in good and due form, have agreed upon the following articles:

ARTICLE 1. It is agreed by the high contracting parties that, in addition to the liberty secured to the United States fishermen by the above-mentioned convention of October 20, 1818, of taking, curing, and drying fish on certain coasts of the British North American colonies therein defined, the inhabitants of the United States shall have, in common with the subjects of her Britannic Majesty, the liberty to take fish of every kind, except shell-fish, on the sea-coasts and shores, and in the bays, harbors, and creeks of Canada, New Brunswick, Nova Scotia, Prince Edward's island, and of the several islands thereunto adjacent, without being restricted to any distance from the shore, with permission to land upon the coasts and shores of those colonies and the islands thereof, and also upon the Magdalen islands, for the purpose of drying their nets and curing their fish: provided that, in so doing, they do not interfere with the rights of private property, or with British fishermen, in the peaceable use of any part of the said coast in their occupancy for the same purpose.

It is understood that the above-mentioned liberty applies solely to the sea fishery, and that the salmon and shad fisheries, and all fisheries in rivers and the mouths of rivers, are hereby reserved, exclusively, for British fishermen.

And it is further agreed, that in order

31.5 cm x 19.8 cm

National Archives of Canada,
Manuscript Division,
MG 24, B 29, Vol. 13, pp. 239-240.

"Blue Book" of Statistics

All colonies within the British Empire annually provided a wide range of statistical and analytical reports to the Colonial Office. Responsibility for compiling the requisite data in the specified format — the "Blue Book" of Statistics — lay with the Provincial Secretary. The information the Secretary amassed served as the basis for planning and policy-making in London and within the colony itself.

The 1855 report on trade is a most instructive document concerning colonial trade and the impact of the Reciprocity Treaty. The Treaty was a commercial success. Both sides imported and exported similar commodities, to the convenience and advantage of both. An American, for example, could purchase products from just across the border, rather than having to transport them from great distance internally within the United States, thus avoiding the expenses and delay of shipping.

The report's statistics indicate that trade overall with the United States, in comparison to 1851, had more than doubled, from $13,000,000.00 to $31,000,000.00. At the same time, contrary to fears that free trade meant the end of a market in Britain, colonial exports to Britain increased by 10 per cent. While there was a temporary falling off of the St. Lawrence carrying trade, it was more than compensated for by increased carrying on Lake Michigan: in 1854 Canadian vessels had transported $8,000,000.00 of cargo; in 1855, they transported $81,000,000.00 of cargo into the American heartland, a ten-fold increase.

Reciprocity also stoked local development. Many small centres along the frontier began to develop their hinterlands as they drew off staples for the American market. Cobourg, for example, pushed a railway back from Lake Ontario to Peterborough, to tap the forest wealth of the backcountry. It became a booming lumber centre, supplying the central American states; with their forests hewn down, these states were then beginning to experience their first lumber shortage. Out of its growing port, Cobourg shipped millions of linear feet of lumber and hundreds of thousands of bushels of wheat across the lake to markets newly opened by reciprocity.

In the opinion of the secretary who compiled this report, reflecting the opinion then current, there could be no question about "the wonderful benefit of reciprocal commerce" which unquestionably functioned "to the mutual accommodation and benefit of the inhabitants of both sides of the line."

Province of Canada: Provincial Secretary. 1855.

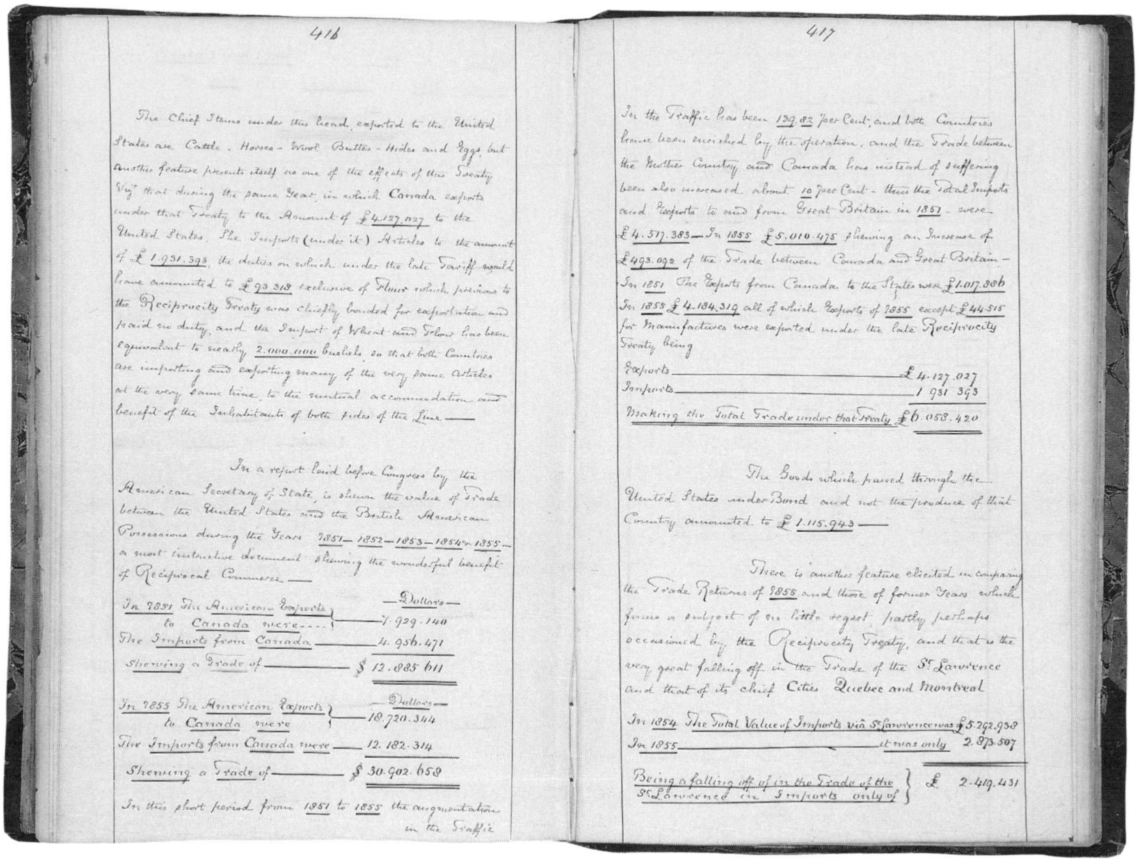

416

The Chief Items under this head, exported to the United States are Cattle. Horses - Wool Butter - Hides and Eggs, but another feature presents itself as one of the effects of this Treaty Viz^t that during the same Year, in which Canada exports under that Treaty to the Amount of £4.127.027 to the United States. The Imports (under it) Articles to the amount of £1.931.393, the duties on which under the late Tariff would have amounted to £93 313 exclusive of Flour which previous to the Reciprocity Treaty was chiefly bonded for exportation and paid no duty, and the Import of Wheat and Flour has been equivalent to nearly 2.000.000 bushels, so that both Countries are importing and exporting many of the very same Articles at the very same time, to the mutual accommodation and benefit of the Inhabitants of both sides of the Line ——

In a report laid before Congress by the American Secretary of State, is shewn the value of Trade between the United States and the British American Possessions during the Years 1851—1852—1853—1854 & 1855— a most instructive document shewing the wonderful benefit of Reciprocal Commerce ——

	Dollars
In 1851 The American Exports to Canada were	7.929.140
The Imports from Canada	4.956.471
Shewing a Trade of	$ 12.885 611

	Dollars
In 1855 The American Exports to Canada were	18.720.344
The Imports from Canada were	12.182.314
Shewing a Trade of	$ 30.902.658

In this short period from 1851 to 1855 the augmentation in the Traffic

417

In the Traffic has been 139.83 per Cent; and both Countries have been enriched by the operation, and the Trade between the Mother Country and Canada has instead of suffering been also increased about 10 per Cent - thus the Total Imports and Exports to and from Great Britain in 1851 - were £4.517.383 — In 1855 £5.010.475 shewing an Increase of £493.092 of the Trade between Canada and Great Britain — In 1851 The Exports from Canada to the States were £1.017.886 In 1855 £4.184.319 all of which Exports of 1855 except £44.515 for Manufactures were exported under the late Reciprocity Treaty being

Exports	£ 4.127.027
Imports	1 931 393
Making the Total Trade under that Treaty	£ 6.058.420

The Goods which passed through the United States under Bond and not the produce of that Country amounted to £1.115.943 ——

There is another feature elicited in comparing the Trade Returns of 1855 and those of former Years which forms a subject of no little regret, partly perhaps occasioned by the Reciprocity Treaty, and that is the very great falling off in the Trade of the St Lawrence and that of its chief Cities Quebec and Montreal

In 1854 The Total Value of Imports via St Lawrence was	£ 5.292.938
In 1855 it was only	2.873.507
Being a falling off of in the Trade of the St Lawrence in Imports only of	£ 2.419.431

32.5 cm x 20.1 cm

National Archives of Canada,
Manuscript Division,
RG 1, E 13, Vol. 33, pp. 416-417.

Annexation of Canada to the United States

William Henry Parker, born ca 1837 in Quebec, inherited lumber interests in both Canada and the United States from his father. An avid sportsman, a "gentleman" who had made the Grand Tour of Europe, Parker wrote this erudite and wonderfully synthesized analysis of the problem then facing the British colonies as they tried to define their relationship with Britain, with the United States and, ultimately, amongst themselves.

Annexation, Parker argued, was redundant — Canada was already open to American capital and talents. Annexation would only lead to subordination, to loss of identity as a people. Canadians (and other colonials as well, it might be added) were still monarchical, and the link with monarchy could not easily be shaken.

The colonies were an expensive burden to the motherland, Parker observed. Neither British people nor their statesmen wished to pay for costly colonial wars in defence of the colonies. Nor did Canada wish to become a second Greece, propped up by foreign bayonets (the British army). Canada wished to preserve her British identity, not to lose it through rash annexation. Self-government, representative institutions and independence would come in due time, as well as separation of the colony from motherland. But until Canada grew into maturity, it was desirable that she hold to the motherland.

The trade, commerce and friendship of the United States were desirable, Parker argued — but so was the protection of Britain, until colonial maturity. To avoid the dislocation of a rapid rupture, to preserve an identity based on British tradition, to mature gradually, and finally to strike out independently — this is what Parker advocated for Canada's future.

This intriguing document captures all the key elements of the annexationist-loyalist debate. It is prophetic in large degree; the scenario of future development that Parker sketched out closely approximates what did happen. And it is still germane to today, as Canadians continue to debate the retention of British-based Canadian values, and the nature of their relationship with the United States.

William Henry Parker. 1855.

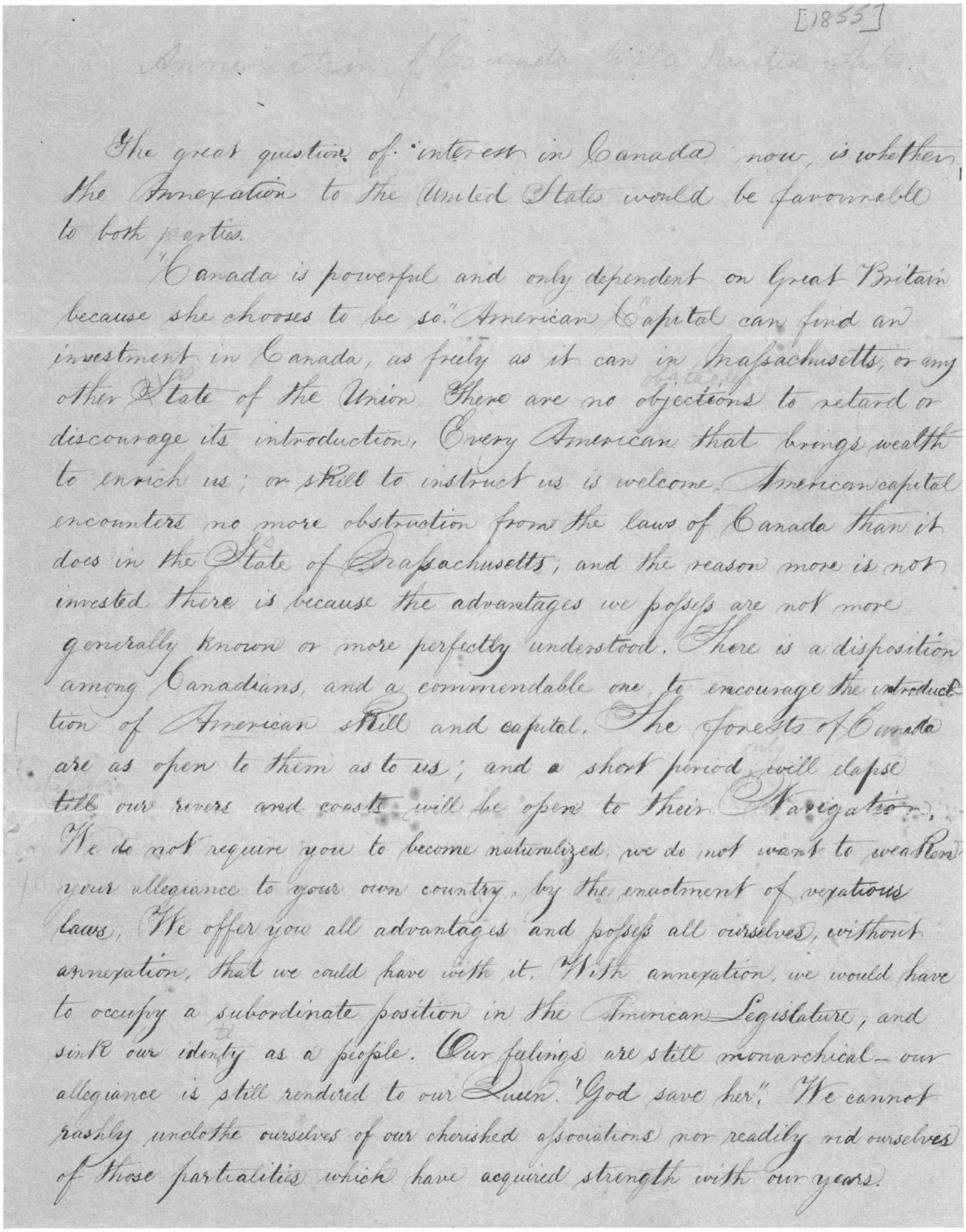

[1855]

Annexation of Canada to the United States.

The great question of interest in Canada now, is whether the Annexation to the United States would be favourable to both parties.

"Canada is powerful and only dependent on Great Britain because she chooses to be so." American Capital can find an investment in Canada, as freely as it can in Massachusetts, or any other State of the Union. There are no objections to retard or discourage its introduction. Every American that brings wealth to enrich us; or skill to instruct us is welcome. American capital encounters no more obstruction from the laws of Canada than it does in the State of Massachusetts, and the reason more is not invested there is because the advantages we possess are not more generally known or more perfectly understood. There is a disposition among Canadians, and a commendable one, to encourage the introduction of American skill and capital. The forests of Canada are as open to them as to us; and a short period only will elapse till our rivers and coasts will be open to their Navigation. We do not require you to become naturalized, we do not want to weaken your allegiance to your own country, by the enactment of vexatious laws. We offer you all advantages and possess all ourselves, without annexation, that we could have with it. With annexation, we would have to occupy a subordinate position in the American Legislature, and sink our identity as a people. Our feelings are still monarchical – our allegiance is still rendered to our Queen. "God save her". We cannot rashly unclothe ourselves of our cherished associations nor readily rid ourselves of those partialities which have acquired strength with our years.

25 cm x 19.7 cm

National Archives of Canada,
Manuscript Division,
MG 24, D 87.

IV

On English-French Political Co-operation in the Province of Canada

In this letter, John A. Macdonald offers to Brown Chamberlain his assessment on the political situation in the United Province of Canada. Chamberlain (1827-1891), a member of the English elite of Montreal, was a publisher of the *Montreal Gazette*, the Canadian Commissioner to the International Exhibition in London in 1862, a member of Parliament (1867-1870) and, finally, Queen's Printer (1870-1891). Macdonald's letter to him reveals the political credo of the most significant politician of the era.

Macdonald recommends to Chamberlain that the English of Montreal lay aside their sentiments of superiority vis-à-vis the French. "You British Lower Canadians never can forget that you were once supreme — that Jean Baptiste was your hewer of wood and drawer of water." It is far better to be realistic and to treat the French with equality:

> "No man in his senses can suppose that this country can for a Century to come be governed by a totally Unfrenchified Government. If a Lower Canadian Britisher desires to conquer, he must 'stoop to conquer.' He must make friends with the French. Without sacrificing the status of his race or language, he must respect their nationality. Treat them as a nation and they will act as a free people generally do — generously."

Contrary to the expectations of English Lower Canadians, Macdonald continues, the French will not disappear. Immigration from Europe has stopped, while the French are spreading into the Eastern Townships and into areas like the St. Maurice, newly opened to colonization. They are filling the factories which are quickly developing in Montreal. The French will survive, and accommodation with them is imperative.

Rejecting other accusations directed against the French, Macdonald maintains that they are no more unruly than the English in Montreal — "you Anglo-Saxons are not bad hands at a riot yourselves." He rejects the charge of French dominance in the civil service lists of Lower Canada; in fact, Anglo-Saxons are over-represented. To Macdonald the French are less dangerous than the "Yankees and Covenanters" (Grits) with their cry of "rep by pop," because of the danger this poses to balance and co-operation in trying to manage Canada.

Macdonald's letter speaks of the political reality of the French Canadians within the United Province of Canada. More significantly, it also advocates acceptance, accommodation and co-operation between the English and French of Canada. To a very large degree Macdonald's realpolitik, as set out in this letter, explains why he grew into the dominant political figure of the watershed Confederation era.

Sir John A. Macdonald. 1856.

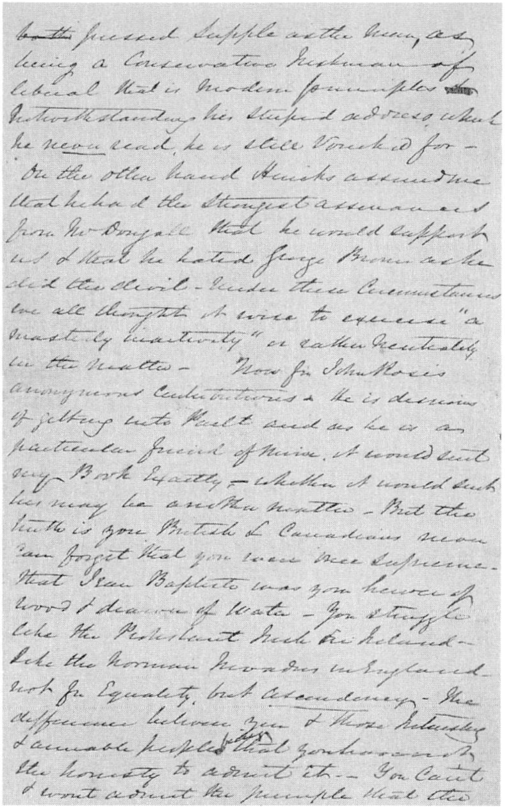

both pressed Supple as the Ministry as
being a Conservative Irishman of
liberal that is modern principles
Notwithstanding his Stupid address which
he never read, he is still Vouched for —
On the other hand Hincks assured me
that he had the strongest assurances
from McDougall that he would support
us & that he hated George Brown as he
did the devil — Under these Circumstances
we all thought it wise to exercise "a
masterly inactivity" or rather neutrality
in the matter — Now for John Rose's
anonymous Contributions & he is desirous
of getting into Parlt and as he is a
particular friend of Mine, it would suit
my Book exactly — whether it would suit
his may be another matter — But the
truth is you British L Canadians never
can forget that you were once Supreme —
that Jean Baptiste was your hewer of
wood & drawer of Water — You struggle
like the Protestant Irish in Ireland —
like the Norman Invaders in England —
not for Equality, but Ascendancy — The
difference between you & those Interesting
& amiable people that you have not
the honesty to admit it — You Can't
& won't admit the principle that the

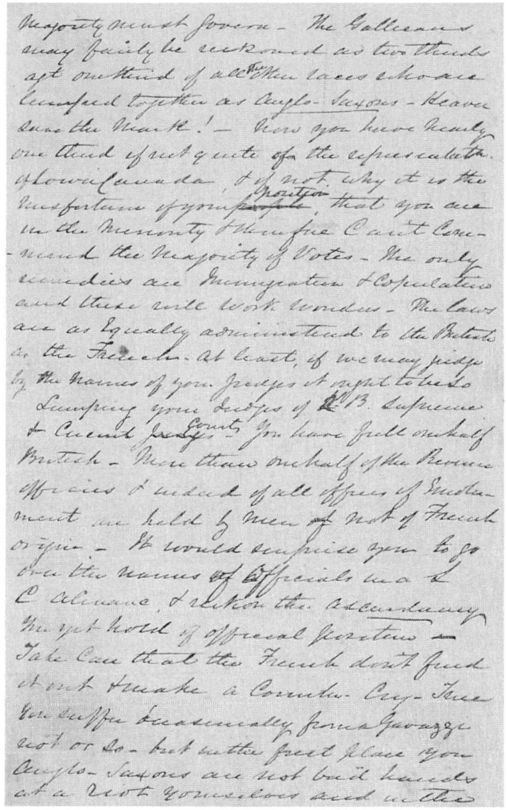

Majority must govern — The Gallicans
may fairly be reckoned as two thirds
agt one third of all the other races who are
lumped together as Anglo-Saxons — Heaven
save the Mark! — Now you have nearly
one third if not quite of the representation
of Lower Canada, & if not, why it is the
misfortune of your ~~people~~ position that you are
in the Minority & therefore Can't Command the Majority of Votes — The only
remedies are Immigration & Copulation
and these will work wonders — The laws
are as Equally administered to the British
as the French — At least, if we may judge
by the names of your Judges it ought to be so
Lumping your Judges of L.C. Supreme
& Circuit ~~Judges~~ Courts — You have full one half
British — More than one half of the Revenue
officers & indeed of all offices of Emolu-
ment are held by men ~~of~~ not of French
origin — It would surprise you to go
over the names of Officials in a L
C Almanac, & reckon the ascendancy
they get hold of official position —
Take Care that the French don't find
it out & make a Counter-Cry — True
You suffer occasionally from a Gavazzi
riot or so — but in the first place you
Anglo-Saxons are not bad hands
at a riot yourselves and in the

20.2 cm x 12.6 cm

National Archives of Canada,
Manuscript Division,
MG 24, B 19, Vol. 2, Item 48.

Seat of Government, Double Shuffle and Political Paralysis

The "seat of government" question disturbed political life throughout the whole Union Period (1841-1867), when Canada West and Canada East, formerly known as Upper and Lower Canada, were united into a single administrative entity known as the United Province of Canada. To the city selected as capital would come the benefits of patronage, of economic stimulus, and of prestige and power.

Understandably enough, sectional interests precluded concession on this point by either Upper or Lower Canada. The compromise was a peregrinating capital. First Kingston (1841-1845), then Montreal (1845-1849) served as capitals; after the burning of Parliament in Montreal, the capital migrated to Toronto (1849-1853) and Quebec City (1853-1858). However, the expenses of constant moving, as well as the accompanying dislocation of government activity, made this arrangement impractical. The debate over the location of the capital, ongoing throughout this period, came to the fore again in 1857; unable to reach a decision, the legislative assembly asked Queen Victoria to decide the issue.

This beautifully penned memorandum, from the Alexander Tilloch Galt papers, captures in detail the acrimony of the capital city debate. But it also reveals how this issue was linked with other significant events of the time. By the time Queen Victoria rendered her decision, choosing Ottawa as capital in 1858, political life in the "two Canadas," raucous and polarized at the best of times, had reached near paralysis. Following the general elections of December 1857-January 1858, two broad political groupings, each consisting of two-partner alliances, were almost equally represented in the province's House of Assembly. Since political parties were still only amorphous agglomerations of individuals rather than organized and controlled groups, there was no certainty that any ministry could long maintain support of the House.

When the Assembly rejected Queen Victoria's choice of Ottawa in 1858 and countered with a resolution that she reconsider and select Montreal as capital, this was construed as an expression of want of confidence in the Macdonald-Cartier ministry, which then resigned. The subsequent Brown-Dorion ministry, (George Brown, leader of the Grits of Canada West, and Antoine-Aimé Dorion, leader of Canada East's Rougistes), fell on a motion of non-confidence several days later. Macdonald and Cartier returned, and through the infamous ruse which has come to be known as the "double-shuffle," (shuffling ministers in cabinet to avoid the necessity of their re-election) managed to survive to 1862. This document records in excruciating detail the constitutional complexities of this political manoeuvre and of the general volatility of provincial politics at that time.

While many legal and government difficulties continued to beset government in the Province of Canada, at least the divisive issue of the seat of capital was removed from the political arena, as construction on parliamentary and governmental buildings commenced in Ottawa in 1859.

Anonymous. 1858.

DOUBLE SHUFFLE 1858

2118

The Seat of Government question in Canada has produced much discussion and difficulty ever since the Union of Upper and Lower Canada in 1841.

The United parliament was first summoned in that year to meet at Kingston by Lord Sydenham — Objections were however raised to the selection of Kingston and it was removed to Montreal in 1844 when Lord Metcalfe was Governor General — It remained there until 1849 when the building which had been occupied temporarily as a parliament House was burnt by a mob, and then, upon resolution of the House of Assembly the alternate system was adopted under which parliament was to meet at Toronto and at Quebec, remaining four years alternately at each place. In 1857 a joint address from the Legislative Council and House of Assembly was passed praying that Her Majesty would be graciously pleased to exercise Her Royal prerogative and fix permanently the Seat of Government for Canada in some convenient place and pledging the Legislature to provide the means for the erection of the necessary buildings at such place as Her Majesty might select.

In the Autumn of 1857 the House of Assembly was dissolved. Colonel Taché the then premier retired from public life and Mr John A Macdonald Attorney General for Upper Canada was charged with the formation of a new Administration. The Elections for the new parliament took place during December 1857 and January 1858 and parliament met on the 25th of February.

The House of Assembly numbers One hundred and thirty members (90 being of English and 40 of French origin) — 122 were present at the opening — the Government Candidate for Speaker was chosen by a majority of 37 — there being with Government 79 Votes against 42 Opposition votes — (the Speaker not voting). The first Amendment moved by Mr Dorion against the address echoing the Speech was negatived by a vote of 40 to 78 giving Mr

32.4 cm x 20 cm

National Archives of Canada,
Manuscript Division,
MG 27, I, D 8, Vol. 5, p. 2118.

IV

Grit Motion on New Ministry and New Union

George Brown (1818-1880) emigrated from Scotland to New York, and then moved to Toronto in 1837. In 1848, he founded the *Globe*, which became an influential newspaper calling for political reform. In 1851, on the contentious matter of state-funded sectarian schools, he championed the separation of Church and State. Partly on this issue, he won a seat in the provincial Assembly. In 1853 he took up the "rep by pop" cry of the Clear Grits. On both issues he earned the animosity of Canada East, which feared domination in the provincial Assembly by Canada West.

This issue also contributed to the disintegration of the Reform party, dominant since the Baldwin-Lafontaine Reform ministry of 1848. With responsible government attained, the Reform movement began to split into radical and moderate wings. By 1854, it was a spent force. While a small core of Reformers survived into the 1860s, Reform moderates gravitated to Macdonald's Liberal-Conservatives in Upper Canada or to Cartier's Bleus in Lower Canada, while Reform radicals swung to the Liberal and Clear Grit movements in Canada West or the Liberal or Rouge movements in Canada East. This significant political reorientation served as the genesis of the future political parties of the Dominion of Canada.

George Brown played a significant role in precipitating a new political spectrum, bringing together radical Reformers and Clear Grits. The latter, influenced by American popular democracy based on "rep by pop," worked out clear-cut positions which they defended in an abrasive manner (hence their name). Agrarian radicals, they wished the annexation of the continental interior to secure unoccupied farmland for future generations.

As provincial politics grew more unmanageable in Canada, Brown, amongst many, began to search for new directions. The Reform Convention of 1859, held in Toronto, drew together liberal and radical political forces; here Brown played a crucial role in the formulation of Grit policy. The future of a United Province of Canada dominated the proceedings. Stymied in their demand for representation by population, feeling that Canada East did not support acquisition of Rupert's Land (a larger and stronger Canada West would not be to its benefit), the Reform Convention resolved that the only way out of political and sectional paralysis was dissolution of the United Province, followed by federal union of all British colonies.

This was the foundation of Brown's political credo. It is reflected in this document, an amendment to a motion that he presented to the Assembly of the Province of Canada in its 1860 session. On the basis of the political program outlined in his 1860 motion, Brown made possible the "Great Coalition" of 1864 in the parliament of the Province of Canada, which eventually led to the Charlottetown Conference and Confederation.

George Brown. 1860.

490

Mr Brown moves in amendment that all after the word "That" in the said motion be struck out, and the following substituted:

"A Committee of nine members be appointed to inquire & report, <u>First</u>, as to the expediency of changing the existing union of Upper and Lower Canada, by the sub-division of the Province into two or more divisions, each governing itself in local & sectional matters, with a general Government and a general Legislature, in which the people shall be represented on the basis of population, for subjects of national or common interests: <u>Second</u>, as to the expediency of inviting the other British Provinces to join such union: <u>Third</u>, as to the expediency of making provision for bringing within the said union such portions of the Hudson's Bay Territories as may from time to time become sufficiently settled: And, <u>fourthly</u>, to suggest for the consideration of this house, such details for carrying into effect said union as may to the said Committee seem expedient."

25.3 cm x 20.2 cm

National Archives of Canada,
Manuscript Division,
MG 24, B 40, Vol. 3, p. 490.

"Map of British North America Comprising Upper and Lower Canada, Nova Scotia, New Brunswick, British Columbia, and the Islands of Prince Edward, Newfoundland and Vancouver. Prepared under the Supervision of the Educational Department for the Use of Public Schools of Upper Canada"

W.C. Chewett's map is a noteworthy cartographic record of its time, reflecting new and interesting geographical information, such as height above sea level and area and depth of each of the five Great Lakes. It shows the uneven sectoral advance of communications in the British colonies; while the Grand Trunk Railway was pushing through the Eastern Townships, and Canada West was developing a large rail network, the Maritimes had but few short lines.

The map very effectively reflects the administrative divisions of the colonies into counties and townships. One can readily notice the legacy of seigneurial land tenure along the North Shore and in the Montreal area on both banks of the St. Lawrence. The irregularity of parishes in these regions is very noticeable in relation to the geometric townships laid out in the British era. New districts under survey and colonization, such as Pontiac and Chicoutimi in Lower Canada, and Nipissing and Algoma in Upper Canada, are demarcated; thus, the map shows the advance of colonization into frontier areas.

The insets mirror the great issues of the era — communications and settlement. The inset of the Northwest demarcates the Thunder Bay-Winnipeg-British Columbia overland route, the proposed railway line through British territory, and points of settlement in British Columbia and Vancouver Island. The British Colonies-United States-Europe inset shows the colonies in relation to Europe, tracing out the trans-Atlantic routes with mileages and distances, as well as the Trans-Atlantic Cable (with several unsuccessful attempts made, but the cable not yet laid). The Newfoundland inset notes the Cormack Track, the main east-west road across Newfoundland, as well as the land portion of the Submarine Telegraph Cable, between St. John's and Cape Ray, along the South Shore.

Communications, settlement, Rupert's Land and the North-Western Territory, as well as the West Coast, are the central concerns of this map. They reveal the objectives — and the biases — of Canada West, of its concern for breaking out past the Lakehead. One senses in this large map, published by the Educational Department of Upper Canada, the province's self-confidence and belief in its central role in the future.

W.C. Chewett & Co. Lith. [1862].

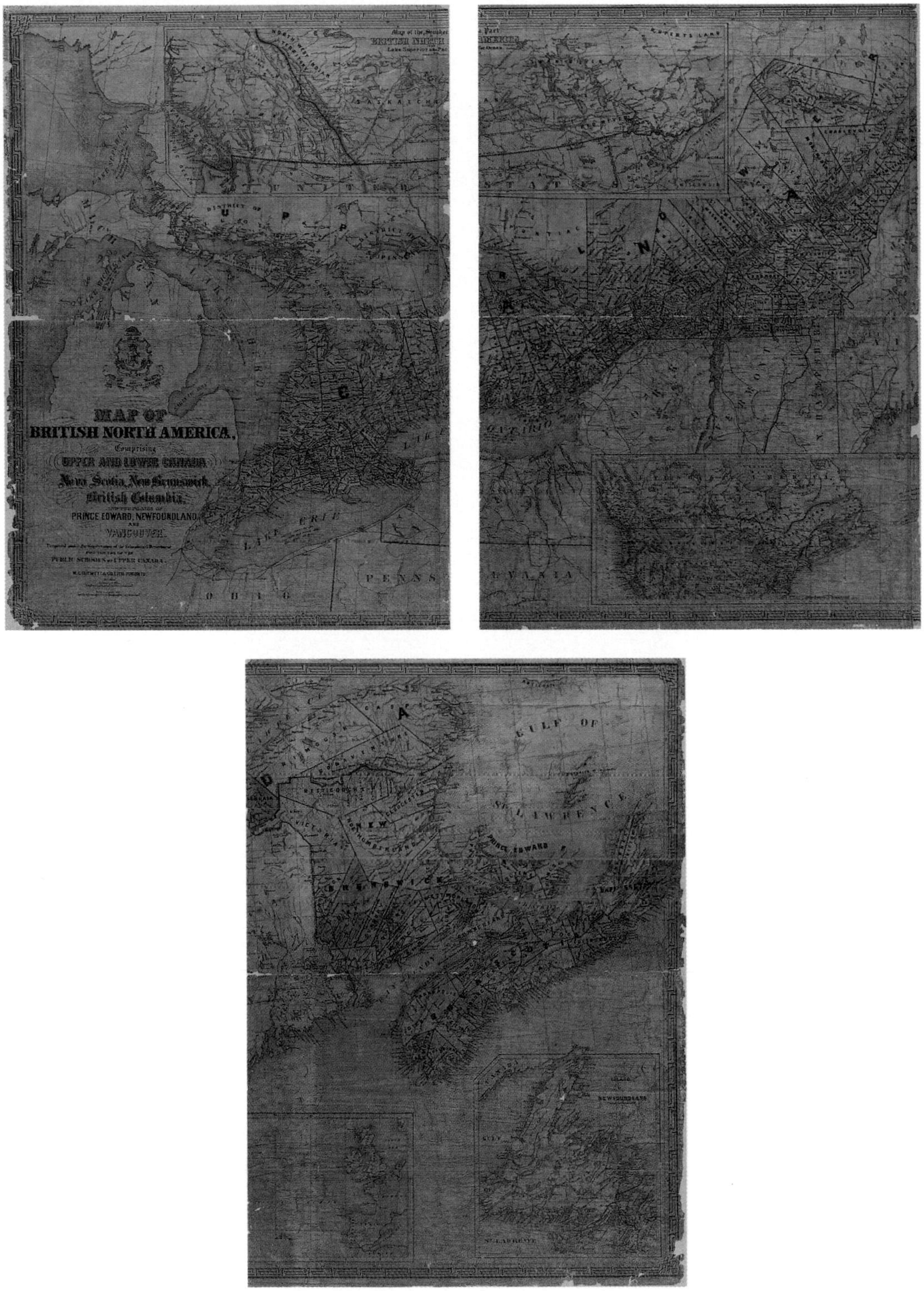

99 cm x 221 cm

National Archives of Canada,
Cartographic and Audio-Visual Archives Division,
NMC-21864.

"Convention at Charlottetown, Prince Edward Island, of Delegates from the Legislatures of Canada, New Brunswick, Nova Scotia, and Prince Edward Island, To Take into Consideration the Union of the British North American Colonies, — September 1, 1864"

The Charlottetown Conference was originally planned by the legislatures of New Brunswick, Nova Scotia and Prince Edward Island to discuss a proposed Maritime Union. The idea was not new, and it had surfaced now and then, especially in difficult times. Nova Scotia and New Brunswick, still piqued at Canada's reneging on a commitment in 1863 to co-operate in the building of an intercolonial railway, were interested in discussing union as a way to achieve this. "Greater Nova Scotians" dreamed of restoring eighteenth-century Nova Scotia, which had included New Brunswick and Prince Edward Island. High officials in the Maritimes, such as Sir Arthur Hamilton Gordon, Lieutenant-Governor of New Brunswick, encouraged local union.

Maritime union was only one of several possibilities. The concept of a union of Canada and the Maritime colonies also had a long pedigree. In fact, in 1858, the Governor-in-Chief of Canada, Sir Edmund Walker Head, had written the Colonial Office requesting authorization to pursue this objective. His successor, Lord Monck, and the Colonial Office, became active promoters of the idea. They saw, in a larger union, a way out of the ongoing political crisis in the Province of Canada. Union was consonant with the British Crown's desire to extricate itself from the burden of managing the British colonies in North America, and providing for their defence. And for purposes of defence, union was imperative against a United States angered at perceived British support of the Confederate states, then on the verge of defeat in the American Civil War.

One can see the hand of the Crown at work in arranging the Charlottetown Conference. One week after the Great Coalition was formed in Canada on 22 June 1864, with union of all British colonies its stated objective, Monck wrote to the Lieutenant-Governors of the Maritime provinces to secure invitations to the conference at Charlottetown for delegates from Canada, and to broaden the conference agenda to include consideration of union of all British North American colonies. Only when this request came did the Maritime provinces themselves fix a date for a conference, till then only loosely considered.

This photograph of the delegates by George P. Roberts was taken on the first day of the conference. Little is known of Roberts, except that he had a photographic studio in Saint John from the early 1860s until the 1880s, and for a while during the 1870s in Halifax. The size of the photograph and its quality, indicating substantial investment in money and time, suggest that Roberts expected the image of the Conference delegates to sell well.

To the delegates, needs of defence, railway-building and economic development suggested union; beautiful autumn weather as the delegates cruised on the steamer *Queen Victoria* put them in a pleasant frame of mind; and visions of unlimited potential in a glorious new union began to dance in delegates' heads. Idealism and bonhommie characterized the conference, where the poetry of union was sung, put to words and adopted in principle. To discuss the mechanics of union, the delegates agreed to meet later in the year in Quebec City.

George P. Roberts. 1864.

21.1 cm x 30.2 cm

National Archives of Canada,
Documentary Art and Photography Division,
C-733.

"International Convention at Quebec of Delegates of the Legislatures of Canada, Nova Scotia, New Brunswick, Prince Edward Island and Newfoundland — 27 October 1864"

This photograph was taken by Jules-Isaï Benoit de Livernois (1830-1865). After trying several business ventures, which included journeying to San Francisco by way of Cape Horn and back, he settled in Quebec City, opening a books and sewing-machine business. Venturing into photography, he was assured of success when he became official Church photographer, which brought him a large clientele. He also began to photograph maps, plans, drawings and paintings of Quebec's past, and to market these images; he in fact became the Garneau of Quebec photography. His reputation earned him the commission to photograph the Quebec Conference; his business acumen led him to realize what a financially rewarding opportunity this might prove to be through the sale of many copies of the photograph.

The Charlottetown Conference had approved union in principle; the Quebec Conference (10-27 October 1864) hammered out the mechanics of that union. The Canadian delegation, hosting the Conference, dominated the proceedings. While Canada's premier, Étienne-Paschal Taché, chaired the sessions, its cabinet, dominated by John A. Macdonald, controlled the agenda and re-wrote resolutions until acceptable to all present.

Some matters, such as the distribution of powers in a federal structure, were relatively easily resolved. Other issues proved more difficult. In the financial realm, colonies feared losing control of customs duties, their largest source of income. Maritime provinces were uneasy about representation by population; with small populations they would lose self-governing status for a small role in a large confederation. To assuage their fears, they were promised a one-third bloc in the second house, the Senate. The schools and language questions worried Quebec and Roman Catholics outside Lower Canada, as well as Protestants in Quebec, who feared that once the new political order came, and educational and cultural matters passed to provincial authority, religious and linguistic intolerance directed at minorities might worsen in each of the separate provinces.

Managed forcefully by the Canadians, the Conference produced the "Seventy-Two Resolutions" that were to be debated in all provincial legislatures. Acceptance of the resolutions was neither swift nor easy in any legislature but that of Canada. Newfoundland's deputies rejected them outright. Only heavy pressure from the Crown ensured acceptance of the resolutions in Nova Scotia and New Brunswick. Prince Edward Island held out until 1873, and Newfoundland until 1949, when it joined on different terms.

It was perhaps understandable that the people of the Maritimes opposed union. With a radically different historical development, they had little in common with centrally-located Canada. Their economic, religious, social and cultural ties were with New England. Their connection with Britain was stronger than with the continental heartland. Except for the Roman Catholic Irish in Maritime cities, they were distinctly English in culture, with their loyalty to the Crown re-stoked by the coming of the United Empire Loyalists: above all things, they were British subjects first. There was a sense of superiority in the Maritimes; they had achieved responsible government first, and their societies were quite free of serious discord, unlike the political maelstrom of Canada. Since their sense of independence had precluded even local union, not surprisingly union with distant Canada was far less desirable.

The "Fathers of Confederation," though inspired by a noble vision, found themselves, in the case of Canada, leading their warring children out of too-close-a-union, and in the case of the Maritimes, leading unwilling children into a forced union.

Jules-Isaï Benoit de Livernois. 1864.

20.3 cm x 30.6 cm

National Archives of Canada,
Documentary Art and Photography Division,
C-6350.

"Bienfaits de la Confédération" in *Le Perroquet*, edition of 4 February 1865

Newspapers of the Confederation period were an influential opinion-making medium. Political vehicles in a demonstrably political age, when people lived their politics with zest, and when politics intruded into many areas of life, newspapers were expected to be partisan, vocal and often extremist in advocating the positions of political groupings and movements.

Political caricature, sometimes cruel and often exaggerated, was a given of the era, both accepted and expected. Charles-Henri Moreau was a master of caricature. He edited *Le Perroquet* which published from 7 January 1865 to 12 August 1865. The newspaper had for its masthead the slogan "Let us laugh for fear of being forced to cry," an appropriate slogan for an accomplished satirist. A satirical, literary newspaper, it was graced with his finely-drawn, powerful, effective and biting caricatures.

In this caricature, as Confederation was debated in the Parliament of Canada, Moreau expressed his reservations about future union. In the image, a father-and-husband, seduced by the new order, has left his wife and children to fend for themselves in the snow and winds of winter. He himself has taken up with a new woman, with the English name of Kate, and loafs back on a divan, enjoying a cigar and wine. In a direct sense, Moreau may be expressing his fear of what Confederation might entail for French culture, based on the family unit and Catholicism. That divorce becomes possible with Confederation damns Confederation as a heinous option. In an indirect sense, Moreau may be commenting on the immorality of *vendus*, those who, for personal gain, desert family and French culture, as expressed in the broken cameo symbolizing love. The *vendu* in this case might be George-Étienne Cartier.

To many people in Quebec, despite the obvious difficulties of forced co-habitation with English Canada West, Confederation as then proposed was undesirable. This was especially the case with Antoine-Aimé Dorion, the Rougiste who in his *L'Avenir* wrote, "this is not the confederation we proposed but simply a legislative union disguised under the name of confederation." He feared that the strong powers accorded to the central government, and the increased number of English-speaking provinces ranged against Quebec, would destroy Quebec's French culture.

Moreau's caricature likely did not represent mainline French-Canadian thinking on Confederation. While the French of Quebec did not greet 1867 with resounding joy, there was a general, cautious acceptance of Confederation, urged on by a Catholic Church and moderate politicians satisfied that the new order left the province control of its culture and destiny.

Charles-Henri Moreau. 1865.

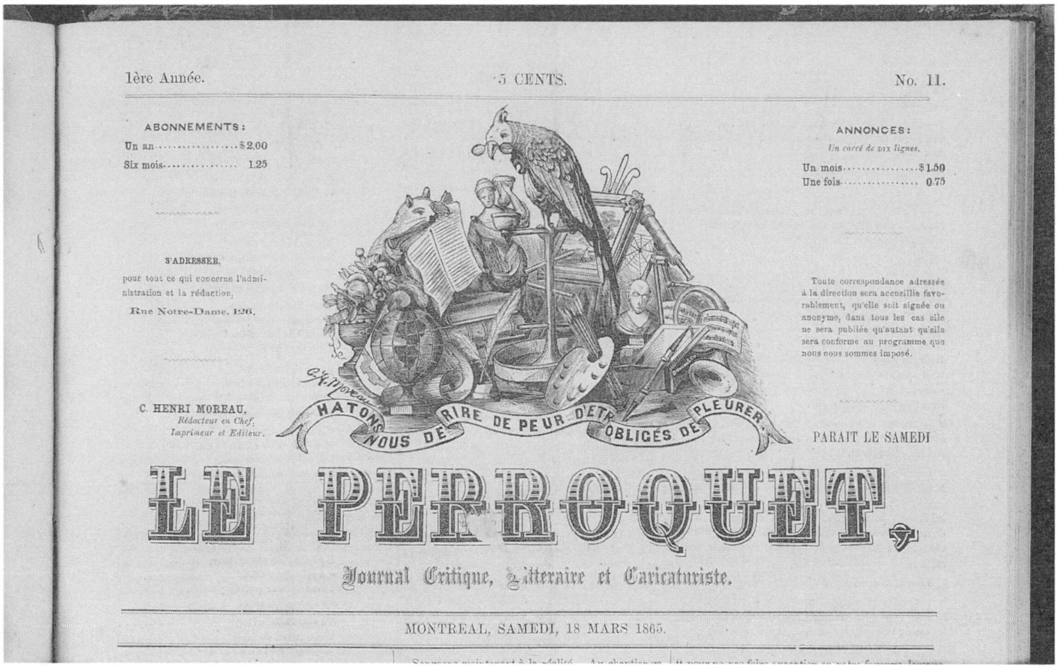

1ère Année. | 5 CENTS. | No. 11.

ABONNEMENTS:

Un an $2.00
Six mois 1.25

S'ADRESSER,
pour tout ce qui concerne l'administration et la rédaction,
Rue Notre-Dame, 126.

C. HENRI MOREAU,
Rédacteur en Chef,
Imprimeur et Editeur.

ANNONCES:
Un carré de dix lignes.

Un mois $1.50
Une fois 0.75

Toute correspondance adressée à la direction sera accueillie favorablement, qu'elle soit signée ou anonyme, dans tous les cas elle ne sera publiée qu'autant qu'elle sera conforme au programme que nous nous sommes imposé.

PARAIT LE SAMEDI

HATONS NOUS DE RIRE DE PEUR D'ETRE OBLIGÉS DE PLEURER.

LE PERROQUET.

Journal Critique, Litteraire et Caricaturiste.

MONTREAL, SAMEDI, 18 MARS 1865.

National Archives of Canada,
Archival Community Programs Division,
C-112903,
[Caricature],
[Banner].

27.4 cm x 20.5 cm
17.7 cm x 24 cm

Resolution Regarding Schools and Language of Instruction

At the London Conference (December 1866-February 1867) delegates from the legislatures of the colonies of Canada, New Brunswick and Nova Scotia met with British officials to finalize the statutes that would unite these colonies. The basis of discussion were the "Seventy-Two Resolutions" adopted at the Quebec Conference. To overcome reservations that certain delegates felt on various points, a number of minor clarifications and alterations were adopted.

For example, the Maritime delegates' fear of being swamped in a future legislature after union manifested itself again. The Conference resolved that regional interests would be protected in the upper house, the Senate, which would have 72 seats. Of these, the Maritimes would receive 24 seats (one-third), divided between Nova Scotia and New Brunswick. Were Prince Edward Island to change its mind and enter the union, Senate seats would be allocated to it out of this Maritime bloc. The number of seats would not change; hence, the influence of the significantly less populous Maritime region would neither increase nor diminish.

The thorny matter of education, at that time closely linked with religion, surfaced again. The Catholics of Canada West and in the Maritime provinces (where they were a minority) wished guaranteed protection for their separate schools. The Catholic bishops of Canada East, as well as the Catholic clergy of Rupert's Land, were concerned about the future of separate schools in those regions. Protestants in Canada East obviously wanted guarantees that they be free to run their separate school system. This critical issue was long debated; the document dislayed here is the result of this debate. In Sir John A. Macdonald's own handwriting, this resolution reciprocally guarantees separate school structures in Canada East and Canada West. Insofar as other provinces are concerned, it makes the "general" (i.e. central) government the final arbiter of the fate of separate or dissenting schools. In the bottom left corner the colonies represented at the Conference are named, with a "yes" annotated to each, signifying their acceptance of the resolution.

Once the discussions were completed, and the "Seventy-Two Resolutions" redrafted to incorporate changes, Macdonald submitted them to the Colonial Secretary, Lord Carnarvon; he, in turn, transmitted them to the British Parliament for consideration.

London Conference. 1866.

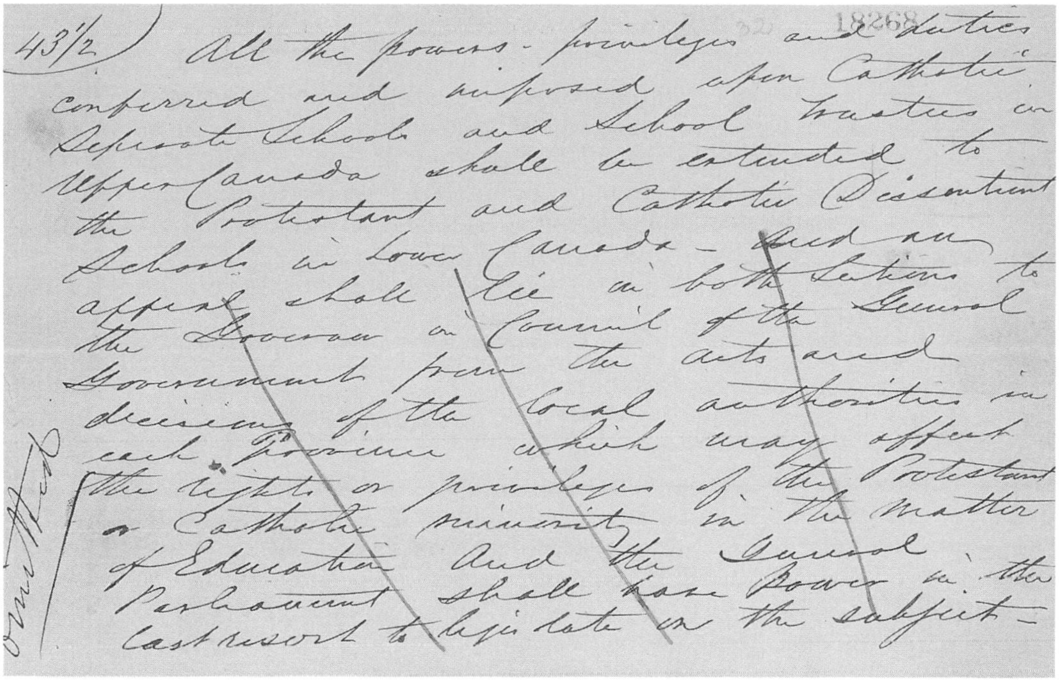

18268

43½) All the powers, privileges and duties conferred and imposed upon Catholic Separate Schools and School trustees in Upper Canada shall be extended to the Protestant and Catholic Dissentient Schools in Lower Canada - And an appeal shall lie in both Sections to the Governor in Council of the General Government from the acts and decisions of the local authorities in each Province which may affect the rights or privileges of the Protestant or Catholic minority in the matter of Education And the General Parliament shall have Power in the last resort to legislate on the subject -

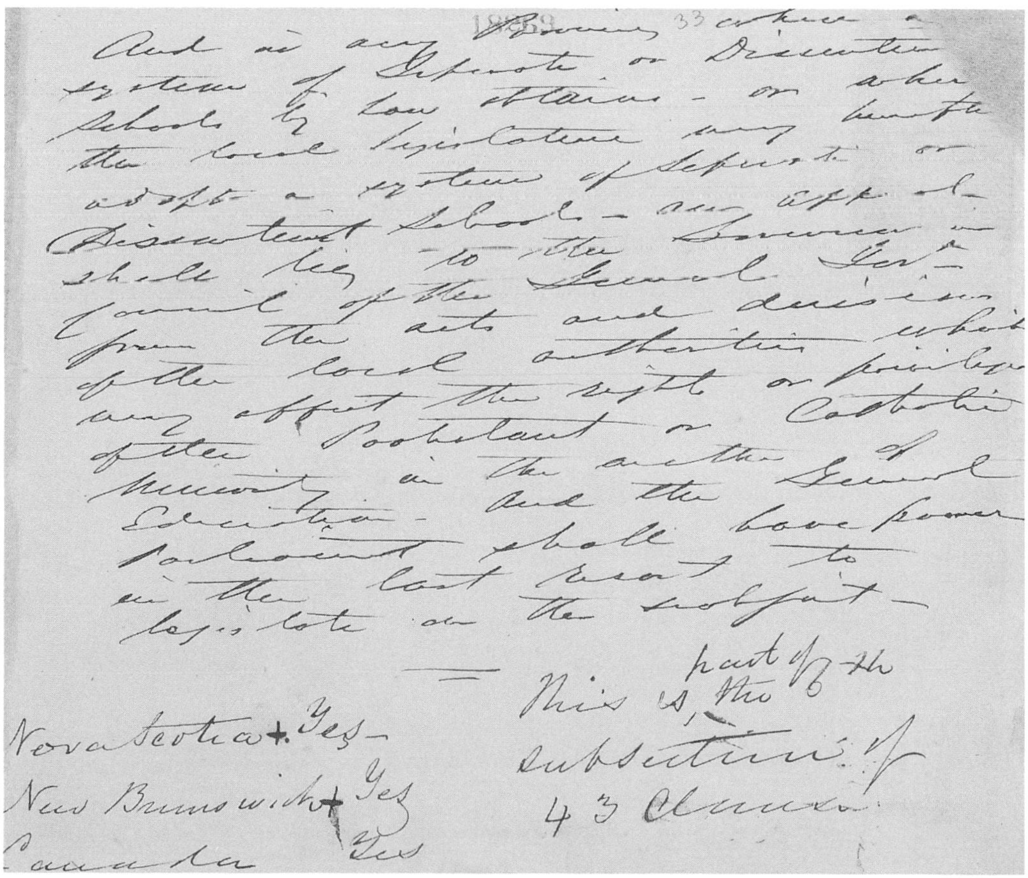

18269

And in any Province where a system of Separate or Dissentient Schools by law obtains - or where the local legislature may hereafter adopt a system of Separate or Dissentient Schools - an appeal shall lie to the Governor in Council of the General Govt. from the acts and decisions of the local authorities which may affect the rights or privileges of the Protestant or Catholic minority in the matter of Education - And the General Parliament shall have power in the last resort to legislate on the subject -

This is, part of the substitution of 43 Clause

Nova Scotia + Yes -
New Brunswick + Yes
Canada Yes

29.3 cm x 19.4 cm

National Archives of Canada,
Manuscript Division,
MG 26, A, Vol. 47(I), pp. 182-183.

IV

"Proclamation of Confederation"

Once the London Conference had done its work of amending and recasting the "Seventy-Two Resolutions" into legislation, they were submitted to the British Parliament as a basis for legislation on North American union. The best efforts of Joseph Howe's Repealers could not dissuade the British Parliament from passage of the legislation.

The legislation passed through the British Houses with very little debate. In fact, fewer than sixteen lords were in their seats for third and final reading of the bill. On 29 March 1867, Queen Victoria gave royal assent to the *British North America Act* (known since 1982 as the *Constitution Act*, 1867), creating the new Dominion of Canada. The Dominion consisted of four provinces — Nova Scotia, New Brunswick, Quebec and Ontario, the latter two separated out of the former United Province of Canada.

The document displayed is Queen Victoria's proclamation declaring the unification of the four provinces into one Dominion of Canada. Dated 22 May 1867, the proclamation fixes 1 July 1867 as the date on which the Dominion of Canada would come into legal existence. The delegates to the Conference had intended to designate the new state the "Kingdom of Canada." Fearing that the monarchism implicit in this designation might irk American sensibilities, the British government insisted on a different title. At the suggestion of Sir Leonard Tilley, Premier of New Brunswick, the delegates agreed upon "Dominion," a concept drawn from the Seventy-Second Psalm.

This proclamation also names the individuals summoned from each province to the Senate of Canada. Given the difficult birth of Confederation, and the regions' fears that their interests would be ignored, it obviously was imperative to have the regional representatives in place as quickly as possible to allay apprehensions about the new union.

Queen Victoria. 1867.

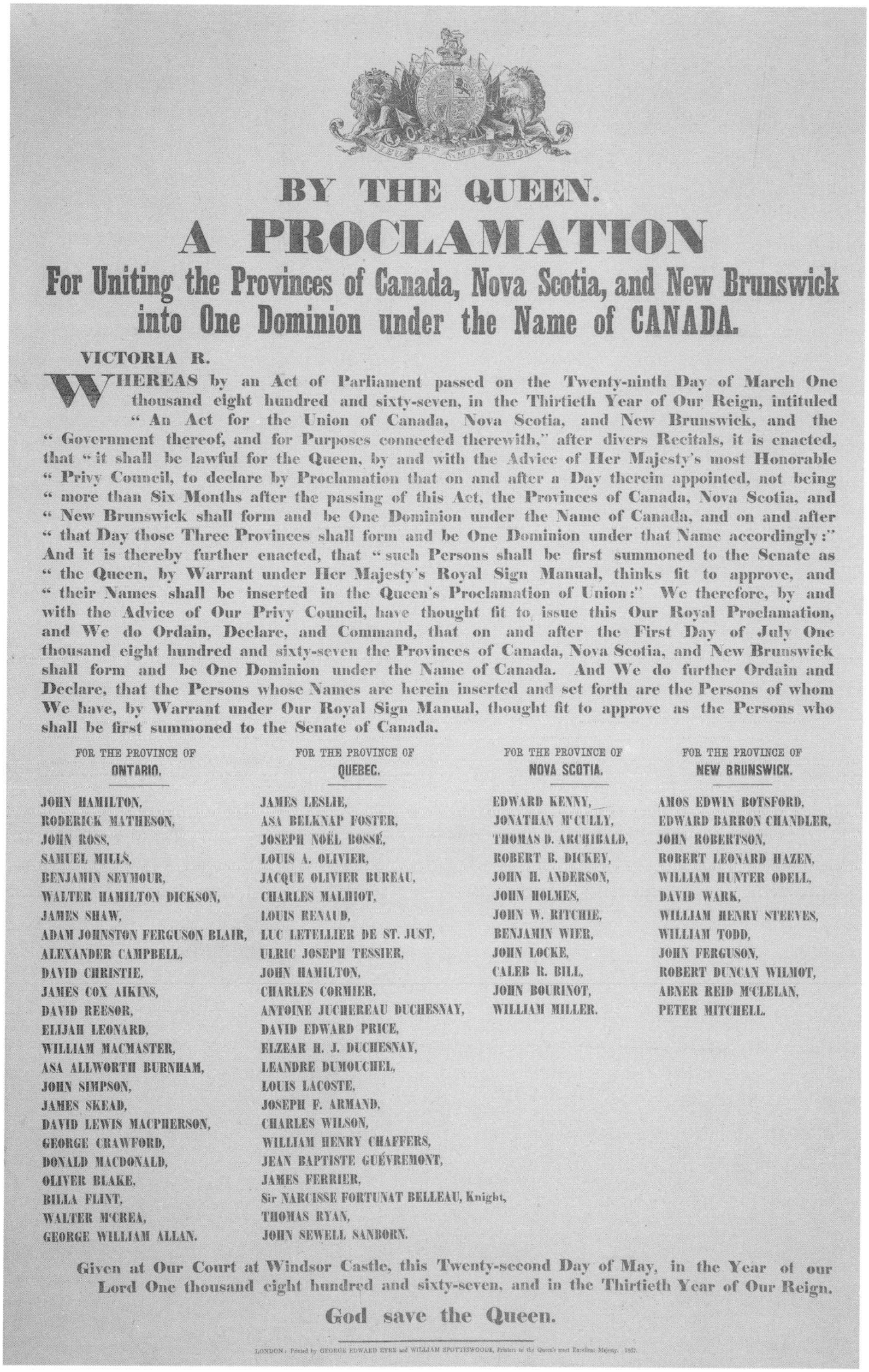

DIEU ET MON DROIT

BY THE QUEEN.

A PROCLAMATION

For Uniting the Provinces of Canada, Nova Scotia, and New Brunswick into One Dominion under the Name of CANADA.

VICTORIA R.

WHEREAS by an Act of Parliament passed on the Twenty-ninth Day of March One thousand eight hundred and sixty-seven, in the Thirtieth Year of Our Reign, intituled " An Act for the Union of Canada, Nova Scotia, and New Brunswick, and the " Government thereof, and for Purposes connected therewith," after divers Recitals, it is enacted, that " it shall be lawful for the Queen, by and with the Advice of Her Majesty's most Honorable " Privy Council, to declare by Proclamation that on and after a Day therein appointed, not being " more than Six Months after the passing of this Act, the Provinces of Canada, Nova Scotia, and " New Brunswick shall form and be One Dominion under the Name of Canada, and on and after " that Day those Three Provinces shall form and be One Dominion under that Name accordingly :" And it is thereby further enacted, that " such Persons shall be first summoned to the Senate as " the Queen, by Warrant under Her Majesty's Royal Sign Manual, thinks fit to approve, and " their Names shall be inserted in the Queen's Proclamation of Union :" We therefore, by and with the Advice of Our Privy Council, have thought fit to issue this Our Royal Proclamation, and We do Ordain, Declare, and Command, that on and after the First Day of July One thousand eight hundred and sixty-seven the Provinces of Canada, Nova Scotia, and New Brunswick shall form and be One Dominion under the Name of Canada. And We do further Ordain and Declare, that the Persons whose Names are herein inserted and set forth are the Persons of whom We have, by Warrant under Our Royal Sign Manual, thought fit to approve as the Persons who shall be first summoned to the Senate of Canada.

FOR THE PROVINCE OF ONTARIO.	FOR THE PROVINCE OF QUEBEC.	FOR THE PROVINCE OF NOVA SCOTIA.	FOR THE PROVINCE OF NEW BRUNSWICK.
JOHN HAMILTON,	JAMES LESLIE,	EDWARD KENNY,	AMOS EDWIN BOTSFORD,
RODERICK MATHESON,	ASA BELKNAP FOSTER,	JONATHAN M'CULLY,	EDWARD BARRON CHANDLER,
JOHN ROSS,	JOSEPH NOËL BOSSÉ,	THOMAS D. ARCHIBALD,	JOHN ROBERTSON,
SAMUEL MILLS,	LOUIS A. OLIVIER,	ROBERT B. DICKEY,	ROBERT LEONARD HAZEN,
BENJAMIN SEYMOUR,	JACQUE OLIVIER BUREAU,	JOHN H. ANDERSON,	WILLIAM HUNTER ODELL,
WALTER HAMILTON DICKSON,	CHARLES MALHIOT,	JOHN HOLMES,	DAVID WARK,
JAMES SHAW,	LOUIS RENAUD,	JOHN W. RITCHIE,	WILLIAM HENRY STEEVES,
ADAM JOHNSTON FERGUSON BLAIR,	LUC LETELLIER DE ST. JUST,	BENJAMIN WIER,	WILLIAM TODD,
ALEXANDER CAMPBELL,	ULRIC JOSEPH TESSIER,	JOHN LOCKE,	JOHN FERGUSON,
DAVID CHRISTIE,	JOHN HAMILTON,	CALEB R. BILL,	ROBERT DUNCAN WILMOT,
JAMES COX AIKINS,	CHARLES CORMIER,	JOHN BOURINOT,	ABNER REID M'CLELAN,
DAVID REESOR,	ANTOINE JUCHEREAU DUCHESNAY,	WILLIAM MILLER.	PETER MITCHELL.
ELIJAH LEONARD,	DAVID EDWARD PRICE,		
WILLIAM MACMASTER,	ELZEAR H. J. DUCHESNAY,		
ASA ALLWORTH BURNHAM,	LEANDRE DUMOUCHEL,		
JOHN SIMPSON,	LOUIS LACOSTE,		
JAMES SKEAD,	JOSEPH F. ARMAND,		
DAVID LEWIS MACPHERSON,	CHARLES WILSON,		
GEORGE CRAWFORD,	WILLIAM HENRY CHAFFERS,		
DONALD MACDONALD,	JEAN BAPTISTE GUÉVREMONT,		
OLIVER BLAKE,	JAMES FERRIER,		
BILLA FLINT,	Sir NARCISSE FORTUNAT BELLEAU, Knight,		
WALTER M'CREA,	THOMAS RYAN,		
GEORGE WILLIAM ALLAN.	JOHN SEWELL SANBORN.		

Given at Our Court at Windsor Castle, this Twenty-second Day of May, in the Year of our Lord One thousand eight hundred and sixty-seven, and in the Thirtieth Year of Our Reign.

God save the Queen.

LONDON: Printed by GEORGE EDWARD EYRE and WILLIAM SPOTTISWOODE, Printers to the Queen's most Excellent Majesty. 1867.

101.6 cm x 63.5 cm

National Archives of Canada,
Government Archives Division,
RG 2, Vol. 5354.

"Two Dates. 1760 and 1867"

Sir Adolphe-Basile Routhier (1839-1920), born in Lower Canada, studied law at Laval University. Named a judge in 1873, he completed his legal career as Chief Justice of Quebec. A prolific and versatile administrator, orator and writer, he authored the French lyrics to *O Canada!* in 1873. He was both general president of the Saint Jean Baptiste Society and a charter member of the Royal Society of Canada.

Routhier personally inscribed the poem displayed here into an album belonging to Marie Reine Josephte Gauvreau, who had married Narcisse Fortunat Belleau (1808-1894), a former premier of Canada (1865-1867) and the first Lieutenant-Governor of Quebec following Confederation (1867-1873).

Routhier's poem adheres closely to the teaching of the historian-theologian Father Henri Casgrain who, in the 1860s, defined the literary values that would dominate French thinking in Quebec for a century. Literature should, according to Casgrain, reflect faithfully the life of a Catholic, religious and moral people, and honour New France of pre-1760 and the reduced homeland of Quebec following Confederation.

Routhier's poem is almost a formulaic reflection of these values. The conquest of 1760 was a time of lament after Montcalm, the immortal hero, was buried in the colours of France — everything but honour had been lost at conquest. Chevaliers and priests, rather than submit to an occupier, returned to France. Abandoned by its natural leaders, would the superb race of New France die out? No, Routhier declaims, because God, who cares for the smallest blade of grass, let a ray shine from his heart upon the French of Canada.

The year 1867, Routhier continues, puts an end to gloom. Out of the tomb of conquest rises a new people, born on the banks of a great river. A people which has long suffered occupation, the French Canadians have survived all obstacles, matured and await their glorious day. That day comes in 1867 when, within the walls of Quebec City, there assembles a French *Parlement*, headed by a governor risen from the common people, who had betrayed neither faith nor honour. After more than a century, he has taken his place; and Routhier exhorts Quebec — "Oh, daughter of France! Oh, my sweet homeland" — to be proud of her child, her own governor.

In writing this poem Routhier exalted Belleau (could one expect anything else, given that he penned it in Madame Belleau's album?). But more importantly, he honoured the office, the symbol of public authority returned to the French of Quebec. His attitudes and perceptions of Quebec's history mirror the general line of the Quebec clergy and explain why the clergy successfully convinced most Quebecers to support Confederation. Confederation, in the context of Routhier's understanding, was a loosening of bonds that had choked French Quebec in its forced union with Ontario, and a decentralization of power. With its own parliament and its own governor, in the sphere of authority allocated to the province, the French "race" was assured its survival.

Sir Adolphe-Basile Routhier. 1867.

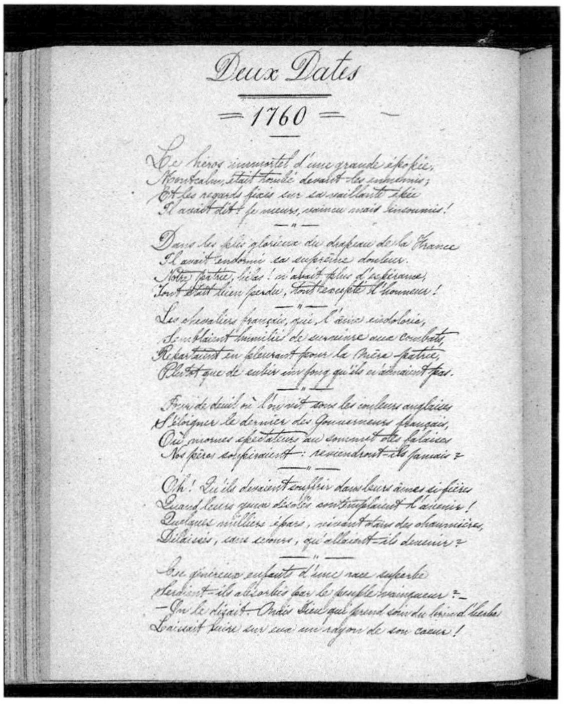

Deux Dates

1760

Le héros immortel d'une grande épopée,
Montcalm, était tombé devant les ennemis;
Et les regards fixés sur sa vaillante épée
Il avait dit: Je meurs, vaincu mais insoumis!

Dans les plis glorieux du drapeau de la France
Il avait endormi sa suprême douleur.
Notre patrie, hélas! n'avait plus d'espérance,
Tout était bien perdu, tout excepté l'honneur!

Les chevaliers français, qui, l'âme endolorie,
Semblaient humiliés de survivre aux combats,
Repartaient en pleurant pour la Mère-patrie,
Plutôt que de subir un joug qu'ils n'aimaient pas.

Jour de deuil où l'on vit sous les couleurs anglaises
S'éloigner le dernier des Gouverneurs français,
Où mornes spectateurs au sommet des falaises
Nos pères soupiraient: reviendront-ils jamais?

Oh! Qu'ils devaient souffrir dans leurs âmes si fières
Quand leurs yeux désolés contemplaient l'avenir!
Quelques milliers épars, vivant dans des chaumières,
Délaissés, sans secours, qu'allaient-ils devenir?

Ces généreux enfants d'une race superbe
Seraient-ils absorbés par le peuple vainqueur? —
— On le disait. Mais Dieu qui prend soin du brin d'herbe
Laissait luire sur eux un rayon de son cœur!

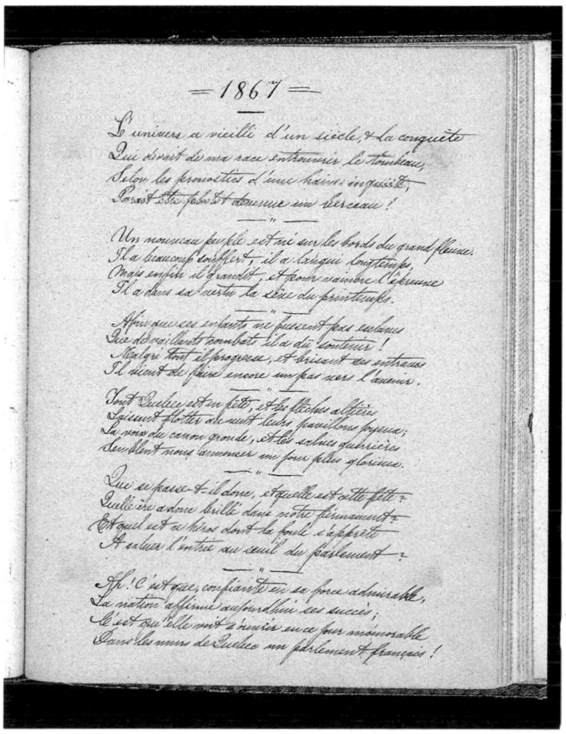

1867

L'univers a vieilli d'un siècle, et la conquête
Qui devait de ma race entrouvrir le tombeau,
Selon les pronostics d'une haine inquiète,
Paraît être plutôt devenue un berceau!

Un nouveau peuple est né sur les bords du grand fleuve.
Il a beaucoup souffert, il a langui longtemps,
Mais enfin il grandit, et pour vaincre l'épreuve
Il a dans sa vertu la sève du printemps.

Afin que ses enfants ne fussent pas esclaves
Que de vaillants combats il a dû soutenir!
Malgré tout il progresse, et brisant ses entraves
Il vient de faire encore un pas vers l'avenir.

Tout Québec est en fête, et les flèches altières
Laissent flotter au vent leurs pavillons joyeux;
La voix du canon gronde, et les salves guerrières
Semblent nous annoncer un jour plus glorieux.

Que se passe-t-il donc, et quelle est cette fête?
Quelle ère a donc brillé dans notre firmament?
Et quel est ce héros dont la foule s'apprête
À saluer l'entrée au seuil du parlement?

Ah! C'est que, confiante en sa force admirable,
La nation affirme aujourd'hui ses succès;
C'est qu'elle voit s'ouvrir en ce jour mémorable
Dans les murs de Québec un parlement français!

27.9 cm x 22.8 cm
27.9 cm x 22.8 cm

National Archives of Canada,
Documentary Art and Photography Division,
[Page titled "1760"] C-30996,
[Page titled "1867"] C-118841.

IV

Canadians Forever. A National Song

Born in England in 1817, William Kirby emigrated with his family to the United States in 1832, and in 1839 moved to Niagara. He married into a United Empire Loyalist family. By profession a literary man, he edited the *Niagara Mail and Empire*, which often supported Sir John Alexander Macdonald, whom Kirby admired and came to know personally. He wrote in 1877 what would become a classic English Canadian novel, *The Golden Dog*. The novel exalts British, more specifically United Empire Loyalist, virtues. In fact, for Kirby, the corruption of New France was overcome only with the arrival of the English, and with the incorporation of Quebec into a state peopled by Englishmen who were given to loyalty, probity and progress.

Loyalty to Britain and the exaltation of Empire suffuse this "song" written in honour of Confederation. In the first stanza there is one mention of France ("Of France and England's martial race"). Beyond that, the "song" is a glorification of Britain, of "loyal fathers," of "British hearts that never fail," of "the glorious Union Jack" and "Victoria's regal throne."

There is also a sense of new growth and perhaps future expansion, as Kirby writes of a Dominion from Cape Race in Newfoundland extending westward "along a hundred bright meridians," "from sun to sun." The Dominion is populated by people of sterling character, freemen of the best British model. Axes ring in towering forests and rifles find their mark. Boatmen sing in cadence as they run rough water, and "loyal yeomen speed the plough" and enjoy the bountiful yield of field and vine, then "rest beneath the maple bough." In a new land, almost-heroic pioneers, sure of themselves and able and hard-working, are busily creating an England anew in British North America. Bucolic and pure, inhabited by loyal yeomen, this utopic "new" England seems straight out of Sir Walter Scott's novels.

Reflecting the attitude of English society in Ontario, Kirby's "song" vibrates with optimism about the future of the newly-created Dominion of Canada.

William Kirby. 1867.

(Copyrighted)

CANADIANS FOREVER.

[The following lines were written in 1867 by the late William Kirby, author of the famous book "Chien d'Or" — Mr Kirby was a … admirer and personal friend of Sir John Macdonald.]

A NATIONAL SONG.

Give thanks to God for all the grace
Bestowed by His Almighty hand;
Of France and England's martial race,
He planted us with firm command
To do and dare,
And guard with care,
This Canada, our native land.
Canadians forever!
No foe shall dissever
Our glorious dominion—
God bless it forever.

It is the land we love the best,
The land our loyal fathers gave;
In battle fires it stood the test,
And valiant heroes died to save—
In summer's glow,
In winter's snow,
A people steadfast, true and brave.
Canadians forever!
No foe shall dissever
Our glorious Dominion—
God bless it forever.

A land of peace for friends we love,
A land of war if foes assail;
We place our trust in God above
And British hearts that never fail.
In feast or fight
And cause of right,
Our word and deed shall aye prevail
Canadians forever!
No foe shall dissever
Our glorious Dominion
God bless it forever.

From Newfoundland at break of day
The cheer is Westward passed along,
A hundred bright meridians play
Like harp-strings to the nation's song.
From sea to sea
United be,
One great Dominion just and strong.
Canadians forever!
No foe shall dissever
Our glorious dominion—
God bless it forever.

Cape Race with lofty beacon lights
Our ocean-gates by tempests blown
And half a world of days and nights,
And lakes and lands is all our own.
From sun to sun
Our waters run,
Niagara midway thundering down.
Canadians forever!
No foe shall dissever
Our glorious Dominion—
God bless it forever.

Our axes in the forests ring,
Our rifles mark the hunters' track
Our boatmen blythe in cadence sing
Upon the rapids' foaming back.
'Tis freedom gives
The joy that lives
Beneath the glorious Union Jack!
Canadians forever!
No foe shall dissever
Our glorious Dominion—
God bless it forever.

By spreading oaks and towering pines
Our loyal yeomen speed the plough,
And reap their fields and dress their vines
And jovial fill the barley-mow.
With sturdy toil
They till the soil,
And rest beneath the maple bough.
Canadians forever!
No foe shall dissever
Our glorious Dominion—
God bless it forever.

Stet

Then deck ~~Victoria's~~ King George's regal throne
With May flowers and the maple tree;
And one for all and all for one,
The watchword of her Empire be,
And heart and hand
United stand,
Confederate and great, and free,
Canadians forever!
No foe shall dissever
Our glorious Dominion—
God bless it forever.

W. KIRBY.

Niagara, Ontario, Sep. 24, 1867.

"Copyrighted"

Editor Mail & Empire.
The free publication in above paper is hereby given — … May 26/11

21 cm x 17 cm

National Archives of Canada,
Manuscript Division,
MG 53, A 56.

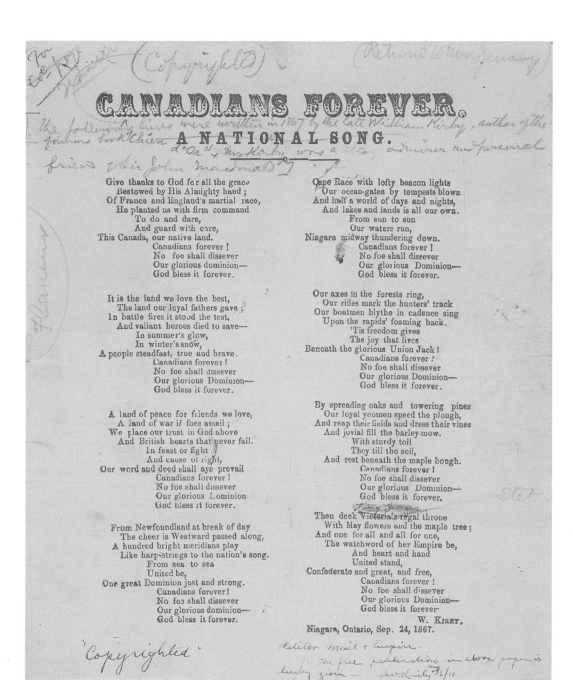

IV

Report of the Repeal Delegation

After the initial bonhommie of Charlottetown and the much stiffer horse-trading of Quebec City, the Maritime provinces began to view Confederation with some doubt. They sensed that they might exchange full self-government for a limited role in a central government. Maritime politics were particularistic, shaped by specific local needs, which would not necessarily receive much sympathy in a federal capital. Additionally, responsible government had come first to Nova Scotia, and Nova Scotians had managed quite well; this gave them, and Maritimers generally, a sense of achievement and pride. Finally, even though Maritimers had experienced some bitter political feuding, over sectarian schools for example, their political life was far less acrimonious than that of the Province of Canada — and they feared being drawn into a political vortex over issues having little to do with them. To many Maritimers, union with Canada presaged political insignificance.

Moreover, culturally and economically, the Maritime provinces had more significant links with the American states of New England. Their trade lay along the coastal axis, and family ties bound people living on different sides of the Canada-United States boundary. Perhaps most significantly, the Maritimes were still emotionally and culturally oriented toward Britain and looked outward toward the sea lanes of the great North Atlantic trading triangle, rather than inland towards the continental interior. The further distant from the centre, the greater the opposition to the idea of Confederation — hence Newfoundland and Prince Edward Island rejected Confederation, and Nova Scotia, under Joseph Howe's leadership, fought a belated struggle against entry into Canada.

Perhaps Howe's ego, bruised by the fact that he had had no role in Confederation, disposed him to oppose union. But there was more to it than this. Howe dreamed of an Imperial Parliament with direct representation from the colonies, and made telling points with his scathing attacks on the back-room politics and political machinations of the "Canadians" in league with Imperial authorities who had foisted Confederation upon Nova Scotia.

The first federal election in 1867 was held jointly with provincial elections. In Nova Scotia only one pro-Confederation candidate (out of 19 members) was elected to the Dominion Parliament, and 36 of 38 seats in the provincial election went to opponents of Confederation. Basing themselves on the voice of their electorate, Howe and other opponents of union fought a spirited battle for repeal of Confederation, and Nova Scotia's withdrawal from Canada.

Since the *British North America Act* was promulgated from London, Howe and three other "repealers" took their struggle to Britain. In 1868, in the nature of a situation report, they prepared this document detailing their struggle for repeal and withdrawl. The pages displayed present some of their arguments against Confederation. British authorities, however, had resolved on colonial union in British North America as the way of future development, and the repeal argument fell on deaf ears in London.

Joseph Howe et al. 1868.

12 REPORT OF

It transfers to the Government at Ottawa powers more extensive than the Queen and the Imperial Parliament in practice ever exercised; and vests in that Government, which the people of Nova Scotia can rarely hope to influence, the entire patronage of the Post-Office and Revenue Departments, and of the Lighthouses and Public Works, constructed at great expense by the people of Nova Scotia.

It transfers the ownership of our Provincial Railways, built at a cost of a million-and-half of pounds currency, to the Dominion, without equivalent or compensation.

It takes from Nova Scotia the regulation of her trade and of her Banking system and Savings' Banks, of her sea-coast and Inland Fisheries, of her Militia, of her Courts and Criminal Law.

It transfers the Customs Laws of Nova Scotia, always amply sufficient for general and local services, and rapidly increasing under a low tariff, to Canada, for a sum which is now no equivalent, and which, being limited in amount, will establish a perpetual drain upon our resources as those revenues expand.

It confers upon the Parliament of Canada the right to burden our trade with the rest of the Empire and with the world at large, for her own advantage, to protect her manufactures and breadstuffs, and to burden our industry by "any mode or system of taxation."

It vests in the Government of Canada the appointment of our Governors, who will thus become the mere tools of the Canadian Administration, instead of being, as they were, the impartial Representatives of the Crown.

Of twelve Senators already appointed by the Canadian Ministers, but one shares the opinions of the people of Nova Scotia, and four at least have been purchased by the distinction to change their opinions and betray their country.

For these and many other reasons that might be stated, this Act of Union has been, and is, most distasteful to the people of Nova Scotia, who believe it to be fraught with evil, uncalled for, and unjust.

But their approval of the Act itself has been aggravated and rendered more intense by the mode in which it was proposed and carried, which the undersigned do not hesitate to characterize as a surprise upon the people of Nova Scotia, and a fraud upon the Imperial Parliament.

Nothing in the condition of the country rendered revolutionary changes necessary. At no time in its history did the people of Nova Scotia demand them, nor was any scheme of Government, resembling the Dominion Act, ever submitted to them at the hustings; yet a Member of the House of Commons, misled, we charitably assume, on the second reading of the Bill assured the House that the policy of Confederation "was brought under the notice of the Electors at every polling-booth, and that at every hustings the issue was distinctly raised." Now that this statement has been "brought under the notice of the Electors at every polling-booth," condemned and negatived "at every hustings," the undersigned trust that it will be frankly withdrawn and that your Honorable House will at once cancel legislation adopted under so gross a misstatement of facts.

REPEAL DELEGATION 13

The Dominion Act was published in this Province in March last. It was discussed in the press, on the platform, and on the hustings until the General Election, which was held on the eighteenth of September.

At that Election the people of Nova Scotia had, for the first time, an opportunity to express their opinions on this scheme of union; and it was condemned with a unanimity and sternness never witnessed before in the decision of a public question in any free country.

In the Counties of Cape Breton, Guysborough, Shelburne, and Victoria, the Anti-Confederate Candidates for the House of Commons were elected by acclamation.

In every other County but one, the Confederates were beaten by large, and in many of them, by overwhelming majorities. In that single County, though a Confederate struggled in by a small majority, followed by a protest for bribery and corruption, the opposition was so strong that one of the gentlemen who signs this Petition obtained a seat.

But one of the Delegates who prepared this Dominion Act was re-elected; but two of the thirty-eight Members of the House who voted approval of it have been chosen; and of fifty-seven Members returned to both Houses, all but four are humble Petitioners to your Honourable House for the repeal of the law so universally condemned.

In the published papers submitted to Parliament, the Lieutenant-Governor, in transmitting an address against Confederation, informed the Right Honourable the Secretary of State for the Colonies that "he believed the attempt to agitate the Province to be a complete failure;" and the Delegates who for many months last year were in communication with the Earl of Carnarvon, made statements that have now been proved to have been as entirely unfounded. Acting upon these statements, Her Majesty's Government and both Houses of Porliament were misled, and have inadvertently done a cruel wrong to a high-spirited people, which it would be a reflection on the justice and magnanimity of both Houses to believe will not be promptly repaired.

Neither Prince Edward Island nor Newfoundland was touched by this Act of Union, and Nova Scotia was only included because it was assumed that those who professed to speak for her, truly represented her interests and opinions. Now that the contrary has been proved, the people of Nova Scotia rely with confidence on the wisdom and justice of your Honourable House. Though this question has so deeply stirred their feelings, the Elections from end to end of the Province have been carried without a blow being struck, a disloyal sentiment uttered, or any necessity, as in Canada, for military interference at the Polls. The people, relying on the high sense of honour which distinguishes British statesmen, and on the protection of Parliament, defeated in a peaceful and orderly manner those who had betrayed them.

The undersigned, elected to represent the people both in the House of Commons and in the Local Legislature, will not dwell upon the consequences of an adverse decision, which they do not anticipate; but ask in their behalf, with all respect, for the repeal of so mchu of the "Act for

30.1 cm x 19.7 cm

National Archives of Canada,
Manuscript Division,
MG 30, D 37, Vol. 22, f. 12, pp. 12-13.

Letter on Public Health, Cholera and Confederation

Cholera was a frightening scourge that rocked the colonies in periodic epidemics (1832, 1849, 1851, 1852 and 1854). An acutely infectious disease of the intestines, often caused by contaminated water, it came with the immigrants who crossed the Atlantic under frightful conditions, which were only moderately improved by legislative intervention of the British Crown in 1855. The epidemics killed at least 20,000 people in the British colonies in North America.

They also caused great anxiety and fear; no one knew how the lethal cholera spread, or how to stop it. This anxiety had disposed the Province of Lower-Canada, in 1833, to open the Grosse Île Quarantine Station, on an island slightly downstream from Quebec City. All vessels put in at the station for medical inspection and clearance; and although a dedicated medical staff did its best to ease immigrant suffering on the island, thousands, particularly the Irish, died there. In large part the threat of cholera and its obvious connection with immigrants lay behind the restrictive immigration measures that the colony imposed in 1850.

Individual towns affected by large immigration also responded to the threat of epidemic. Saint John, for example, whose dockyards attracted many Irish, passed new ordinances concerning cleanliness and urban hygiene. The city was inspected for filthy sites, which were cleaned up; the keeping of farm animals (it was common to keep pigs in towns then) was disallowed; house-to-house searches detected persons who were ill, and doctors commenced their treatment. The epidemics, along with the quickening urban growth which was producing the first working-class slum areas, aroused public officials to an awareness of the need for public hygiene. From this time onward municipal sanitation became a public concern as city and town administrations moved to require toilet facilities in urban dwellings, to prohibit the dumping of household wastes, as well as slaughterhouse remains, indiscriminately into streets, yards and elsewhere.

Saint John may very well have been a leader in this regard because of people like Dr. William Stenning Harding, who wrote this letter both about cholera in the 1850s, and about public health within the new political context of Confederation. Dr. Harding (1814-1902), son of the first mayor of Saint John and a graduate of the University of Edinburgh's medical school, worked as a quarantine officer, performing "heroic service" against cholera and diphtheria. He was pleased that, with the coming of Confederation, the effective system of quarantine, as devised by the former Province of Lower-Canada, could be systematically expanded throughout the whole Dominion.

The letter evidences a touch of self-interest, as Harding promoted himself for a new federal position as a quarantine officer. Interestingly he points out that the true danger of cholera is its contagious aspect, hence the wildfire nature of the epidemics. In fact, in 1856 a medical conference of Saint John doctors had concluded that cholera was a contagious disease, a fact denied by all governmental authorities until the International Cholera Conference came to that finding in 1866.

Harding's letter reveals much about the level of public health at the time, the medical profession and the struggle against a fearsome death that killed, quickly and indiscriminately, thousands of people in the colonies and immigrants on their way to new hopes and homes.

William Stenning Harding. 1867.

St. John April 16th 1867

My Dear Mr. Boyd

After you had kindly complied with my request and examined certain evidence bearing on the prevention of disease, the completed terms of Confederation were published. Under the new law Quarantine regulations for all the ports of the Dominion will be solely under the direction of the General Govt. The powers for such have been exercised for many years in Canada by the General Govt. of Canada. The discovery of this clause of the Confederation Act was very gratifying to me, because I believe its principle correct, and because it will provide us with a system of prevention which recognises the fact – and states it in round terms – that Cholera is to be expected to come in ships. This, being precise and definite is more satisfactory than what has been recorded here, by our Board of Health, as the maximum of knowledge on the subject, viz, that the whole world has "vainly endeavoured" to find out the mode of progression of Cholera, that its "wanderings are misterious". In consequence of this view, not being known as a contagious disease, no code of instruction has been issued here, as in Canada, which states or in any way signifies that it may be expected to come in a ship, and therefore no mention is made of quarantine restriction for its prevention.

I have been looking forward to Confederation as a means of promoting the growth and prosperity of this country, and not anticipating any thing in connection with it of special bearing on myself I now perceive however that it will greatly facilitate, or perhaps I may say, certainly enable me to obtain an appointment to act in those matters with which I have become so much identified – identified as explained to you.

At Quebec there are three medical men under appointment by the General Govt. to carry out the Quarantine laws. Two of them, during the season of navigation, reside at Gross-Isle, and one at Quebec City. The duty of all is to prevent if possible the introduction of certain specified diseases – three or four in number, Cholera of course is one of them. At St. John two, or sometimes three, "Visiting Physicians" or "Health Officers" have every year been appointed by the Common Council

23 cm x 18.6 cm

National Archives of Canada,
Manuscript Division,
MG 27, I, D 15, Vol. 19.

Great Seal Deputed of Canada

The new state required new symbols, as a formal outward expression of its existence, as a representation of its traditional and legal authority devolved from the British Crown, and for general purposes of government. The Great Seal is one such symbol.

This intricately-incised casting was produced in England by members of the Wyon family, which had earned a distinguished reputation for its skilled medal-making. Until the Great Seal's delivery to Canada, the Dominion government employed a temporary great seal featuring the Royal Arms of England. Upon receipt of the permanent seal, this temporary seal was to have been defaced and returned to London; it survives, and is held by the Archives nationales du Québec.

The intaglio (female) matrix of the first permanent Great Seal of Canada, shown here, is one-sided. It depicts Queen Victoria seated beneath a triple Gothic canopy, holding a sceptre with cross in her right hand, and in her left hand an orb with cross. Under each of the side canopies are two shields each, bearing the arms of the four provinces originally united at Confederation. These provincial arms were granted in 1868. The Royal Arms of the Realm appear at the foot of the monarch. The seal bears the date of Confederation, and a scroll above the canopy bears the motto *Dieu et Mon Droit.* The inscriptions, translated from Latin, read "Victoria, by the Grace of God Queen of Great Britain, Defender of the Faith," and "Seal of Canada."

Originally, the seal was to be a much simpler design. A royal warrant of 1868 had intended that the seal consist of the provincial arms of the four founding provinces. Some of the Fathers of Confederation wished the seal to reflect more aptly the nature of the government and society which they were designing — a country with a strong central government closely linked with Imperial Britain. Hence the imposing throne and canopy, and the symbols of power — sceptre and orb — wielded by the overseas monarch. At the same time, however, the provincial arms surrounding the central symbol of power continue to remind one that the Dominion is a federation of provinces as well.

This first Great Seal was made of silver. It proved too soft a metal to easily impart its impression to documents requiring an imprimatur. Hence, subsequent seals, prepared with the accession of each new monarch, were made of fine steel.

Alfred Benjamin and Joseph Shepherd Wyon. 1869 [-1905].

12.7 cm (diameter) silver

National Archives of Canada,
Documentary Art and Photography Division,
C-6792.

Canadian Confederation Medal

Sir John A. Macdonald, while in Britain in 1867, made arrangements for the creation of a special commemorative medal to mark the advent of Confederation. On the advice of Lord Monck, the Governor-General, Macdonald turned to the firm of J.S. and A.B. Wyon, Chief Engravers of the Royal Seals, who also engraved the Great Seal Deputed of Canada. Both Macdonald and the Queen approved the obverse and reverse designs of this medal, once they felt that they were "in keeping with the historic dignity of the occasion."

The medal, three inches in diameter, bears a portrait of Queen Victoria on the obverse side, surmounted by the motto, "Victoria, by the Grace of God Queen of Great Britain, Defender of the Faith." The Queen, as a sign of great favour, sat for this likeness. The reverse side shows an allegorical group of female figures. The leading figure, Britannia, with trident in right hand and her left hand resting on a lion, presents the Charter of Confederation to the four sister provinces joining together into the Dominion of Canada. The four sisters each hold an implement of livelihood, symbolizing the chief source of their respective province's wealth and economic activity. Ontario holds a sickle and sheaf of corn, Quebec a canoe paddle, Nova Scotia a miner's spade (for the Cape Breton coal fields) and New Brunswick a lumberman's axe. Encircling the whole scene is the motto, "Canada Reorganized 1867, Youth and Ancestral Vigour."

The only Confederation medal cast in gold was presented to the Queen. Fifty medals were struck in silver for distribution amongst the Fathers of Confederation and high dignitaries. Finally, 500 medals were made of bronze for presentation to members of the House of Commons and the Senate, delegates to the Charlottetown and Quebec Conferences not present at the London Conference (whose attendees received silver issues), members of colonial parliaments before Confederation, and to approximately 100 institutions in Canada.

Over the next several decades, some remaining medals were granted to individuals in the nature of recognition for distinguished service to Canada. As well, a variant of this medal, with the addition of an extra border and a loop so that the medal could be worn, was granted to Indian chiefs ceding land to the Dominion in the numbered Western Treaties. The medal thus symbolically admitted Indian chiefs and their tribes into Confederation, and sealed the cession of Indian lands into the Dominion land reserve.

Held by some experts to be among the finest examples of the art of medal-making, the Confederation medal, much like the Great Seal, symbolized a historic moment for the former colonies of British North America as they joined their fortunes into a common future.

Alfred Benjamin and Joseph Shepherd Wyon. 1867.

7.6 cm (diameter)
7.6 cm (diameter)

National Archives of Canada,
Documentary Art and Photography Division,
[Obverse] C-14988 Bronze,
[Reverse] C-81609 Bronze.

“Parliament Buildings, Ottawa. Centre Block. GRI-3”

The construction of the original Parliament Buildings commenced in late 1859, following Queen Victoria’s designation of Ottawa as the new capital of the United Province of Canada. At that time, Ottawa was a dynamic lumber town, with a large trade in squared timber. In the 1850s the hydro-power of the Chaudière and Rideau Falls began to drive milling operations of global significance. Through the Grand Trunk Railway, Ottawa was linked into the American markets. Economic dynamism alone was insufficient to secure Ottawa’s selection as the capital — its strategic location was more decisive. Located away from the American frontier, it was safer than other centres from attack. Additionally, it was a compromise choice, on the border between the two sections of a quarrelling United Province of Canada.

The architects Thomas Fuller and Chilion Jones won the design competition for the Parliament Building. The government’s choice of Fuller and Jones’ Gothic Revival style building was not surprising, as the British Houses of Parliament, completed only seven years earlier, had been built in Gothic Revival. The drawing displayed here is Plan No. 10 of the contract dated 18 April 1863, a detailed side cross-section from tower to library. It is a design re-worked from the original, and signed by Thomas Fuller and Charles Baillairgé who, in 1863, replaced Jones as one of the supervising architects.

The Gothic Revival Centre Block pictured here reflects many of the stock elements of that style as characterized in the pointed arches, lancet windows with tracery, turrets, exposed and prominent buttresses and variegated stonework. The library resembles a chapter house attached through a cloistered walkway to a Gothic cathedral. While inspired by the British Houses, the Parliament Buildings were not a copy since, by 1859, architectural tastes had changed to allow a freer interpretation and assemblage of Gothic motifs and features.

This cross-section of the original building does not deal with structural engineering; hence, we cannot see such engineering novelty as interior iron framing, among the first such uses in North America. The drawing, however, does offer very interesting comment on interior finish work. It bears such notations as “panels of ground glass,” “concrete and cement floor” and “iron door.” It is these iron doors to the library, and the wrought iron dome added later, which saved this structure from the disastrous fire of 1916, in which the original Centre Block burned. Lighting was an important consideration in this pre-electric era, hence the “panels of ground glass,” especially in the clerestory windows of the roof. Because ground glass was opaque it provided privacy, while at the same time it allowed natural light to illuminate the interior.

Completed in 1866, the building housed the last session of the Parliament of the United Province of Canada.

Thomas Fuller and Chilion Jones. 1863.

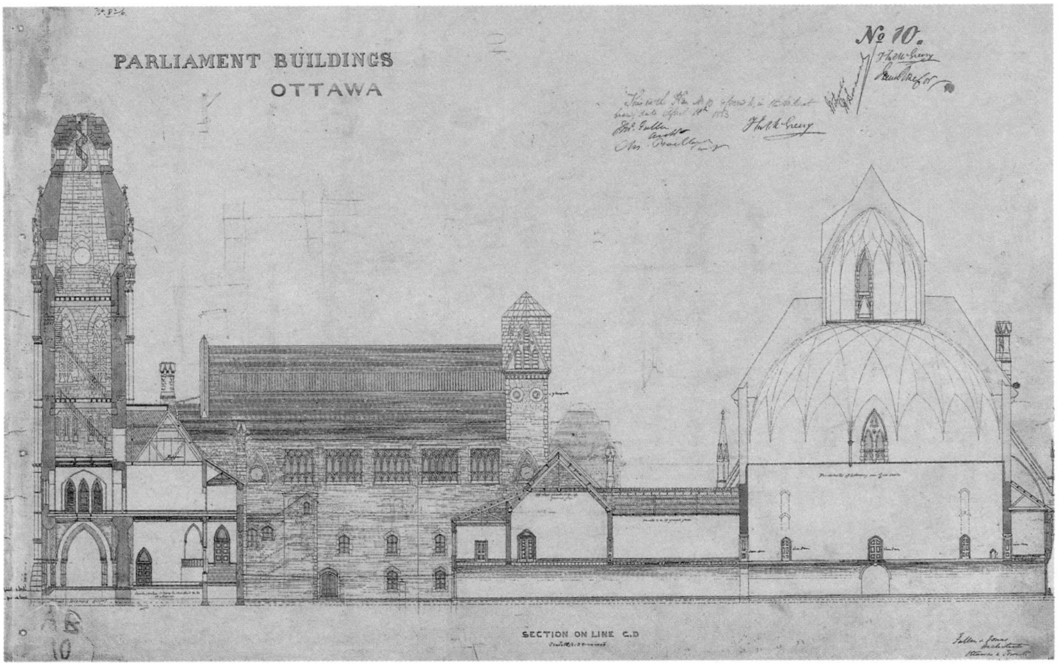

57 cm x 95.5 cm

National Archives of Canada,
Cartographic and Audio-Visual Archives Division,
NMC-19003.

"Parliament Buildings. Main Front. View from Sparks Street"
and also
"Centre Block"
and also
"Parliament Buildings, Ottawa..."

Samuel McLaughlin (1826-1914) came to Canada from Ireland. He took up photography in the 1850s. During 1858-1860 he published Canada's first photographic album, *The Photographic Portfolio*, consisting of views in and around Quebec City. Because of his proven photographic ability, especially in images of buildings, he became official Government photographer in September 1861. In that month, construction of the Parliament Buildings halted when money ran out; in fact, substantial corruption characterized much government activity at this time, including the building of Parliament. In the ensuing embarrassment and confusion, it seemed wise to John A. Macdonald's government to document construction of the buildings, and to assemble visual evidence to disarm an enraged opposition and angry electorate. An ongoing visual record would be vital to exoneration in any future investigation. Hence McLaughlin was hired by the Department of Public Works.

In the photograph "Main Front..." we see the main facade of the Centre Block, and to the right a portion of the East Block (the East and West Blocks were designed by Stent & Laver). The central tower is temporarily capped. Derrick-like structures on the left side of the roof drew up materials, such as the wooden beams to truss the corner towers and the wooden planking to sheath the trusses. Before the Parliament Buildings stand temporary wooden sheds to house material. To the bottom right of the main building is a winching boom, with piles of lumber neatly stacked beside it. In mid-ground is a permanent wooden dwelling, with vines weaving up along door-frame and verandah post, and a child's swing in the yard. In the foreground, where there seems to be a precipitous trench, is Wellington Street, between two rows of fences; the peculiar effect is due to foreshortening by the camera lens.

The Notman studio image reflects the wonderful detail of the Gothic Revival architectural style, evident in the intricate masonry of windows and walls and in the wrought iron decorative roof work. The rough lawn and the temporary wooden stairs leading to the Centre Block indicate that work on the site is still in progress.

Alexander Henderson's "Parliament Buildings..." is a splendid view of Barrack's Hill from the river side, atop which sit the new structures (the Library has not yet been started). To the left the Rideau Canal joins with the Ottawa River. There is a rich symbolism in this photograph, with river, canal and Parliament Buildings — the past and future of Ottawa — knotted together in one image. The photograph details how the Parliament Buildings received their lumber supply. Massive rafts of squared timber, each with its own temporary housing, lie beached near a sawmill that processed them. Some distance from the mill, draught horses labour up a winding road, drawing sawn planks to the builders on the Hill.

These photographs record a significant achievement, the construction by native engineers of a wonderful public building complex built in a grand style, symbolizing the birth of a new political entity and its youthful aspirations for the future.

Samuel McLaughlin.	ca 1865.
Alexander Henderson.	ca 1866.
Notman Studio.	ca 1869.

28.4 cm x 36.5 cm
19 cm x 11.9 cm
18.3 cm x 22.6 cm

National Archives of Canada,
Documentary Art and Photography Division,
[McLaughlin] PA-181436,
[Henderson] PA-138699,
[Notman Studio] C-4539.

Power of Central Government

The *British North America Act* of 1867 created a federation, dividing powers between the central government in Ottawa, and the provincial governments. Section 91 of the *Act* accorded to the federal authority significant powers, such as defence, post office, trade and commerce, weights and measures, currency and coinage, Indian affairs, criminal law, communications and so on. To the provinces it granted authority over property, local works, municipalities, education, private law matters (contracts and torts) and so forth.

The powers given the federal authority were manifestly broad, strengthened by the "peace, order and good government" provision of Section 91 which many at the time viewed as bringing under federal purview all "residuary" matters not conferred upon the provinces. The central authority was strengthened even further by the explicit primacy which the *Act* granted to the federal government in areas where it shared power with the provinces, such as immigration. Finally, the *Act* also authorized the federal government to disallow any provincial act virtually at will.

The intent and distribution of powers of the *British North America Act* would be challenged later by politicians, historians and legal theorists. But there is little doubt that Sir John A. Macdonald, who virtually by himself designed the *British North America Act* — aided by Alexander Tilloch Galt in economic matters, George-Étienne Cartier in provincial-central relations and Judge James Robert Gowan in matters of law and justice — was an uncompromising centrist, as set out in the document shown here, a letter to Macdonald's acquaintance, Brown Chamberlain.

Expecting a conflict with "states rights" people, Macdonald writes to Brown,

> "By a firm yet patient course, I think the Dominion must win in the long run. The powers of the General Government are so much greater than those of the United States, in its relations with the Local Government, that the Central power must win."

It was Macdonald's contention that, in dealing with the provinces, the federal power need treat them no differently than a municipal corporation, such as Montreal or Quebec City.

With the example of the American Civil War fresh in mind, Macdonald and many of the fathers of Confederation feared a loose union. Additionally, only a strong central authority could hold together regions as disparate as the colonies which came into Confederation. And only a powerful centre could undertake the costly and crucial task of railroad-building, a stipulation of the *British North America Act.* Without such central authority, Macdonald feared collapse and surrender to "Yankee Covenanters" to the south.

Sir John A. Macdonald. 1868.

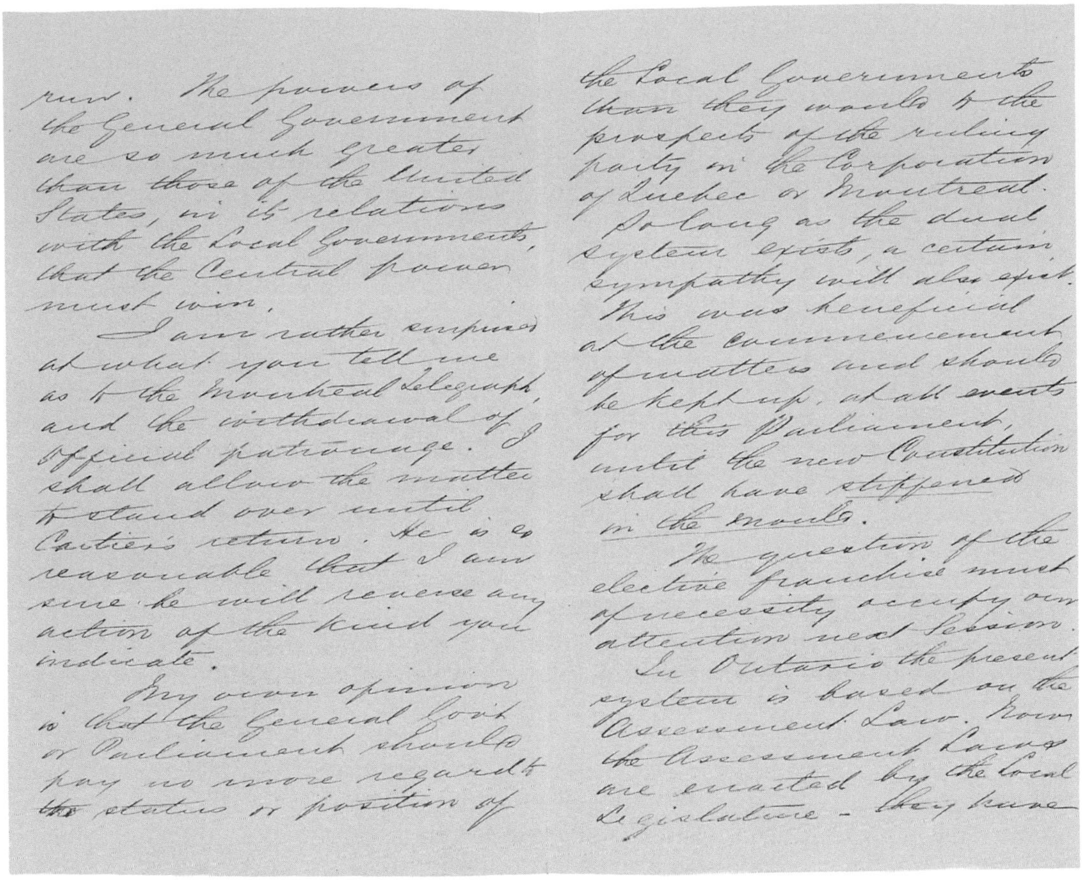

rum. The powers of the General Government are so much greater than those of the United States, in its relations with the Local Governments, that the Central power must win.

I am rather surprised at what you tell me as to the Montreal Telegraph, and the withdrawal of official patronage. I shall allow the matter to stand over until Cartier's return. He is so reasonable that I am sure he will reverse any action of the kind you indicate.

My own opinion is that the General Gov't or Parliament should pay no more regard to the status or position of the Local Governments than they would to the prospects of the ruling party in the Corporation of Quebec or Montreal.

So long as the dual system exists, a certain sympathy will also exist. This was beneficial at the commencement of matters and should be kept up, at all events for this Parliament, until the new Constitution shall have stiffened in the mould.

The question of the elective franchise must of necessity occupy our attention next Session. In Ontario the present system is based on the Assessment Law. Now the Assessment Laws are enacted by the Local Legislature - they have

20.3 cm x 12.7 cm

National Archives of Canada,
Manuscript Division,
MG 24, B 19, Vol. 3, Item 35.

Proclamation of Federal By-election, County of Huntingdon

Once Confederation was proclaimed by Queen Victoria, it was necessary to have an operational House of Commons as soon as possible. The members of the first session of the first parliament were elected on the basis of provincial constituencies; it would have taken far too long to conduct a census and draw up federal ridings. In fact, one can construe the first federal election as four local plebiscites held after the fact in the four confederating provinces. Save for Nova Scotia, which almost wholly defeated pro-Confederate candidates, the electorates of the other three provinces returned a large majority of pro-Confederates, i.e. members of Macdonald-Cartier's Liberal-Conservative party.

Although the two major political parties were well on the road to clear definition on the basis of political creeds and human values, the electoral mechanism was dated and subject to manipulation by the governing party. Until the election of 1878, election campaigns were relatively decentralized, often managed under pre-Confederation regulations and practices. General elections were spread out over many weeks. This allowed the governing party to schedule voting in constituencies in a manner favourable to its election effort; for example, it could hold electoral contests in "safe" seats, hoping that victory there would create a bandwagon effect elsewhere. This also allowed a defeated candidate to stand for election immediately in another riding. Moreover, voting by a show of hands, in constituencies where electorates were numerically small, allowed for intimidation, bribery and other forms of electoral persuasion, which was more or less the norm of the day.

Macdonald's Liberal Conservatives won the general election held in August-September 1867. The victorious candidate in Huntingdon was Sir John Rose (1820-1888). Prominent in banking and railways, and former holder of key ministerial posts in pre-1867 Canada, Rose was called to the first cabinet. Parliamentary procedure of the time required cabinet ministers to resign their seats and stand for re-election, which is what Rose did. This summons to the electors of the riding, issued in November 1867, calls such a by-election, in effect to confirm a minister of the first federal cabinet. Rose carried the by-election, and held the seat until his resignation from Parliament in 1869.

Canada: Privy Council. 1867.

92

116767

PROCLAMATION!

ELECTORAL DISTRICT OF

HUNTINGDON

PROVINCE OF QUEBEC,

TO WIT:

Public Notice is hereby given to the Electors of the Electoral District of Huntingdon, that in obedience to Her Majesty's Writ to me directed, and bearing date the eighteenth day of the month of November, in the year of our Lord one-thousand-eight-hundred-and-sixty-seven, I require the presence of the said Electors at the PUBLIC SQUARE, of the Village of HUNTINGDON, in the said Electoral District, on the

TWENTY-EIGHTH DAY OF THE MONTH OF NOV.

INSTANT, AT ELEVEN O'CLOCK A.M.,

for the purpose of electing a Person to represent them in the House of Commons of Canada; and that in case a Poll shall be demanded and allowed in the manner by law prescribed, such Poll will be opened on the fifth and sixth days of the month of December next, from nine o'clock in the forenoon to five o'clock in the afternoon, in the

Village of Huntingdon, at the Court House.
Parish of St. Anicet, at the office of I. I. Crevier, N. P.
Township of Dundee, at the Village of Dundee.
Township of Elgin, at Oak Creek School-house.
Township of Franklin, at Cantwell's Corners.
Township of Godmanchester, at Stark's School-house.
Township of Havelock, at Vicars.
Township of Hemmingford, at Scriver's Corners.
Township of Hinchinbrooke, at the Town Hall.

Of all which every person is hereby required to take notice and to govern himself accordingly.

Given under my hand, at Huntingdon, on this nineteenth day of the month of November, in the year of Our Lord one-thousand-eight-hundred-and-sixty-seven, and in the thirty-first year of Her Majesty's Reign.

Returning Officer.

DISTRICT ELECTORAL DE

HUNTINGDON

PROVINCE DE QUEBEC,

SAVOIR:

Avis Public est par la présente proclamation donné aux Electeurs du District Electoral de Huntingdon qu'en obéissance au Bref de Sa Majesté a moi addressé, en date du dix-huitieme de l'année de Notre Seigneur, mil huit cent soixante-et-sept, je requiers la présence des dits Electeurs à la PLACE PUBLIQUE dans le Village de HUNTINGDON, dans le dit District Electoral,

LE VINGT-HUITIEME JOUR DU MOIS DE NOVEMBRE

COURANT, AONZE HEURES DU MATIN,

afin d'elire une PERSONNE pour les représenter dans la Chambre des Communes du Canada:—et qu'en cas de demande et d'octroi d'un Poll en la maniére voulue par la loi tel Poll sera ouvert, les cinquieme et sixieme jours du mois de Decembre prochain de neuf heures du matin a cinq heures du soir, dans le

Village de Huntingdon, dans l'Audience.
Paroisse de St. Anicet, au Bureau d' I. I. Crevier, N. P.
Township de Dundee, au village de Dundee.
Township d'Elgin, a la Maison d'Ecole Oak Creek.
Township de Franklin, au Coin Cantwell.
Township de Godmanchester, a la Maison d'Ecole Stark.
Township de Havelock, Vicars.
Township de Hemmingford, au Coin Scriver.
Township de Hinchinbrooke, a la Salle du Township.

Et du contenu de la présente Proclamation toute personne est requise de prendre connaissance, et de se gouverner en consequence.

Donne sous mon Seing, à Huntingdon, ce dixneuvieme jour du mois de Novembre de l'année de Notre Seigneur, mil huit cent soixante-et-sept, et dans la trente-et-unieme annee du Régne de Sa Majesté.

Officier Rapporteur.

31.3 cm x 43.9 cm

National Archives of Canada,
Manuscript Division,
MG 26 A, Vol. 258, p. 116767.

Great Seal and Armorial Bearings

No armorial bearings were assigned, at the time of proclamation of Confederation, as symbols of authority to the Dominion government. However, in 1868, Queen Victoria granted and assigned armorial bearings to each of the four provinces which entered Confederation, "for the greater honour and distinction of the said provinces."

This document, a contemporary copy of the original warrant, was certified on 21 September 1868 by the Registrar of the College of Arms in London. It granted Ontario arms consisting of a maple sprig with three leaves, topped by the Cross of St. George. Quebec's coat-of-arms consisted of two fleur-de-lis, a lion and also a maple sprig with three leaves. Nova Scotia received arms consisting of a salmon and three thistles in flower, while New Brunswick was accorded armorial bearings made up of a lion and an ancient galley. These coats-of-arms, graphically represented in this document, were intended for use on seals, shields, banners, flags and other symbols of provincial authority.

This warrant also authorizes a "Great Seal of Canada," consisting of the coats-of-arms of the four provinces quarterly (all four combined into one shield). This was the original design for a great seal rejected by Sir John A. Macdonald as lacking sufficient governmental majesty. Thus, another great seal, shown elsewhere in this exhibition, was designed. This combination of provincial armorial bearings, however, came informally to serve as the Dominion government's coat-of-arms. As other provinces later entered Confederation, their provincial arms were added to the original four, and the federal shield grew unwieldy. In 1921, a coat-of-arms designed specifically for the federal government replaced what had, through usage, become a symbol of Dominion authority.

United Kingdom: Privy Council. 1869.

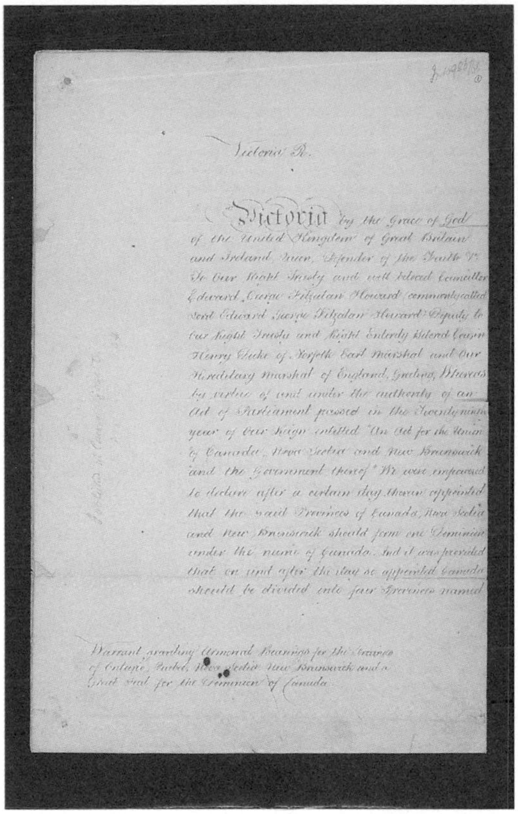

Victoria R.

Victoria by the Grace of God of the United Kingdom of Great Britain and Ireland Queen, Defender of the Faith &c. To Our Right Trusty and well beloved Councillor Edward George Fitzalan Howard commonly called Lord Edward George Fitzalan Howard Deputy to Our Right Trusty and Right Entirely beloved Cousin Henry Duke of Norfolk Earl Marshal and Our Hereditary Marshal of England, Greeting. Whereas by virtue of and under the authority of an Act of Parliament passed in the Thirtieth year of Our Reign intituled "An Act for the Union of Canada, Nova Scotia and New Brunswick and the Government thereof" We were empowered to declare after a certain day therein appointed that the said Provinces of Canada, Nova Scotia and New Brunswick should form one Dominion under the name of Canada. And it was provided that on and after the day so appointed Canada should be divided into four Provinces named

Warrant granting Armorial Bearings for the Provinces of Ontario, Quebec, Nova Scotia, New Brunswick and a Great Seal for the Dominion of Canada

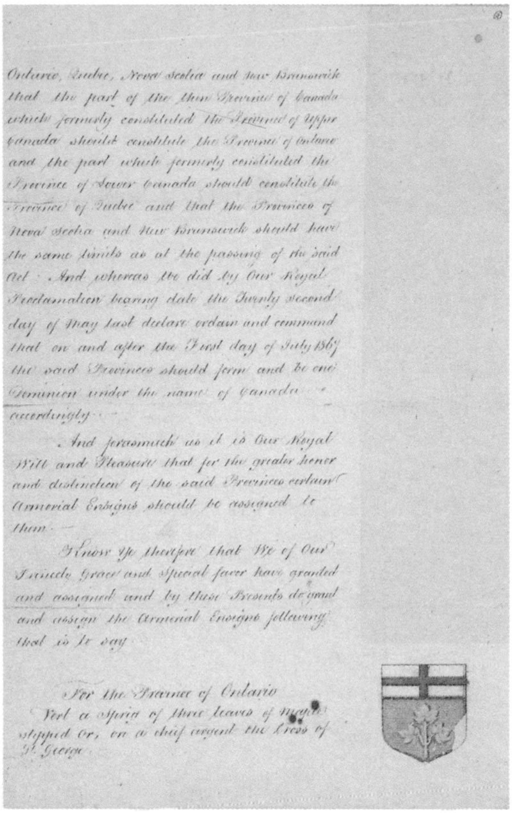

Ontario, Quebec, Nova Scotia and New Brunswick that the part of the then Province of Canada which formerly constituted the Province of Upper Canada should constitute the Province of Ontario and the part which formerly constituted the Province of Lower Canada should constitute the Province of Quebec and that the Provinces of Nova Scotia and New Brunswick should have the same limits as at the passing of the said Act. And whereas We did by Our Royal Proclamation bearing date the Twenty second day of May last declare ordain and command that on and after the First day of July 1867 the said Provinces should form and be one Dominion under the name of Canada accordingly.

And forasmuch as it is Our Royal Will and Pleasure that for the greater honor and distinction of the said Provinces certain Armorial Ensigns should be assigned to them.

Know Ye therefore that We of Our Princely Grace and Special favor have granted and assigned and by these Presents do grant and assign the Armorial Ensigns following that is to say

For the Province of Ontario
Vert a Sprig of three leaves of Maple slipped Or, on a chief argent the Cross of St. George

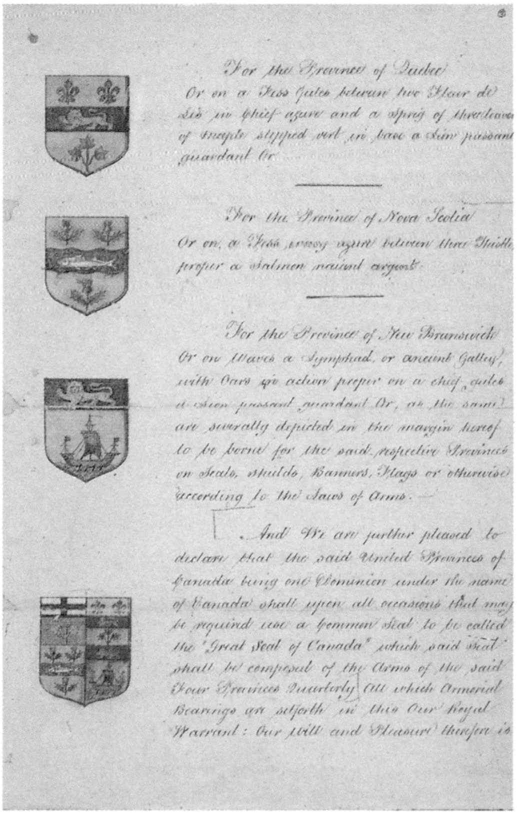

For the Province of Quebec
Or on a Fess Gules between two Fleur de Lis in chief azure and a sprig of three leaves of Maple slipped vert in base a Lion passant guardant Or

For the Province of Nova Scotia
Or on a Fess wavy azure between three Thistles proper a Salmon naiant argent

For the Province of New Brunswick
Or on Waves a Lymphad, or ancient Galley, with Oars in action proper on a chief gules a Lion passant guardant Or, as the same are severally depicted in the margin hereof to be borne for the said respective Provinces on Seals, Shields, Banners, Flags or otherwise according to the Laws of Arms.

And We are further pleased to declare that the said United Provinces of Canada being one Dominion under the name of Canada shall upon all occasions that may be required use a Common Seal to be called the "Great Seal of Canada" which said Seal shall be composed of the Arms of the said Four Provinces Quarterly All which Armorial Bearings are set forth in this Our Royal Warrant: Our Will and Pleasure therefore is

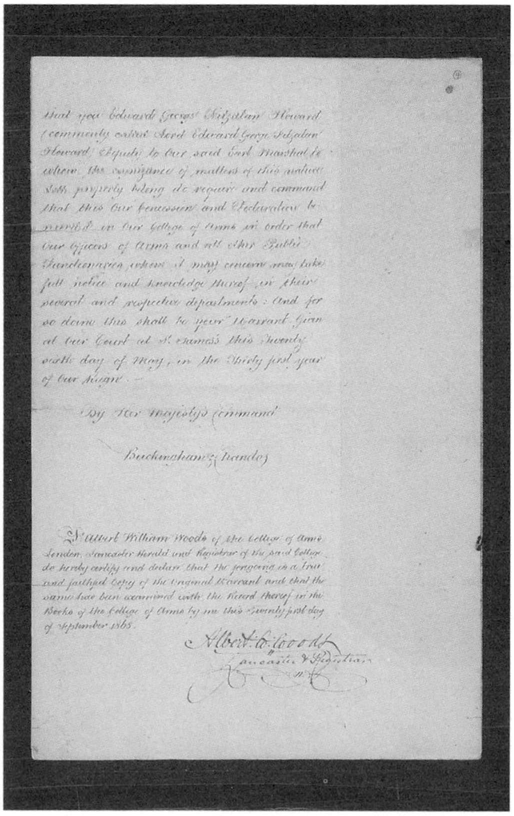

that you Edward George Fitzalan Howard (commonly called Lord Edward George Fitzalan Howard Deputy to Our said Earl Marshal to whom the cognizance of matters of this nature doth properly belong do require and command that this Our Concession and Declaration be recorded in Our College of Arms in order that Our Officers of Arms and all other Public Functionaries whom it may concern may take full notice and knowledge thereof in their several and respective departments: And for so doing this shall be your Warrant Given at Our Court at St. James's this Twenty sixth day of May, in the Thirty first year of Our Reign. –

By Her Majesty's Command

Buckingham & Chandos

I Albert William Woods of the College of Arms London, Lancaster Herald and Registrar of the said College do hereby certify and declare that the foregoing is a true and faithful Copy of the Original Warrant and that the same has been examined with the Record thereof in the Books of the College of Arms by me this Twenty first day of September 1868.

Albert W. Woods
Lancaster & Registrar

40.6 cm x 19 cm

National Archives of Canada,
Government Archives Division,
RG 2, Vol. 25 A.

IV

Assassination of Thomas D'Arcy McGee, Coroner's Jury Findings

Thomas D'Arcy McGee, born in Ireland in 1825, migrated to Boston, where he worked as an editor. In 1845 he returned to Ireland to edit a nationalist paper, and participated in the rebellion of 1848. He fled to the United States, and a decade letter moved to Montreal at the request of the Irish community of that city.

In Montreal, he founded a newspaper, the *New Era*, which began to advocate a "new nationality" in the New World. His paper became the tribune of union, which would spur growth and create a distinctly Canadian people. Hence, he supported a transcontinental railway, acquisition and settlement of Rupert's Land and protective tariffs to foster home industry. In his program, he was closer to Grit and Reform Party positions, and initially co-operated with George Brown. But he quickly gravitated to Sir John A. Macdonald and Cartier, who had a more comprehensive vision of future union.

Elected from Montreal to the provincial legislature in 1858, he participated in the "Great Coalition" leading to the Charlottetown Conference, and in both the Charlottetown and Quebec Conferences. His powers of oratorical and the lyricism of his prose convinced many to support Confederation. A writer of Irish history and author of 300 poems, he could rightly be called the bard of Confederation.

He also became the first political victim of Confederation. McGee always strove to improve the lot of the Catholic Irish, both in Ireland and in North America. But the community was politically rent, and the adherents of the Fenian movement saw betrayal of the Irish cause in McGee's political and cultural activity. The Fenians, dedicated to winning Irish home independence, proposed to achieve their objective by revolution and armed seizure of Canada, which they would then barter for Irish home rule. McGee, completely opposed to such a program and tactics, tirelessly and effectively criticized the Fenians. In all likelihood, it was a Fenian who, in one of the few acts of political assassination in Canadian history, murdered him in Ottawa in 1868.

This document, with jurors' signatures and seals, records the findings of the coroner's jury called on 8 April, the day following McGee's death, to investigate the assassination.

City of Ottawa: Coroner's Jury. 1868.

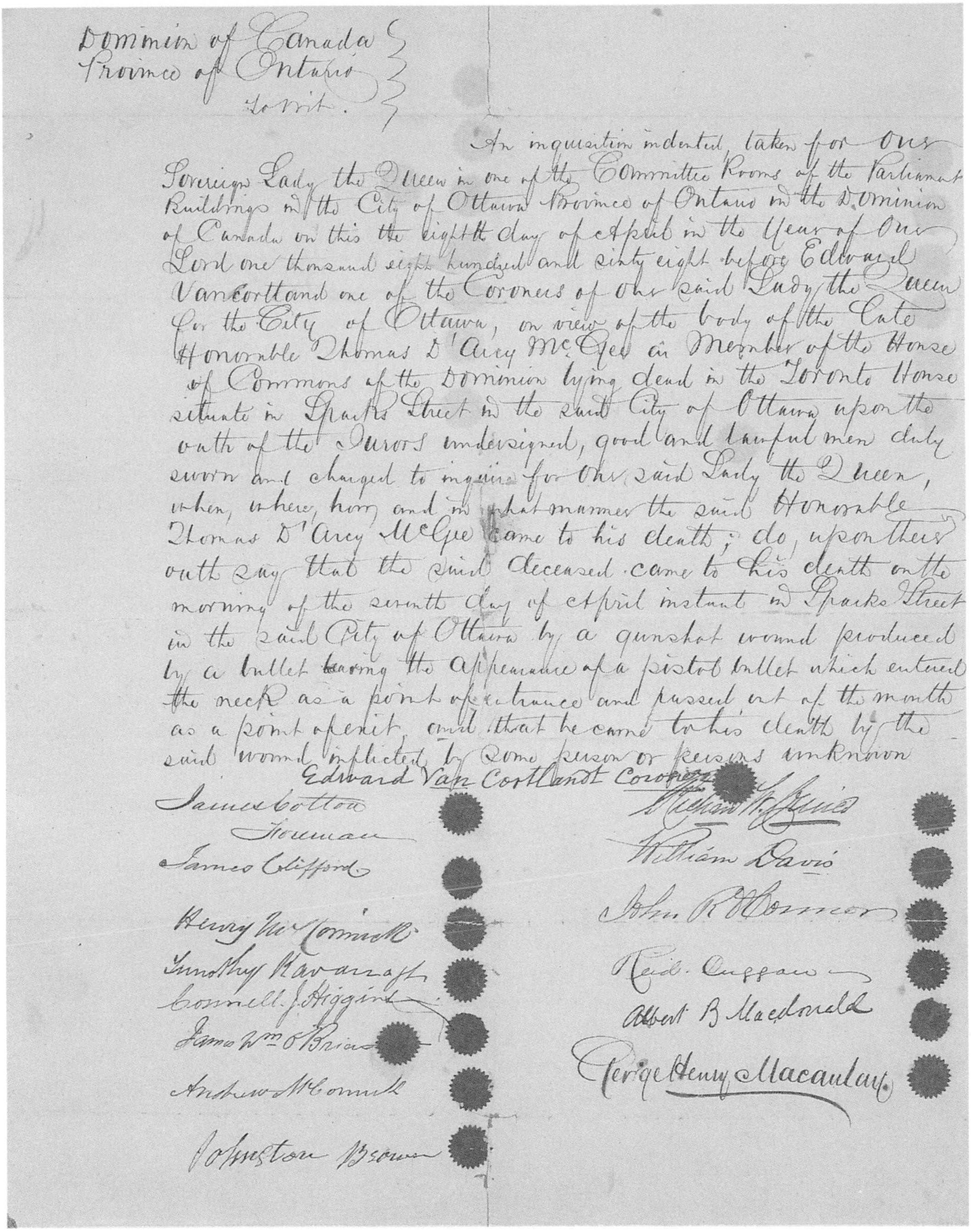

Dominion of Canada }
Province of Ontario }
To wit. }

An inquisition indented, taken for Our Sovereign Lady the Queen in one of the Committee Rooms of the Parliament Buildings in the City of Ottawa Province of Ontario in the Dominion of Canada on this the eighth day of April in the Year of Our Lord one thousand eight hundred and sixty eight before Edward Vancortland one of the Coroners of Our said Lady the Queen for the City of Ottawa, on view of the body of the Late Honorable Thomas D'Arcy McGee a Member of the House of Commons of the Dominion lying dead in the Toronto House situate in Sparks Street in the said City of Ottawa upon the oath of the Jurors undersigned, good and lawful men duly sworn and charged to inquire for Our said Lady the Queen, when, where, how and in what manner the said Honorable Thomas D'Arcy McGee came to his death; do, upon their oath say that the said deceased came to his death on the morning of the seventh day of April instant in Sparks Street in the said City of Ottawa by a gunshot wound produced by a bullet having the appearance of a pistol bullet which entered the neck as a point of entrance and passed out of the mouth as a point of exit, and that he came to his death by the said wound inflicted by some person or persons unknown

Edward Van Cortlandt Coroner

James Cotton
Foreman
James Clifford
Henry McCormick
Timothy Kavanagh
Connell J. Higgins
James Wm O'Brien
Andrew McCormick
Johnston Brown

[illegible]
William Davis
John R. O'Connor
Richd. Duggan
Albert B Macdonald
George Henry Macaulay

42 cm x 33.5 cm

National Archives of Canada,
Manuscript Division,
MG 27, I, E 9.

Commission to Sir John Young, Baron Lisgar

Sir John Young, Baron Lisgar (1807-1876) was named Governor-General of Canada in 1869, a post he held until 1873. His tenure of office saw the completion of Confederation (except for Newfoundland and the Arctic Islands), as Manitoba and the rest of Rupert's Land and the North-Western Territory, British Columbia and Prince Edward Island all entered the union by 1873.

Lisgar, a very active Governor-General, assumed office at a time when the young Dominion was threatened by Fenians in the settled central and Maritime provinces, and in the Red River region by Fenians and Metis led by Louis Riel. He very ably helped to dispel Canadian-American tensions occasioned by the Fenian raids into Canada, and soothed American displeasure at Canada's acquisition of the continental interior. While he wholeheartedly promoted Confederation, he realized that the manner of Manitoba's entry into the union could leave behind a legacy of ill-will. For this reason he strove to mediate the conflict between Ottawa and those inhabitants of the Red River region who had taken up arms against the Crown. His proclamation of 6 December 1869 to those participating in the Red River disturbances offered a pardon to all who desisted from further disorders.

While Lisgar was Governor-General of Canada, the Hudson's Bay Company surrendered title to Rupert's Land to the Dominion of Canada. The Company and the Colonial Office had been negotiating terms of the surrender since the early 1860s. After Confederation, Dominion representatives joined these negotiations. Finally, on 19 October 1869, all parties agreed to the terms of surrender: the Company would transfer its charter territory to the Crown in return for £300,000 sterling, title to the land on which its establishments stood and one-twentieth of the territory's fertile areas, which would be opened for occupation and sold to settlers.

Both the Company and Britain wished to hand over the territory as quickly as possible. The Dominion government, however, for reasons of international law, did not wish to assume authority over this region until it was pacified. Thus, until the territory was actually admitted into Confederation, the Hudson's Bay Company was responsible — however amorphous its sovereignty — for Rupert's Land. To avoid an executive vacuum between April 1869 and August 1870, when the Dominion finally took title to the Company's lands, the Company appointed Lisgar its representative as Governor-in-Chief of Rupert's Land. This commission is one of several documents of empowerment to Lisgar. By virtue of it, Lisgar combined in himself both the offices of Governor-General of the Dominion and Governor-in-Chief of Rupert's Land, a symbolic as well as real affirmation of unified sovereignty with executive authority to act in the resolution of the Red River Rebellion.

Hudson's Bay Company. 1869-1870.

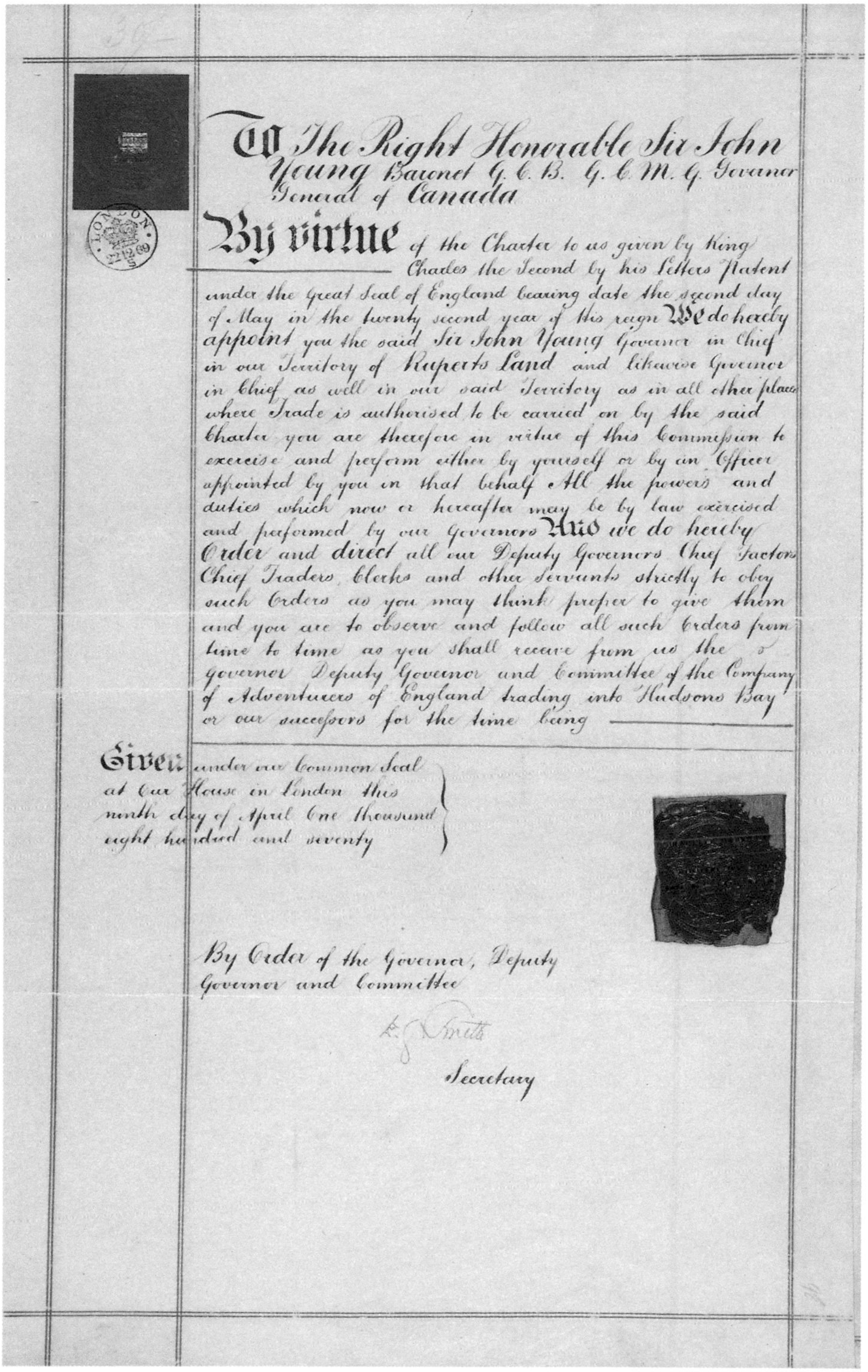

To The Right Honorable Sir John Young Baronet G. C. B. G. C. M. G. Governor General of Canada

By virtue of the Charter to us given by King Charles the Second by his Letters Patent under the Great Seal of England bearing date the second day of May in the twenty second year of his reign We do hereby appoint you the said Sir John Young Governor in Chief in our Territory of Ruperts Land and likewise Governor in Chief as well in our said Territory as in all other places where Trade is authorised to be carried on by the said Charter you are therefore in virtue of this Commission to exercise and perform either by yourself or by an Officer appointed by you in that behalf All the powers and duties which now or hereafter may be by law exercised and performed by our Governors And we do hereby Order and direct all our Deputy Governors Chief Factors Chief Traders, Clerks and other Servants strictly to obey such Orders as you may think proper to give them and you are to observe and follow all such Orders from time to time as you shall receive from us the Governor Deputy Governor and Committee of the Company of Adventurers of England trading into Hudsons Bay or our successors for the time being

Given under our Common Seal at Our House in London this ninth day of April One thousand eight hundred and seventy

By Order of the Governor, Deputy Governor and Committee

Secretary

46.5 cm x 20 cm

National Archives of Canada,
Manuscript Division,
MG 27, I, B 2.

Dispatch to Governor Douglas at Vancouver Island Regarding Gold Rush, Administrative Measures and Security

With the discovery of gold in the Fraser River Valley in 1857, and the inrush of thousands of miners, Great Britain reoriented its whole policy vis-à-vis British Columbia. Sir Edward Lytton, the Colonial Secretary, enunciated this new policy to Governor James Douglas in a number of memoranda of 1858, one of which is presented here. Douglas, a "Scotch West Indian," son of a Scottish merchant and a "free coloured woman," had entered the employ of the North West Company. After its merger in 1821 with the Hudson's Bay Company, Douglas stayed on, rising through Company ranks. When Britain leased Vancouver Island to the Hudson's Bay Company in 1849, Douglas became the Company's chief agent there. In 1851 he was also named Governor of the Crown colony of Vancouver Island.

When gold-seekers came in the spring of 1858, the first wave 25,000-strong, Britain moved rapidly to assert her claim against possible American expansion. She cancelled the remaining year left on the Hudson's Bay Company's lease of the West Coast, created the new colony of British Columbia and offered Douglas the post of Governor, requiring him to sever his relationship with the Company.

In this memorandum, Lord Lytton assesses Douglas' actions, evaluates policies and offers suggestions to the new governor. He approves Douglas' appointments of revenue officers and gold commissioners to raise money for administrative purposes and to regulate gold claims and mining. He proposes to send legal and justice officials from Britain, to avoid the suspicion that "local interests" might be promoted. He approves Douglas' measures to establish good relations with the Indians, with the gold commissioners setting aside Indian reserves to avoid miner-Indian warfare. Surveying and postal services are required — Lord Lytton allows Douglas latitude to take necessary measures here as required.

The memorandum, while empowering Douglas to act decisively to protect British interests, also advises him to realize that he no longer acts for the Hudson's Bay Company, which never had any authority on the West Coast other than the right to trade with native people. Lytton also informs Douglas that he "will be empowered to govern, and to legislate, on [his] own authority," but "as a temporary measure only." Douglas, with a penchant for authoritarian action, was gently but firmly reined in and, on the pages displayed, instructed to work towards establishing institutions of popular government in British Columbia.

Gold rushes rarely occasioned lasting change. In the case of the Pacific coast, however, the gold rushes galvanized Britain to action to secure the coast against loss to the United States. To Britain's great good fortune, in Governor Douglas she found a person equal to the task.

United Kingdom: Colonial Secretary. 1858.

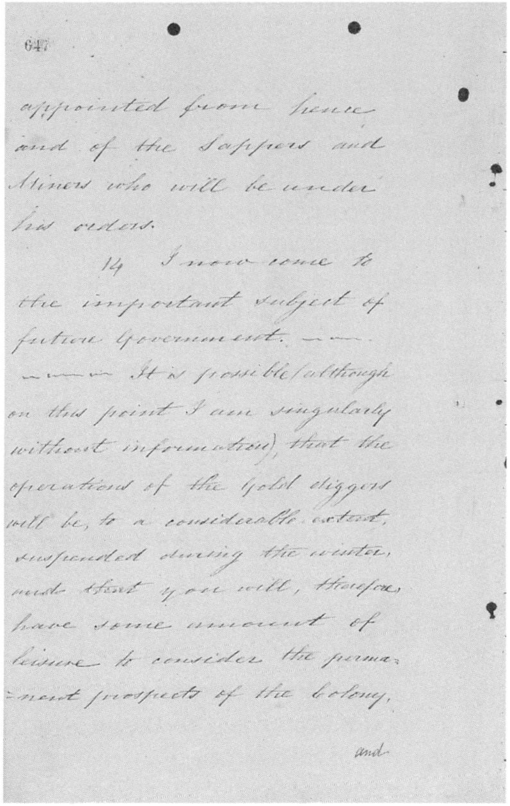

647

appointed from hence and of the Sappers and Miners who will be under his orders.

14 I now come to the important subject of future Government. —— It is possible (although on this point I am singularly without information) that the operations of the Gold diggers will be, to a considerable extent, suspended during the winter, and that you will, therefore have some amount of leisure to consider the permanent prospects of the Colony,

and

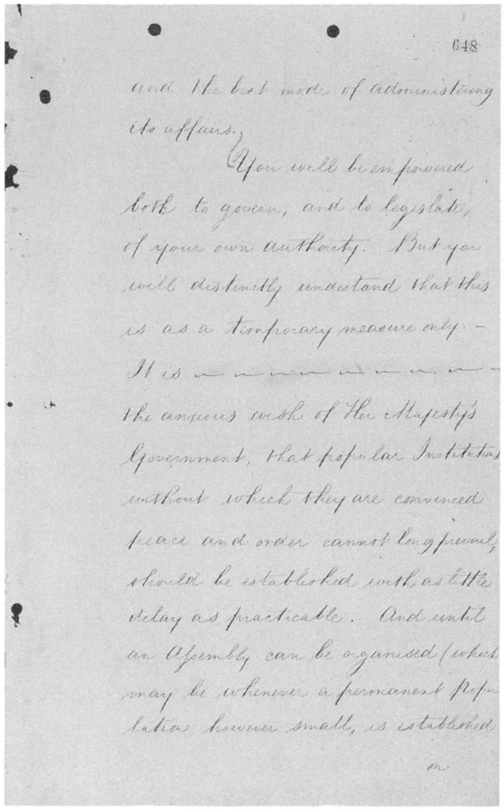

648

and the best mode of administering its affairs.

You will be empowered both to govern, and to legislate, of your own authority. But you will distinctly understand that this is as a temporary measure only. — It is —— the anxious wish of Her Majesty's Government, that popular Institutions without which they are convinced peace and order cannot long prevail, should be established with as little delay as practicable. And until an Assembly can be organised (which may be whenever a permanent population however small, is established

on

31.8 cm x 19.8 cm

National Archives of Canada,
Manuscript Division,
RG 7, G 8, C, Vol. 1, pp. 647-648.

"The Abandoned"

This unique photograph of a steamer run aground summarizes the fickleness of British Columbia's gold-based economy in the late 1850s-1860s. An inscription on the reverse side of this image reads, "The Abandoned / an old steamer run on shore as being of no further use, the population having decreased so rapidly in consequence of Columbia gold fields — engines of course taken out." A close inspection of the wheelhouse reveals, in barely-discernible letters, that the vessel was named *Alexandra.* The smokestack is gone, probably removed at the same time that the engines were salvaged.

The *Alexandra* was probably born of, as well as a victim of, the gold rush phenomenon of the second half of the nineteenth century. The discovery of "placer" gold, small particles of gold freely suspended in water which could easily be retrieved by amateurs, drew tens of thousands to California in 1848. As the California fields gave out, miners moved northwards, first into the Fraser River country (1850s), then into the Cariboo (1860s). The gold rush phenomenon was an expression of substantial changes in human life, of a communications and transportation revolution — mass newspapers and the telegraph, railways and particularly steamboats, which could work the coasts and often go far inland along rivers that led to gold fields.

Before her ungracious abandonment, the *Alexandra* perhaps plied the rivers leading to gold fields, or the ferry routes among the channel islands, or worked the Victoria-Vancouver run. However, the gold of the Fraser River gave out quickly. When prospectors found gold in the interior, on the Horsefly River in 1860 and around Barkerville in 1862, the population of the coastal region depleted rapidly as thousands rushed to the new gold diggings. The *Alexandra*'s days were done. Despite the capital invested in the vessel, there was nothing else to do but run the ship aground, dramatic evidence of the sparseness of settled Europeans in British Columbia, and the migratory penchant of much of its gold-seeking population.

Anonymous. ca 1862.

20.3 cm x 27.2 cm

National Archives of Canada,
Documentary Art and Photography Division,
PA-124069.

"Goldmining Asturias Claim 1867 or 1868"

Born in England in 1838, Frederick Dally arrived in Victoria in 1862 when the Cariboo gold rush was in full force. After working as a merchant, in 1866 he turned to photography. He is best known for his 1867-1868 photographs of the Cariboo Road and the workings in the Cariboo gold fields. This image is a photograph out of that series, depicting a gold-dig more intensive than primary panning for gold.

Once the easily-worked alluvial gold had been recovered by panning or surface-sluicing in sandbars and gravel-beds, Pacific gold fields were quickly abandoned — unless gold nuggets were discovered, or "underground pay streaks," veins of gold to be worked. As Dally's photograph shows, using pick and shovel, miners have opened up pits and excavated soil which is gold-bearing. With a spring as a source of water, they wash this soil through their sluiceworks, separating gold particles and nuggets from the gravel and muck as it makes its way down the sluices.

Extracting gold through this method was more costly in labour and financial terms than alluvial panning, and often required partnerships and more permanent dwellings, which in turn required regular supply and administration. Hence the phenomenon of gold towns springing up, such as Barkerville in the Cariboo gold fields. To supply the town and its miners, a company of Royal Engineers built the Cariboo Road, linking Barkerville with Yale in the Fraser River valley; the road was 650 kilometres long, most of it blasted from solid rock.

The method of extracting gold through sluiceworks and surface mining caused significant environmental damage. One can see in this photograph the clear-cutting of forest which gave miners access to gold-bearing soil on a denuded hillside. Miners could then freely work the soil and gravel through sluiceworks. But after they were done, erosion would continue the destructive work already evident in the photograph.

Frederick Dally. ca 1867-1868.

18.1 cm x 22.7 cm

National Archives of Canada,
Documentary Art and Photography Division,
C-26181.

Crimean War Medal *and* Canadian General Service Medal

The Crimean War (1854-1856), fought in a distant theatre (Crimean Peninsula and Caucasus region of Russia), pitted Britain, France and the Ottoman Empire against the Russian Empire. Although not directly threatened, the British colonies in North America were affected by this war, fought half-a-world away.

The war immediately roused a great patriotic fervour amongst the colonials. The provinces offered to raise and equip an infantry regiment to serve overseas, an offer graciously declined by the Crown. However, many colonials did go overseas, enlist and serve in the Crimean theatre. Lieutenant Alexander Dunn of the 11th Hussars, for his participation in the charge of the "Light Brigade" at Balaclava, was the first "Canadian" to receive the coveted Victoria Cross. Other Canadians received the Crimean War Medal, shown here in both *verso* and *recto*.

The *recto* image of Queen Victoria was struck from the die of an earlier medal; the *verso*, the figure of "Fame" bearing a wreath to honour a hero, was designed by Benjamin Wyon, a member of the famed Wyon family of medal makers. The unknown recipient of one of the medals displayed, judging by the clasps awarded for actions, participated in all the major engagements of the Crimean War (Azov, Sevastopol, Inkerman, Balaclava and Alma).

The Crimean War not only fired patriotism; it also posed very starkly the question of defence of the British colonies. As Britain gathered her regular forces for the Crimea, the colonies were left with approximately two thousand British regulars to defend them. The "sedentary" militias of New Brunswick, Nova Scotia and the Province of Canada, organized earlier on volunteer and territorial (county) principles, were little more than paper forces. The sobering realization of their defencelessness, the heightened sense of militarism of the war years and mounting patriotism disposed the British colonies to organize effective militia forces. The Province of Canada, for example, passed Militia acts in both 1855 and 1856 which provided for cavalry, artillery and infantry units, and which provided for the purchase of equipment and for training.

The militias born at this time would later defend Canada against Fenian raids in 1866 and 1870, and participate in the 1870 Red River campaign. Interestingly, a military decoration to honour veterans of these actions came into existence only in 1899. In 1897, in connection with Queen Victoria's sixtieth jubilee, several prominent Canadians agitated for a "Canadian" military decoration, and received Queen Victoria's approval for such an award — hence the Canadian General Service Medal.

The *recto* of this medal was drawn from the India Medal of 1895, designed by T. Brock. The *verso*, designed by George W. de Saulles, shows a Canadian ensign wreathed by maple leaves, surmounted by the word "CANADA." It was suspended from a red ribbon with a broad white centre stripe. In 1899-1902, 16,000 such medals were struck in silver at the Royal Mint in London, and presented, *ex post facto* and always with a bar, to veterans who defended against the Fenian raids (1866, 1870) and participated in the Red River Expedition (1870).

Of the two full-size General Service Medals shown here, one was presented to Private Hugh John Macdonald, the son of Canada's first Prime Minister, the other to Lieutenant Wilfrid Laurier, later Canada's seventh Prime Minister. This medal became distinctly Canadian when, in 1914-1915, 17,000 copies were struck at the Canadian Mint in Ottawa.

Alfred Benjamin Wyon, T. Brock and George W. de Saulles. 1855, 1899.

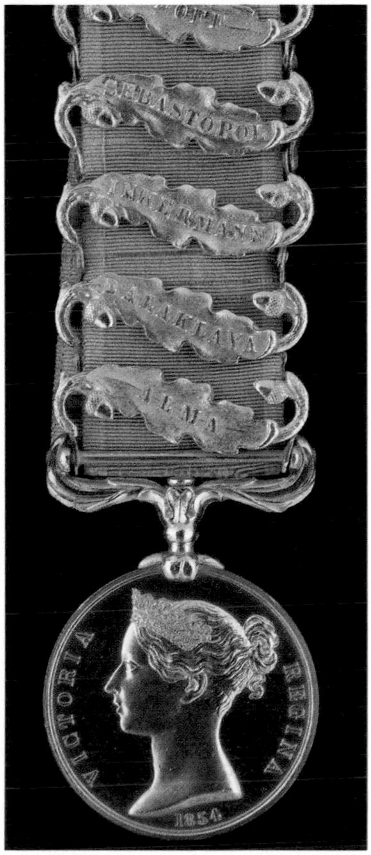

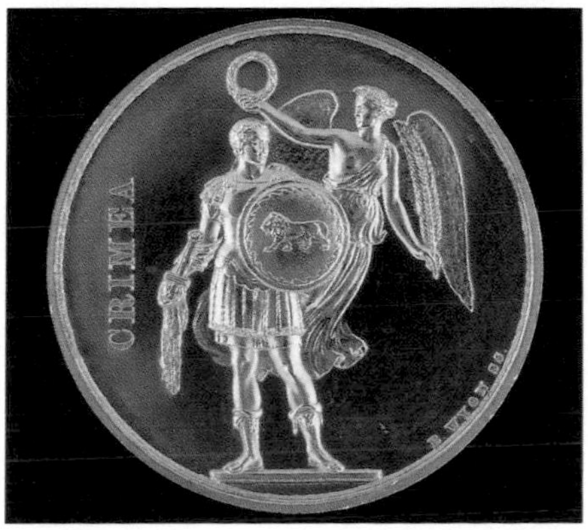

National Archives of Canada,
Documentary Art and Photography Division,
[Large Canada General Service Medal, Obverse] C-62124, 36 mm (diameter) (Silver)
[Large Canada General Service Medal, Reverse] C-53769, 36 mm (diameter) (Silver)
[Small Canada General Service Medal, Obverse] C-62144, 18 mm (diameter) (Silver)
[Small Canada General Service Medal, Reverse] C-62145, 18 mm (diameter) (Silver)
[Crimean War Medal, Obverse] C-138580, 36 mm (diameter) (Silver)
[Crimean War Medal, Reverse] C-138581. 36 mm (diameter) (Silver)

"British Troops on the March — Canada, 1862"

Printed by Leighton Brothers (London, England) this print depicts the march of British reinforcements from Saint John along the Madawaska Road to the citadel of Quebec.

The American Civil War had commenced in 1861; events south of the border necessarily affected the British colonies in North America. In November 1861 Captain Wilkes of the USS *San Jacinto*, on his own responsibility, intercepted the British mail-packet *Trent* in the Bahama Channel and seized two Confederate delegates on their way to Britain to negotiate British support for the Confederacy. Since Union forces had violated British neutrality, this incident enraged British public opinion; war between Britain and the United States, with potentially disastrous consequences for the colonies, seemed possible. To bolster its garrisons there, Britain rushed almost 12,000 troops to the British North American colonies.

The troops arrived too late in the season to steam into the Gulf of St. Lawrence. Consequently, they had to be moved overland to Canada, the probable theatre of operations in the event of war. They landed in Saint John, New Brunswick. A snow road, the Madawaska as it was called, was put into the best shape possible; and the troops set out through forest and hip-deep snow for the citadel. In this coloured wood engraving, we see the regular troops, hauling baggage sleds, weaving through the mid- to back-ground. In the foreground stand Canadian and Indian guides. Unlike the troops, they are dressed in skins, and supplied with snowshoes and toboggans, aboriginal inventions. Between 11 January and 9 March 1862, a force of 6,780 men with 18 guns passed into Canada by this route.

The war scare, as it began to envelope Britain and the colonies in 1861, made intercolonial co-operation on defence imperative. Nothing could better serve this end than a railway linking Maritime provinces and the Province of Canada. Had such a railway existed — it had certainly been talked about for many years — the winter march of the British Regulars, with its attendant suffering for the men involved, would have been unnecessary.

Unknown Artist. 1862.

31.8 cm x 44.1 cm

National Archives of Canada,
Documentary Art and Photography Division,
C-40906.

IV

Engagement with Fenians

The Fenian Brotherhood was organized by Irish-Americans in 1857. A reflection of Old World politics in the New World, its aim was to win Irish independence from Britain. While one wing favoured an uprising in Ireland, another hoped to achieve Irish independence through pressure upon Britain's North American possessions. By 1865, Fenians had a substantial treasury and 10,000 American Civil War veterans organized into "clubs." In 1866 they moved against the British colonies. A raid into New Brunswick in April failed. Another Fenian group crossed over the Niagara frontier in June and, after engaging a detached column of Canadian militiamen at Ridgeway, made good their escape. Yet another group crossed the Quebec frontier at Missisquoi Bay on 7 June and, several days later, withdrew.

This letter, written by Captain Ramsay Weston Phipps of the Royal Artillery, describes the Canadian response to this incursion of 7 June. The letter, dated 11 June, recounts the movements of Canadian militia and British Regulars in the St. John's-St.Armand-Pigeon Hill region of the Eastern Townships, and their futile search for an enemy who was in no mood to fight. Horsemen, gun batteries and militiamen went back and forth through the area, but the Fenians had slipped away. "It was a great disappointment," writes Phipps to his mother; "chance had thrown into my hands the only battery that were likely to be engaged, and here was nothing to fight."

In an interesting notation, Phipps observes that a United States cavalry officer allowed mounted Canadian guides to cross a parcel of American territory in search of Fenians. This was probably the result of President Andrew Johnson's condemnation of the Fenians on 6 June, which denied them safe refuge on the American side of the border and ordered American military forces to seize Fenian ordnance.

Following these events, the Fenian menace receded, although it did not go away altogether. The failed raid upon New Brunswick was crucial in swinging that province to favour Confederation. Leonard Tilley, ably supported by Crown officials working under instructions from the Colonial Office, won passage of the "Seventy-Two Resolutions" through New Brunswick's assembly. Defence against external threat lay in union, and a railway to bind the colonies into one commercial and defensive entity.

Captain Ramsay Weston Phipps. 1866.

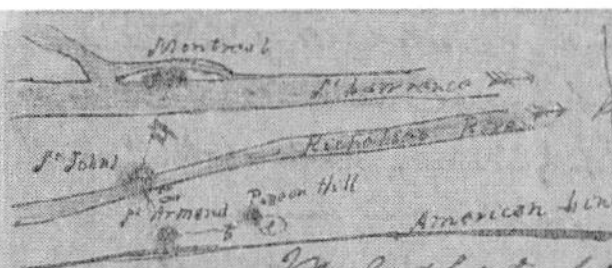

Camp St. Armand
June 11/66

Dear Mother

My last hasty letters and, perhaps, the Newspapers will have told you the end of all this scare. The whole thing has been too absurd, and I suppose we ought to be well laughed at: here we have been concentrating and guarding, and goodness knows what, all for a few scoundrels that might have been sent off by a troop of Cavalry. I give you the description of all we have done, ridiculous as it cannot seem: a sham fight is real service compared to it.

On June 8th at six in the evening, whilst I was in camp at St. Johns a report was made that the Fenians were advancing on St. Armand, a tiny village, two miles from the frontier, where some Volunteers had been quartered till they came back in a panic. It was settled to send a force up there, and by half past seven o'clock a Division of the Battery (two guns, about 40 Men and 30 horses) under your humble servant, with a Subaltern, were in the train, the Carriages and Horses being put in quickly. We had to go about twenty eight miles to St. Armand picking up on the road the Infantry consisting of 200 Men of 25 Regt and about the same number of Volunteers who were at St. Alexandre about halfway; an Officer of the 25 commanded the whole.

brought out milk, and water, and doughnuts, or meat cakes. When we got within two miles of Pigeon Hill we heard that all Fenians had left it and were crossing the frontier. The guns were ordered to the front, and trotted off in hopes of getting a slap at them. They soon passed all the out pickets and went on till stopped by an order to keep in sight of the Rifles who were hurrying up. We thus got first into the hamlet were I ~~knew that~~ I had orders to stop for the main body. Hearing that the "Guides" a troop of Montreal Volunteer Cavalry, composed of gentlemen, well mounted and armed had been brought up to St. Armand, and would arrive in a few seconds, I proposed to follow them at their own pace, leaving my [illegible] to keep at a distance at a walk: at the same time sending for leave to do so.

In a few moments about forty of the Guides came trotting past the Infantry and I went after them but to our mutual disappointment we were stopped in a few yards and sent different directions.

All Fenians left were reported in a wood, two miles off, touching the frontier. The Guns and Rifles were to advance straight to the frontier while the Guides rode round the wood: the Infantry to meet them on the frontier, then turn back and search the wood, entering it from

21 cm x 13.4 cm

National Archives of Canada,
Manuscript Division,
MG 24, F 44.

"Action Near Freleysburg (Frelieghsburg, Québec). Precipitate Retreat of the British Vol. Cavalry 99 Strong, Near Freleysburg, Canada East on the 8th of June 1866"

This handcoloured lithograph, drawn on stone by John McNevin and printed by A. Brown of New York, is a most interesting exercise in Fenian propaganda. The information under this depiction advises the reader that fifteen men under Major P. O'Hara of the 3rd Massachusetts Infantry, "Army of Ireland," put to flight 99 British cavalrymen, and captured the enemy standard.

While the depiction of this battle is quite dramatic, with Fenians rising in ambush out of grass, wheatfields and bush, and putting to flight a much larger number of mounted opponents, there is only one difficulty with it as a historical record — the event never occurred. There was no red-coated cavalry militia in Canada East in 1866. The print was circulated by the Fenian Brotherhood in 1866 to bolster the spirits of its adherents, and to enlist men and raise money for its cause.

After John McNevin. 1866.

11.75 cm x 42.4 cm

National Archives of Canada,
Documentary Art and Photography Division,
C-11731.

IV

"Halifax Harbour, Point Pleasant Defences. Fort Ogilvie"

Coastal defence had an importance in the latter half of the nineteenth century that could be compared to missile and air defence today. Rapid advances in weapons technology — steam-driven armoured warships, long-range rifled artillery and torpedoes — threatened seaports with swift and devastating surprise attacks. To a naval power like Britain, control and defence of colonial seaports was crucial.

Halifax had always been a cornerstone of British Imperial and colonial defence plans. Its harbour gave British warships secure anchorage, while its position on the isthmus of Nova Scotia, jutting out eastward into the Atlantic, put it astride the great sea routes linking North America, the West Indies and Europe. As successive improvements in weapons repeatedly rendered existing fortifications obsolete, frequent re-assessments of the defences of Halifax harbour were followed by large scale construction and re-construction of the forts and batteries around the harbour. A massive improvement of harbour defences began in the 1860s, continuing unabated virtually until 1906, when the last British troops withdrew from Canada.

The drawings shown here were prepared by Lieutenant Hamilton Tovey of the Royal Engineers, and reflect improvements to the overall plan of strengthening harbour defences to meet the increased threats of the 1860s. Fort Ogilvie, originally a battery in the woods at Point Pleasant overlooking the entrance to Halifax Harbour, had been built in 1793. During the American Civil War the fort was entirely rebuilt and enlarged to accept rifled muzzle loaders (RMLs). With the other defence works in place at Halifax at that time — amounting to some 167 heavy guns — complete, overlapping coverage of the inner harbour was possible; the naval anchorage was secure.

Fort Ogilvie would again be rebuilt in the 1890s. The renewed structure and other Halifax defensive works would continue to contribute to the defence of Halifax and Canada right up to World War II, when Fort Ogilvie came to house anti-aircraft installations.

Lieutenant Hamilton Tovey. 1867.

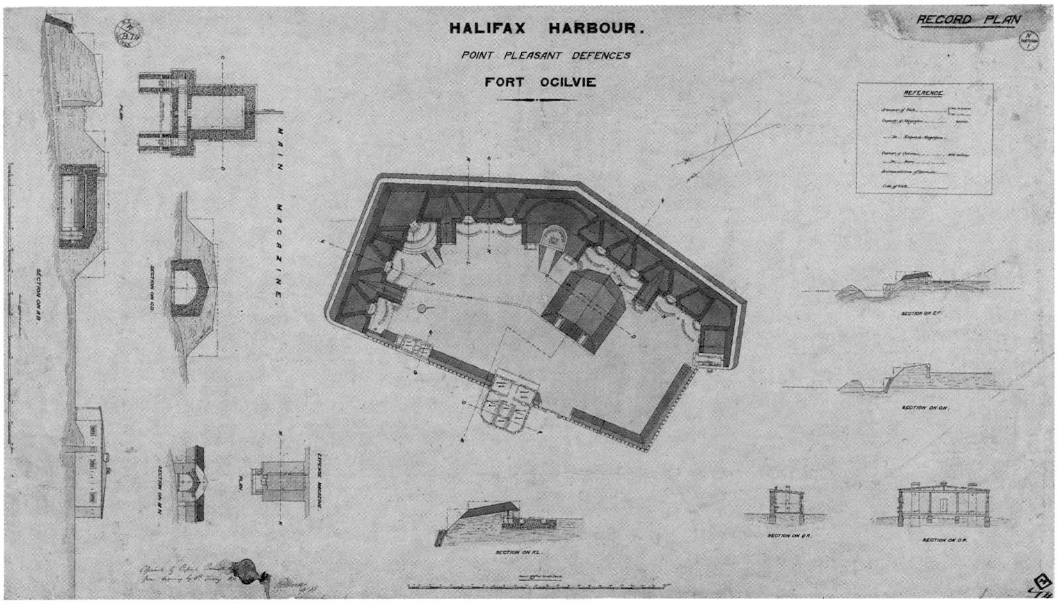

67 cm x 121 cm

National Archives of Canada,
Cartographic and Audio-Visual Archives Division,
NMC-10893.

Treaty of Washington. Macdonald's Fears of British Betrayal of Canadian Interests

As the decade of the 1860s drew to a close, both Britain and the United States recognized the need to resolve a number of outstanding issues which disturbed relations between them and, necessarily, affected the new Dominion of Canada. This led to the Washington Conference of 1871.

Americans still harboured much ill-will against Britain (and, thus, against Canada) from the Civil War years. There had been the "Trent Affair." In addition, British shipyards had built privateers such as the *Alabama* for the Confederacy, which had disrupted Union shipping and caused heavy losses; Americans demanded compensation for these losses. Americans also wanted access to Canadian and Newfoundland inshore fisheries. Their right to fish had expired when the United States, in revenge for perceived British and Canadian support of the Confederacy, had in 1866 abrogated the Reciprocity Treaty of 1854. The San Juan Island dispute, an ongoing irritant, also came under consideration at the Conference.

The Imperial Commission to the Washington Conference was led by Lord Elgin, the original architect of the Reciprocity Treaty; it included Sir John A. Macdonald, Prime Minister of Canada. Macdonald was there to represent the Dominion's interest, for Canada, bordering on the United States, would be most affected by the outcome of the British-American negotiations. But he could accomplish little on behalf of Canada. The Americans, for example, refused to admit to the agenda Canada's claims to compensation for damages caused by Fenian raids, or to consider reciprocity. Britain, very anxious to settle all outstanding issues for the sake of tranquillity, was prepared to concede to the United States all down the line.

Since most concessions were at Canada's expense, Macdonald held out against signing the Treaty of Washington. In the letter displayed here, Lord Elgin entreats Macdonald to add his name to the document. Viewing matters from the Imperial vantage, Eigin points out that the Treaty "is fair and honourable," the best possible under the circumstances. Macdonald's signature was mandatory. Without it, Elgin continues, the American Senate would not likely approve the Treaty. Delicately pointing out to Macdonald that he is a member of an Imperial High Commission, which had been instructed by Her Majesty's Government to accept the terms of the Treaty in the overall interests of the Empire, Elgin in fact advises Macdonald that he has no recourse but to sign.

On 8 May 1871, the Treaty was approved. Canada opened her inshore fisheries to the United States, for which she received access to the American market for her fish products, and a cash settlement. Canada would also lose San Juan Island in 1872. To soften the harshness of the Treaty, Britain extended to Canada loan guarantees to underwrite a transcontinental railway.

While harsh toward Canada, the Treaty was of fundamental importance. It signalled an end to British-American hostility; tension between Britain and the United States always bore a direct threat to Canada. The Treaty accepted the borders of the new Dominion of Canada and allowed Britain to remove most of her regular forces from Canada (except for naval garrisons in Halifax and Esquimalt), a victory both for the British taxpayer and the American patriot.

Lord Elgin. 1871.

68381

Copy

Private

253

H. M's High Commission
Washington
May 6th 1871.

My dear Sir John

I have been thinking over the conversation which took place between us yesterday, & I am anxious to repeat to you the arguments which I then employed with a view to impress upon you the importance of your name being attached to the Treaty, which we hope to sign on Monday next.

It is not necessary for that purpose that I should enter into any consideration in detail of the merits of that Treaty. I believe it to be one, which taken as a whole, & regarded as it ought to be, as a broad settlement of the many differences which have lately sprung up between Gt. Britain & the United

68382

States, is fair & honourable to all parties & calculated to confer very important advantages upon our respective Countries.

I should doubtless have desired to see it differently framed in some parts; but all negotiations unless carried on under the shadow of a triumphant army, are necessarily compromises, & I am convinced that the arrangement to which we have come, is the best that under the conditions of the problem before us we could have secured.

Believing this I am naturally most anxious not to run any risk of the Treaty being rejected by ~~the~~ Senate & I cannot doubt that the absence of your signature would lead to that result. It would be a very serious matter if the signature of any member of the Commission were wanting, but any of our names could I think be more safely spared than yours.

Sr

22.4 cm x 17.8 cm

National Archives of Canada,
Manuscript Division,
MG 26, A, Vol. 167, pp. 68381-68382.

IV

Examination of Sir George-Étienne Cartier Regarding the St. Alban's Raid

The Treaty of Washington did not immediately resolve all outstanding issues between Britain and the United States. Some issues went to arbitration. For the *Alabama* claims the United States received $15,500,000.00 in damages in Geneva in 1872. In the same year the San Juan Island issue, adjudicated by the German Emperor, resulted in the award of the island to the United States. The Treaty created the Washington Claims Commission to investigate other remaining contentious issues, and to recommend solutions. One such issue was the St. Alban's Raid of 1864.

The raid had occurred on 19 October 1864. A group of Confederate agents, working out of Canada, had raided the town of St. Alban's in Vermont, and there robbed banks in an amount exceeding $80,000.00. Their release by a Montreal police magistrate on technical grounds shocked Canadian officials and enraged Americans, who took this action as further proof that Britain and her colonies were inimical to the Union government of the United States. Americans had long complained that the colonies turned a blind eye to the activities of Confederate agents on their soil; in their minds, the release of the raiders proved it.

The British provinces, in their turn, had their grievances against the American Union states. While the Reciprocity Treaty had still been in force, and trade had been very active during the Civil War, American customs officials had often hindered colonial merchants and shippers to the point of Treaty infractions. There had been cases of American customs officials firing at British colonials, and impressment of British nationals into Union forces had occurred often. Tensions had risen so high that, for several months following the St. Alban's raid, the United States government had required British colonials to present passports for entry into the United States.

This was the historical context within which this document was created. George-Étienne Cartier, as Attorney-General for the province of Canada East in 1864, when the raid had occurred, was asked to clarify and explain why Canadian judicial officials released the raiders, along with the money they had stolen. A most interesting document, Cartier's deposition and the annexes to it reveal the intricacies of the event, of the technicality by which the raiders had been released, and the Canadian government's determined and successful efforts to re-arrest the raiders and recover the stolen money. Canadian officials, through the Governor-General and the British Minister in Washington, had striven to satisfy the demands of the United States; the American Secretary of State, William Seward, had been pleased to recognize this.

The St. Alban's Raid was but one event of many which strained relations between the British colonies (and later Canada) and the United States. Following the Treaty of Washington, however, and the work of the Washington Claims Commission, relations gradually normalized. Only with better relations with the United States could the disarming of the Canadian-American border begin.

Washington Claims Commission. 1873.

86260

Washington Claims Commission

Examination of Sir G. E. Cartier Bart.

Will you state what was done within your own knowledge by Lord Monck, yourself and your colleagues with respect to the Raid of St. Albans or any other raid or outrage committed or intended to be committed by the Southern Refugees in Canada against the territory or Citizens of the United States of America and what steps were taken to prevent or repress such raids outrages or intended raids and outrages and what was done for the arrest and punishment of any such Refugees who took part in such Raids or outrages subsequent thereto.

I herewith produce as part of my evidence.

"North America.
Novr. 1. 1865.
"Correspondence respecting the attack on St. Albans Vermont &
"Naval force on the North American Lakes with Appendices presented
"to both Houses of Parliament by command of Her Majesty 1865"
marked and hereafter referred to as Paper A.

also

Return to Addresses of the Legislative Assembly of Canada dated respy. 6 Feby & 11 August 1865 for copies of papers relating to St. Albans Raiders' affair and for copy of Report of F. W. Torrance Esq. on case of C. J. Coursol Esq. Judge of the Session of the Peace Montrcal marked and hereafter referred to as paper B. also

Return to an Address of the House of Commons of Canada dated 26 April 186 for copies of all correspondence with the Imperial Government relating to the outlay incurred by Canada in defence of the Frontier of the United States in 1863-4 and also arising out of the threatened Fenian Invasion. Subsequently as constituting a

40.1 cm x 31.6 cm

National Archives of Canada,
Manuscript Division,
MG 26, A, Vol. 203, p. 86260.

"'Manitobah' Settler's House and Red River Cart"

William George Richardson Hind, born in England in 1833, emigrated to Toronto in 1852, where he maintained an art studio. In 1861, as official artist, he accompanied his brother, Henry Youle Hind, on the Moisie River Expedition. Following the expedition, he joined the famed "Overlanders" of 1862.

The Overlanders, lured by the gold of the Cariboo, were organized by Thomas and Robert McMicking of Welland county in Canada West. Groups of individuals from Canada and England made their way to Fort Garry by various routes. Once there, the approximately 150 trekkers formed up in a train of Red River carts and made their way over the prairies. Led through the Rockies by Indian guides, they descended the dangerous Fraser River by raft with the loss of only six lives. Most stayed in the Cariboo only a short time, establishing themselves successfully in other occupations.

The trek was a notable achievement. Until then most people drawn by west coast gold had taken the usual time-consuming routes — by ship around the treacherous Cape Horn, or by steamer to Panama, overland to the Pacific and then by steamer up the coast. The Overlanders demonstrated that transcontinental land travel by settlers was possible, but only with great hardship; British North America was in dire need of a developed land route.

On this trek Hind prepared approximately 160 sketches and oils, including the one displayed here. This oil painting reflects much that was symbolic and characteristic of the interior. The land of the prairie stretches away unbroken, and is coming under the plow. The thatched house on the left is probably of wattle-and-clay, perhaps a "first home" on the prairie. The house on the right, however, is of wood, constructed in the Red River style. Since wood on the prairie was scarce, and long, thick logs unavailable, whole walls could not be built out of continuous logs laid horizontally atop each other and notched at the corners. Houses were built of squared uprights, with short squared timbers set between them, and tied across with lintels at the top. In this oil we also see the ubiquitous Red River cart, an almost totemic attribute of much of the graphic record of Rupert's Land.

Perhaps Hind meant this oil to do no more than record the "Manitobah" countryside in his time. But one might also see in the painting an interesting, perhaps prophetic, symbolism in the conjoining of the Red River cart driven by a man with dark, possibly Metis, features, and fenced settlers' houses alongside plowed fields fronting on the open prairie.

William George Richardson Hind. ca 1862.

25.1 cm x 37.7 cm

National Archives of Canada,
Documentary Art and Photography Division,
C-13965.

Journal of Events in Red River

William Begg (1839-1897) went to Red River in 1867 as agent for manufacturing concerns in Hamilton. He settled there and ventured into business with local merchants. In the 1870s he published trade magazines and edited the *Daily Nor'wester* and *Daily Herald.* Later he worked for the Canadian Pacific as immigration agent, and in British Columbia as a newspaper editor.

While in the Red River colony, Begg maintained a daily journal; the one shown here may well be a contemporary copy written by Begg himself. It is a detailed, immediate record, recalling the course of the Red River Rebellion as it unfolded. Perhaps even more interesting is Begg's "Preface," in which he accounts for the long-term as well as short-term causes leading to the "open and decided" resistance of 1868-1870.

Chief among these causes, Begg points out, was the Canadian government's ignorance of the real conditions in the North-West Territories. Additionally, the Canadian government made no effort to inform the 14,000 inhabitants of Red River of what it intended to do — hence "dame rumour had full sway," and the inhabitants came to fear loss of freedoms so long enjoyed. The "Ontario men," self-styled paladins of a Canadian manifest destiny, came into the colony. As they agitated for union, which they understood as annexation of Rupert's Land to Ontario, they mounted a crude smear campaign against the Hudson's Bay Company. This, in Begg's estimation, backfired. Local inhabitants knew the truth about the Company's administration; they came to see these representatives of their future as dishonourable, and "annexation to Canada became a byeword of ridicule."

Several other immediate events had contributed to Canada's bad reputation among Red River's inhabitants. The grasshopper plague of 1867-1868 had devastated the region. As a relief project, Canada had hired local people for the building of the Dawson Road. It had hoped to win credit in the Red River area for concern shown about the well-being of the local populace, and at the same time to prepare a road for the expected rush of settlers into Rupert's Land once the territory was turned over to the Dominion. But the Canadian supervisors, Begg recounts, had abused the locals by fiscal improprieties, and had harmed Canada's reputation.

Finally, Colonel John Stoughton Dennis commenced his survey of the North-West Territories in August 1869, before locals were even consulted and before the Red River region even entered Confederation. This, Begg suggests, was the final straw — the survey was, in the very least, "arbitrary and presumptuous."

All of this was too much to bear. One portion of the population, the Metis, raised a force of 600 men and in October of 1869 blocked William McDougall, the designated Lieutenant-Governor, from entering the colony. The Red River Rebellion had commenced.

William Begg. 1869-1870.

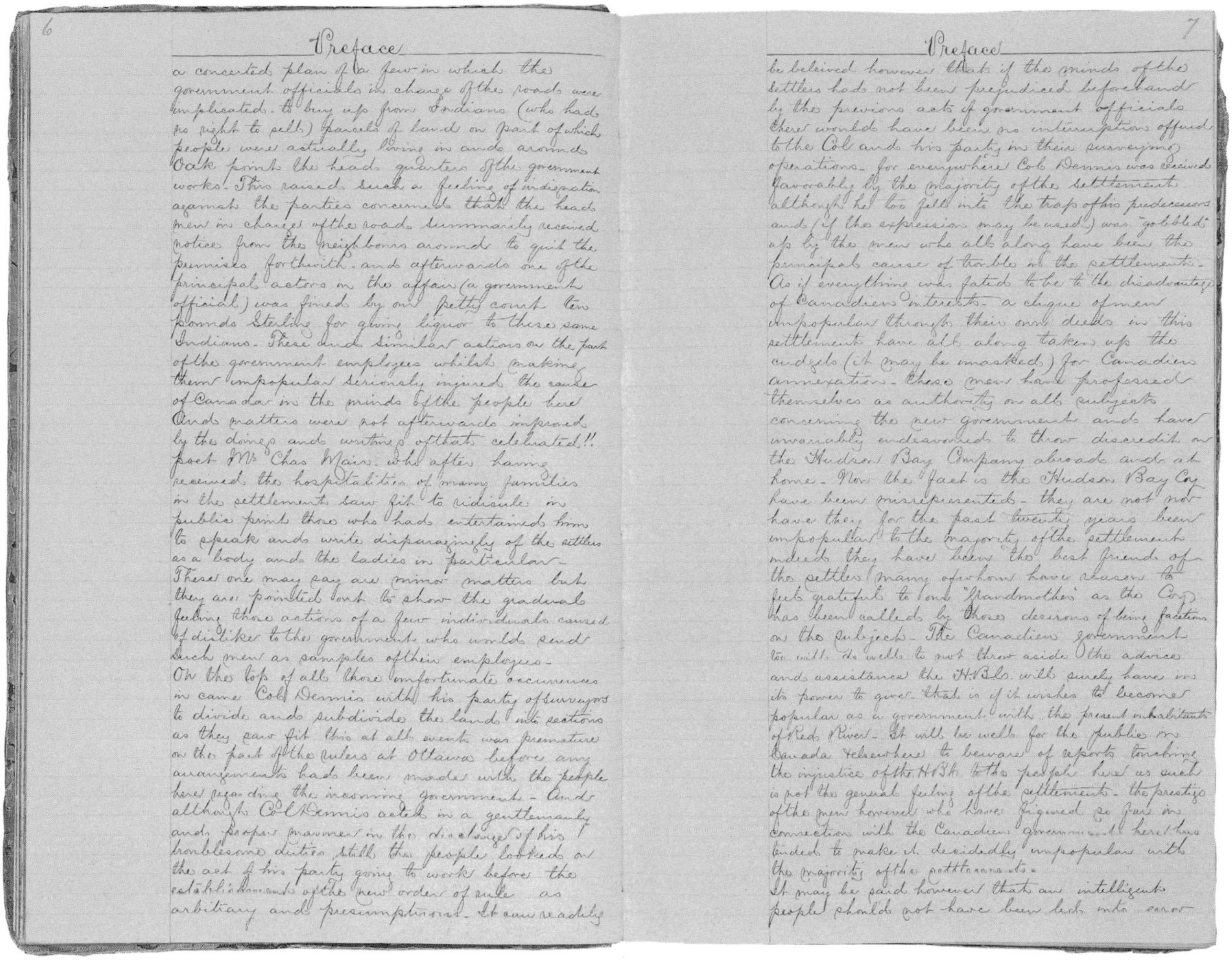

6

Preface

a concerted plan of a few in which the government officials in charge of the roads were implicated. to buy up from Indians (who had no right to sell) parcels of land on part of which people were actually living in and around Oak point the head quarters of the government works. This raised such a feeling of indignation against the parties concerned that the head men in charge of the road summarily received notice from the neighbours around to quit the premises forthwith. and afterwards one of the principal actors in the affair (a government official) was fined by our petty court ten pounds Sterling for giving liquor to these same Indians. These and similar actions on the part of the government employees whilst making them unpopular seriously injured the cause of Canada in the minds of the people here And matters were not afterwards improved by the doings and writings of that celebrated!! poet Mr Chas Mair. who after having received the hospitalities of many families in the settlement saw fit to ridicule in public print those who had entertained him to speak and write disparagingly of the settlers as a body and the ladies in particular.

These one may say are minor matters but they are pointed out to show the gradual feeling these actions of a few individuals caused of dislike to the government who would send such men as samples of their employees.

On the top of all those unfortunate occurrences in came Col Dennis with his party of surveyors to divide and subdivide the lands into sections as they saw fit this at all events was premature on the part of the rulers at Ottawa before any arrangements had been made with the people here regarding the incoming government. And although Col Dennis acted in a gentlemanly and proper manner in the discharge of his troublesome duties still the people looked on the act of his party going to work before the establishment of the new order of rule as arbitrary and presumptuous. It can readily

7

Preface

be believed however that if the minds of the settlers had not been prejudiced beforehand by the previous acts of government officials there would have been no interruption offered to the Col and his party in their surveying operations. for everywhere Col Dennis was received favorably by the majority of the settlement although he too fell into the trap of his predecessors and (if the expression may be used) was "gobbled" up by the men who all along have been the principal cause of trouble in the settlement.

As if everything was fated to be to the disadvantage of Canadian interests. a clique of men unpopular through their own deeds in this settlement have all along taken up the cudgels (it may be masked) for Canadian annexation. these men have professed themselves as authority on all subjects concerning the new government and have invariably endeavoured to throw discredit on the Hudson Bay Company abroad and at home. Now the fact is the Hudson Bay Coy have been misrepresented. they are not nor have they for the past twenty years been unpopular to the majority of the settlement indeed they have been the best friend of the settlers many of whom have reason to feel grateful to our "Grandmother" as the Coy has been called by those desirous of being facetious on the subject. The Canadian government too will do well to not throw aside the advice and assistance the H.B.Co. will surely have in its power to give. that is if it wishes to become popular as a government with the present inhabitants of Red River. It will be well for the public in Canada & elsewhere to beware of reports touching the injustice of the H.B.Co to the people here as such is not the general feeling of the settlement. the prestige of the men however who have figured so far in connection with the Canadian government here has tended to make it decidedly unpopular with the majority of the settlements.

It may be said however that an intelligent people should not have been led into error

37 cm x 24 cm

National Archives of Canada,
Manuscript Division,
MG 29, C 1, pp. 6-7.

"Fort Garry"

In this watercolour, William Armstrong depicts Fort Garry, the focal point of the Red River Rebellion of 1870. Executed in soft browns and greens, the scene is tranquil, belying the gathering tensions which would erupt in late 1869 in armed opposition to the new Dominion of Canada.

In 1822, the Hudson's Bay Company had built Fort Garry, located strategically at the forks of the Red and Assiniboine Rivers, on a site formerly occupied by the North West Company's Fort Gibraltar. The great flood of 1826 had damaged the post so severely that the Hudson's Bay Company had erected a new centre, Lower Fort Garry, some 30 kilometres downstream on the Red River, where the ground was higher. However, the confluence of the Red and Assiniboine was a much more natural location for administrative and trade purposes. Consequently, the Company had returned to that point in 1836, building Upper Fort Garry near the site of the original Fort Garry. It is now within the city limits of Winnipeg.

Out of its headquarters in this post, the Hudson's Bay Company administered its vast reserve, both its chartered Rupert's Land and territories further west and north which it managed by license from the British Crown. As ardent annexationists, such as the "Ontario men" and "Canada Firsters," began to dream of and agitate for union of the British colonies and expansion westward, they attacked the Company. Its rule was harsh, they argued; the Company was despotic, and kept its subjects in a form of economic and political servitude.

A majority of residents of the Red River Settlement, it seems, felt otherwise. They were governed by a Council named by the Company; but the Company took care to canvas popular opinion before nominating councillors to the Council of Assiniboia. In the Company's lands a system of law and jurisprudence responsive to local needs was evolving; in place of lawyers and suits, the residents more often had recourse to arbitration. In times of crisis, like the grasshopper plague of 1867-1868, the Company did all in its power to assist its "subjects" in the Red River colony. In a word, most locals felt themselves free in every respect, and had little quarrel with the "good grandmother" who had wardship over them.

But the "grandmother" wished to be relieved of her wardship of the vast interior lands, and so transferred responsibility to a new guardian, the Dominion of Canada. In the process, everyone — Company, Colonial Office and the Dominion — neglected to ask the inhabitants how they felt about the intended new order.

William Armstrong. 1869.

20.2 cm x 40.6 cm

National Archives of Canada,
Documentary Art and Photography Division,
C-10514.
Gift of Mrs. William McDougall, 1933.

"Protests of the Peoples of the North-West"

The Red River uprising was originally a French Metis affair; few English "half-breeds" joined in. But, as William Begg observed at the time, English half-breeds did not oppose the Metis, refused to rally to the designated Lieutenant-Governor, William McDougall and, in the event that McDougall would have imposed reprehensible measures, were prepared to take up arms and support the Metis.

The Metis, in addition to fearing loss of land, lifestyle and rights, were uneasy about union with Canada because of cultural factors. Roman Catholic and French-speaking, they could expect little sympathy from an English-speaking, Protestant-dominated Ontario, which treated "their" land as its future inheritance. In Louis Riel, the Metis found a leader to express their concerns and lead their movement.

Riel (1844-1885), born in the Red River Settlement, studied in St. Boniface, then at the Sulpician College in Montreal. Not suited for the priesthood, he returned to Rupert's Land. As the Metis' fears rose throughout 1869 with the impending transfer of Rupert's Land to Canada, they resolved to take direct action. In October they halted Colonel Dennis' survey and formed a National Council of the Metis of Red River. In November they occupied Fort Garry. In December they proclaimed a "Provisional Government," headed by Riel. In January of 1870 this Provisional Government and a new "List of Rights" were endorsed by a convention made up of an equal number of representatives from French- and English-speaking inhabitants of the colony.

Neither the Dominion government nor the Provisional Government of the Metis wished open conflict. After establishing contact, the two sides agreed on negotiations, and in March three delegates left Red River bound for Ottawa. Somewhat earlier, on 4 March, Thomas Scott, a Protestant "Ontario man" agitating for union, had been executed by Riel's government for treason. This event had angered Ontario and especially the powerful Orange Order to which Scott had belonged. Ontario's seizure of these delegates in transit to Ottawa elicited from Riel the "Protestations" displayed here.

In this decree, Riel indicts the "trouble-makers" from Ontario for disturbing the Red River, for forcing him to make an example of Scott. The "Ontario men" do not work for the good of the British Crown, nor do they adhere to British principles of justice and parliamentary government. The Red River, Riel affirms, remains loyal to the Crown, and is not yet subject to Canada, with whom it is just discussing union — hence, his protest against this unlawful seizure by Ontario.

The delegates were released and continued to Ottawa. Riel's Provisional Government had earlier decided that only if Rupert's Land entered Confederation with provincial status could local rights be guaranteed, and had empowered its delegates to negotiate provincial status as a requisite for union. The result was the *Manitoba Act*, setting the date of 15 July 1870 for the entry of the Red River colony into Confederation. Only a very small portion of the former Rupert's Land was designated as the province of Manitoba by this *Act*. Nonetheless the Metis entered Confederation with their religious rights assured in schools, their language secured in the provincial legislature, and their right to land ensconced in law.

Louis Riel. 1870.

PROTESTATION

DES PEUPLES DU NORD-OUEST.

Le present etat d'excitation contre nous en certaines parties du Canada nous fournit une belle occasion de montrer la difference de leurs principes et des notres. Est ce que tant de journaux Canadiens et tant de personnes qui les approuvent s'exercent contre nous simplement et sincerement dans l'interet de la Confederation? Est ce dans l'interet de l'Angleterre? S'il en est ainsi, comment se fait-il que Snow, Dennis, McDougall, et tant d'autres objets de sympathie principalement en Haut-Canada aient pris des voies assez detournees, et aient assel cherche à tromper le peuple pour le jeter dans un mecontentement aussi grand que general? Les hommes du Haut-Canada, avec les quels nous avons evite toutes sortes de melee durant les derniers six mois, ont cherche a nous diviser à nous surexciter les uns contre les autres, à nous amener dans l'horrible collision d'une guerre civile! La guerre civile n'a-telle pas ete proclamee au milieu de nous? Et ceux qui l'ont ose, n'auraient-ils pas usurpe d'une maniere infame le nom de sa Majeste? Tant d'etrangers que nous avons ete contraints, à differentes epoques, de faire prisonniers n'ont ils pas ete remis genereusement en liberte? Lorsque nous savions qu'ils se hateraient de faire contre nous le mal qu'ils soulevent aujoud'hui dans le Haut-Canada, en se parjurant. Et parce-que l'un de ceux qui par obstination continuraient à trouble la paix publique qu'eux seuls ont compromise au milieu de nous et que nous faisons tant d'efforts pour maintenir dans le Nord-ouest nous a force à faire de faire de lui un exemple que d'autres pussent apprendre, ils veulent nous de'clarer la guerre; pendant que Sir John A. McDonald, le Premier est oblige de dire en justice que le Canada n'apas de juridiction dans ce pays. Non! Ces gens la n'ont pas travaille et ne travaillent pas dans l'interet de l'Angleterre! Ils ne s'occupent de la Confederation qu'autant qu'ils la croient necessaire a la reussite de leurs plans dont l'objet est trop personnel et trop exclusif pour etre juste! Ces personnes par un grand manque d'honnetete et de loyaute ont ambitionne sur nous une superiorite tout-a-fait condamnable, par ce que pour l'obtenir, ces faux sujets Anglais n'ont voulu et ne veulent respectes les droits de personne dans une colonie Anglaise. Ils se sont flattes du coupable espoir de pouvoir associer leurs projets egoistes avec ceux de la politique Imperiale pour l'Amerique Britannique du Nord. C'est une chose qu'ils ont oubliee: La politique d'un gouvernement ayant à s'occuper des interets generaux de la societe, sans distinction de langage, d'origine, sans distinction de croyance est toujours incompatible avec les vues etroites de l'interest individuel, lorsque celuici, au lieu d'en imposer a l'autre ne lui est pas entierement subordonne. Ils auraient du le savior: le seul moyen d'assurer l'existence et l'extention de la Confederation est de placer sur un pied egal et liberal les Provinces de l'Amerique Britannique du Nord. S'il est vrai que la Compagnie de la Baie d'Hudson a neglige l'avancement politique de ce pays, le peuple, lui, aussitot qu'il l'a pu, a du agir. Il s'est forme un gouvernement, et ce gouvernement qui se dit lui meme provisoire ne veut pas que le Nord-Ouest entre dans la Confederation, avant que dans ce pays aussi toutes les classes des hommes civilises n'aient recu la garantie d'etre sur un meme noble pied degalite.

Dans le mois d'octobre dernier, lorsque les premiers representants du peuple de la Riviere-Rouge se sont d'abord publiquement assembles pour prendre, au nom de leurs constituants, le titre et les fonctions de "Protecteurs des droits des peuple.

Ils declarerent :—

1°. Qu'ils etaient sujets loyaux de sa Majeste la Reine d'Angleterre.

2°. Qu'ils etaient redevables a la Compagnie de la Baie d'Hudson du bien qu'ils pouvaient avoir recu sous son gouvernement quelle que fut la nature de ce gouvernement.

3°. Que la Compagnie de la Baie d'Hudson se retirant du gouvernement de ce pays, ils etaient prets a passer par ce changement la. Mais en meme temps s'etant etablie, ayant vecu sur ces terres qu'il a aide la Compagnie de la Baie d'Hudson a ouvrir, le peuple de la Riviere-Rouge, ayant acquis de cette facon des droits incontestables dans ce pays proclamait hautement ces droits.

4°. Que le peuple de la Riviere-Rouge ayant jusqu'a ce temps maintenu et supporte le gouvernement de la Compagnie de la Baie d'Hudson, sous la couronne d'Angleterre, Snow et Dennis ont meconnu le droit des gens en venant etablir ici des travaux au nous d'une autorite etrangere sans payer le respect du a l'autorite alors existant dans le pays.

5°. La Colonie de la Riviere-Rouge ayant toujours ete soumise a la couronne d'Angleterre, s'etant developpee a part a travers toutes les chances de sa situation, ces representants declarent au nom de leurs constituants, qu'ils feraient tout en leur pouvoir pour faire respecter en leur faveur toutes les prerogatives si liberalement accordees par la couronne d'Angleterre a n'importe quelle colonie Anglaise.

Ces principes ont ete publies en Canada dans le mois de Novembre dernier. Ils sont encore comme ils etaient alors la ligne de conduite du gouvernement Provisoire. Le drapeau Anglais qui flotte sur nos tetes rendra donc aux yeux du monde ce grand temoignage en notre faveur. Pleins de confiance en ces principes qui font notre force, nous ne voulons pas qu'ils soient sujets loyaux de sa Majeste la Reine d'Angleterre ceux qui ont voulu nous faire la guerre jusqu' ici, et qui voudraent encore nous la faire a cause de la conduite que nous avons tenue sur ces resolutions. Pour nous ruiner, et a fin de s'elever sur nos ruines, ils nous ont toujours comptes au rang des barbares. Cependant nos grandes difficultes ne nous ont jamais fait appeler à notre secours le dangereux element des tribus sauvages. Au contraire, tandisque nous n'epargnons rien pour les maintenir dans le calme, eux autres viennent d'envoyer a travers notre pays ou leur gouvernement n'a pas de juridiction, des emissaires dans le but criminel de nous creer des ennemis parmi les Indiens. Mais nous esperons que la Province nous aidera a completer la pacification du Nord-Ouest; nous esperons que l'autorite de la couronne d'Angletere facilitera le denoument des grandes complications qui ont ete causees par une grande imprudence Politique.

Des peuples que le progres et la civilisation remplissent d'ambition d'un cote nous environnent et de l'autre de nombreuses nations sauvages qui vivent dans l'attente et l'apprehension. Le peuple de la Riviere-Rouge a ete forme a meme ces deux grandes divisions pour leur servir d'intermedaire. En effet nous sommes lies avec les deux par le sang et les habitudes. Et celui qui fait monter et descendre les peuples, suivant ce qu'il valent dans la balance de la justice, sait combien nous avons ete outrages.

La Province d'Ontario en arretant nos delegues que le Gouvernement Federal avait invites par trois commissions speciales vient de faire un acte contre lequel nous protestons au nom de tout les peuples du Nord-Ouest. Nous denoncons l'opprobre d'une parielle demarche a tous les peuples civilises nous en appelons au droit des gens que le Haut-Canada a toujours meconnu quand il s'est agi de nous, que le Gouvernement Federal n'a pas lui-meme assez protege mais qu'il est de notre honneur de reclamer devant Dieu et devant les hommes de toutes les manieres qui nous sont et nous seront possibles.

LOUIS RIEL.

45.2 cm x 26.4 cm

National Archives of Canada,
Manuscript Division,
MG 27, I, F 3, Vol. 1.

Letter to George-Étienne Cartier on Metis Needs

Although the *Manitoba Act* responded to most Metis demands and halted disturbances, the Dominion government nonetheless resolved to dispatch a military force to Red River. In April 1870 there was a motion before the United States Congress on annexation of Red River. Fenians were active again. In May they were turned back by Canadian militia at Eccles Hill in Quebec, but were threatening to invade through Red River. In this disturbed situation, Ottawa resolved to show flag and force in both Manitoba and the North-West Territory. Under Sir Garnet Wolseley, 400 British regulars and 800 Canadian militiamen made the arduous trek from Fort William to Red River along the river-portage systems at the head of Lake Superior and the Dawson Road. Riel fled to the United States, returning later in the year to raise a force against a threatened Fenian invasion, and then staying on quietly in his home village of St. Vital.

Almost from the outset, promises made to the Metis were ignored by central authorities. This is evidenced by Joseph Royal's letter to George-Étienne Cartier. Royal was a well-educated spokesman of the Metis, and the founder of the newspaper *Le Métis.* After meeting with Cartier, on his return to Manitoba he wrote the letter displayed here, setting out Metis needs. For governor, Royal wrote, the Metis need a man out of Quebec, who knows the French language. They require judges, several of whom should also be from Quebec. Since the large majority of inhabitants of the North-West Territory are of French and Roman Catholic origin, they should, Royal argues, have representatives on the Governor's Council. The land promised the Metis should be distributed. The public buildings twice promised by Ottawa, such as legislature, justice building, prison and city hall, have not been built. And the promised Winnipeg-St. Boniface bridge over the Red River has not even been started. The Metis of Manitoba pay their taxes, and are in a province which has entered Confederation — yet their benefits from Ottawa are less than what the capital is offering distant British Columbia.

The letter reflects the disregard in which the Metis felt Ottawa held them; it did not rush to secure to them their rights following the *Manitoba Act* of 1870. The lands promised the Metis were lost to new settlers and troops who came in 1870 and later. Beaten and threatened by newcomers, the Metis packed and moved, largely westwards. Those who stayed were, by various stratagems, deprived of their lands. Of the approximately 10,000 Metis in Manitoba in 1870 out of a population of 14,000, perhaps two-thirds left over the space of several years following Manitoba's admission into Confederation. Immediately after the Red River was pacified, the central government, preoccupied with other issues, disregarded its commitment to a people that fell between the cracks. Consequently Royal's requests were already, in their own time, beyond realization.

Joseph Royal. 1872.

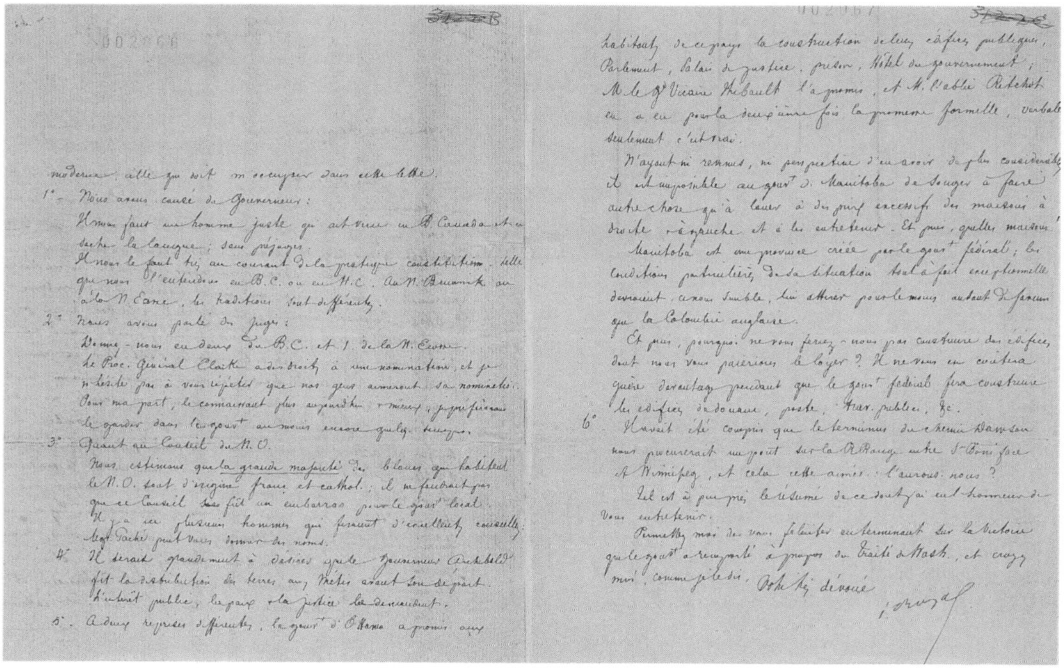

002066

modérée, telle qu'on doit m'occuper dans cette lettre.

1° Nous avons causé du Gouverneur:
Il nous faut un homme juste qui ait vécu en B. Canada et en sache la langue; sans préjugés.
Il nous le faut très au courant de la pratique constitutionnelle telle que nous l'entendons en B.C. ou en H.C. Au N. Brunswick ou à la N. Écosse, les traditions sont différentes.

2° Nous avons parlé des juges:
Donnez-nous en deux du B.C. et 1 de la N. Écosse.
Le Proc. Général Clarke a des droits à une nomination, et je n'hésite pas à vous répéter que nos gens aimeront sa nomination.
Pour ma part, le connaissant plus aujourd'hui et mieux, je préférerais le garder dans le gouvt au moins encore quelq. temps.

3° Quant au Conseil du N.O.
Nous estimons que la grande majorité des blancs qui habitent le N.O. sont d'origine franç. et cathol.; il ne faudrait pas que ce Conseil fût un embarras pour le gouvt local.
Il y a ici plusieurs hommes qui feraient d'excellents conseillers; Mgr Taché peut vous donner des noms.

4° Il serait grandement à désirer que le Gouverneur Archibald fît la distribution des terres aux Métis avant son départ. L'intérêt public, la paix et la justice le demandent.

5° A deux reprises différentes, le gouvt d'Ottawa a promis aux

002067

habitants de ce pays la construction de leurs édifices publiques, Parlement, Palais de justice, prison, Hôtel du gouvernement; M. le Gr Vicaire Thibault l'a promis, et M. l'abbé Ritchot en a eu pour la deuxième fois la promesse formelle, verbale seulement c'est vrai.

N'ayant ni revenus, ni perspective d'en avoir de plus considérables, il est impossible au gouvt de Manitoba de songer à faire autre chose qu'à louer à des prix excessifs des maisons à droite et à gauche et à les entretenir. Et puis, quelles maisons!

Manitoba est une province créée par le gouvt fédéral; les conditions particulières de sa situation tout à fait exceptionnelle devraient, ce nous semble, lui attirer pour le moins autant de faveurs que la Colombie anglaise.

Et puis, pourquoi ne nous ferez-vous pas construire des édifices, dont nous vous paierions le loyer? Il ne vous en coûtera guère davantage pendant que le gouvt fédéral fera construire les édifices de douane, poste, trav. publics, &c.

6° Il avait été compris que le terminus du chemin Dawson nous procurerait un pont sur la R. Rouge entre St Boniface et Winnipeg, et cela cette année: l'aurons-nous?

Tel est à peu près le résumé de ce dont j'ai eu l'honneur de vous entretenir.

Permettez-moi de vous féliciter en terminant sur la victoire que le gouvt a remportée à propos du Traité de Wash., et croyez-moi, comme je le dis, votre tout dévoué

[illegible]

25.3 cm x 20.5 cm

National Archives of Canada,
Manuscript Division,
MG 27, I, D 4, Vol. 5, pp. 2066-2067.

"Men's Lodge Division P. at Elbow of North Saskatchewan Sept. '71"

Charles George Horetzky, born in Scotland in 1838, came to Rupert's Land as an employee of the Hudson's Bay Company. He was at Fort Garry during the Red River Rebellion. An amateur photographer, he was hired in 1871 for the Canadian Pacific Railway survey, which commenced laying out the route to British Columbia in that year. This photograph was taken during that survey.

In this image we see the sweep of the flat prairie, and the majesty of the broad Saskatchewan River in the background. A belt of shrubbery and trees lies between the river and the camp in the foreground. To the left stands a teepee, an indication that the surveying party, consisting largely of European Canadians, has turned to the ways of the prairie. Six people relax at the campsite, one of them sitting on the shaft of a Red River cart.

The carts were used by all travellers through the prairies — by Metis, by Indians, and by people of European ancestry. They were the product of local adaptation to particular conditions. The carts were of all-wood construction; no metal was used in their manufacture. The wheels were concave towards the cart, and almost the height of a human being; thus, because they splayed outwards from the hub, they did not sink as deeply into prairie mud, and there was enough wheel to ride through the spring and fall mud flats that passed for roads. There was no lubrication at hub and axle; constant dust and dirt blown by wind would have rapidly mixed with grease and destroyed hub and axle. Consequently, a cart train was audible for miles around as wood wore on wood, squealing and groaning under heavy loads drawn over primitive roads. All travellers throughout the plains who left written records recalled the unending, and to them torturous, shrieking and groaning of the Red River cart.

In its time and place, the cart was an effective vehicle. The young Dominion, eager to lay down a rapid and effective link from sea to sea to bind its provinces and territories, devoted all its energies to a transcontinental railway — and the reliable Red River cart served surveyors well on the western plains as they laid out the route of this undertaking.

Charles George Horetzky. 1871.

15.1 cm x 19.9 cm

National Archives of Canada,
Documentary Art and Photography Division,
PA-9170.

"Plan of the Province of Manitoba on Mercator's Projection"

This map was prepared by Colonel John Stoughton Dennis (1820-1885), soldier and surveyor. He began his surveying career in 1843, when he was commissioned a surveyor in the Department of Crown Lands of the Province of Canada. Placed in charge of surveying Rupert's Land in 1869, his activity spurred on the Red River Rebellion. In 1871 he was named Dominion Surveyor-General, and was largely responsible for mapping the prairies and determining the form of the western township.

This manuscript map indicates just how small Manitoba originally was at the time of its entry into Confederation. But it also provides a wealth of other information about the region and its inhabitants. There is a population census of the settled points of Manitoba. The four electoral divisions are indicated, with the breakdown of population by origin. Colour coding indicates what townships were intended for French Metis and for English "half-breed" land grants.

The map also defines the form of the township which became the standard unit throughout the whole western prairie under the Dominion Lands Survey system. Modified from American practice, the township was fixed at six miles square, and subdivided into 36 sections of 640 acres each; each section was then further subdivided into quarter sections of 160 acres each, which were the basic granting unit. There was a road allowance around every section. The river banks along which the Metis had traditionally fronted their holdings were exempted from this survey grid. Townships were numbered northwards from a base line along the 49th parallel; ranges of townships were numbered east and west from the original Fort Garry meridian. Five other meridians were established as the survey moved westward.

The commencement of the survey, and the survey system adopted, were signal events. Only after the land had been measured out could settlement of the prairies begin; and only settlement could justify and economically sustain a railway. Only then would the North-West Territories be secured against outside threat and the Dominion reach from sea to sea.

Colonel John Stoughton Dennis. 1871.

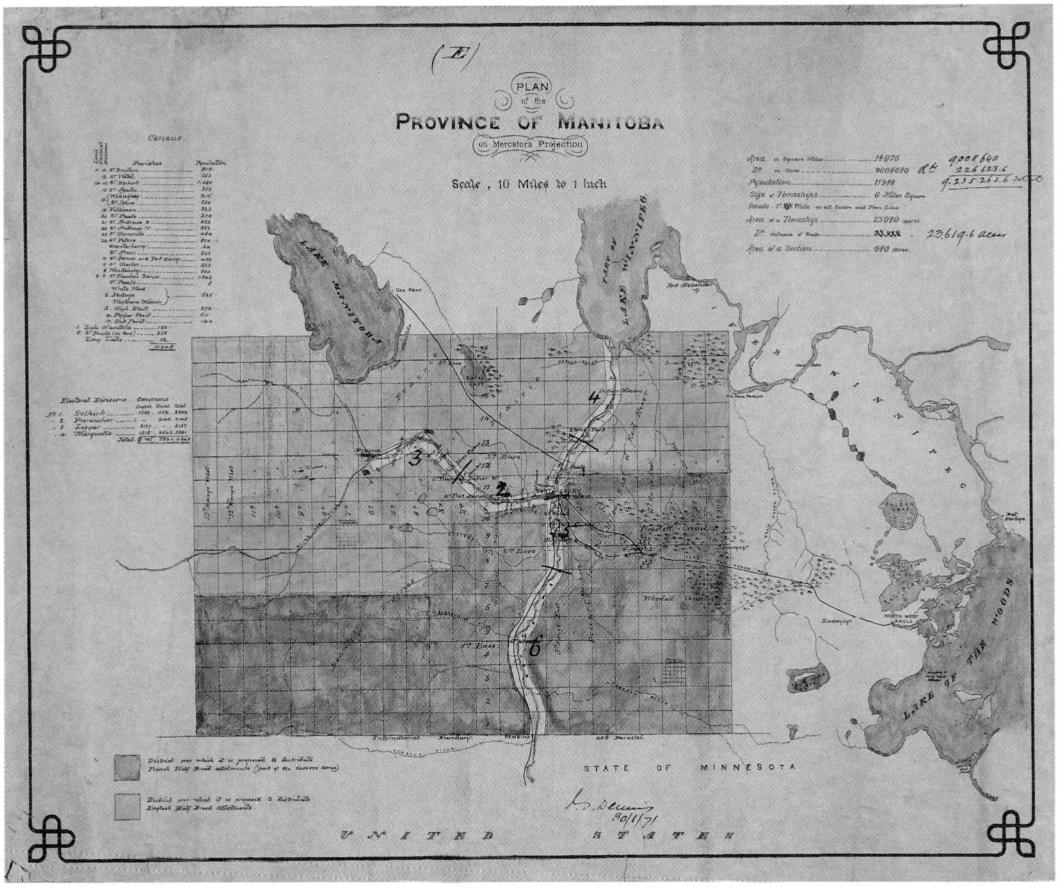

55 cm x 66.3 cm

National Archives of Canada,
Cartographic and Audio-Visual Archives Division,
NMC-105735.

Indian Treaty No. 255 — Western Treaty No. 1

With the Red River Settlement pacified, the North-West Territories transferred to the Dominion government and the mechanics of the Dominion Survey in place, there remained the matter of aboriginal right in land. The British Crown, on transferring Rupert's Land and the North-West Territory to the Dominion government, required Ottawa to assume wardship over the native people, to commit itself to their "protection" and "well-being." This included compensation for cession of their rights in land.

The Canadian government turned to the system of treaty negotiation developed in Upper Canada, best represented in the Robinson-Huron and Robinson-Superior Treaties of 1850. Western Treaty No. 1, shown here, is the first Indian treaty negotiated by the Dominion government, and the first of eleven "numbered" treaties which would extinguish Indian right in land over most of the North-West Territories by 1923. By the terms of this Treaty, the Chippewa and Swampy Cree surrendered over 40,000 square kilometres in the area from the international border near Lake-of-the-Woods, north through the southern portion of Lake Winnipeg and then southwesterly to the 49th parallel.

In return the Chippewa and Cree received reserves on the basis of 160 acres per family of five, an annuity of $3.00 per person and rights to fish and hunt in ceded land as long as it remained unoccupied. The Indians, however, sought more security for the future than had been the case in the Robinson Treaties. They won a promise from the Dominion government to build and maintain schools on reserves wishing to have them. The government also agreed to provide the Indians with farm implements, seed grains, farm animals and instruction in farming, and to prohibit the sale of liquor on Indian lands. The native people sensed that the day of the hunt was done, and strove to secure their survival by adaptation to new conditions and a new livelihood, farming.

In negotiating Treaty No. 1, and the subsequent western treaties, 35,000 Indians of the plains realized that their choices were limited. They had to make the best of their situation. Settlers were sure to come; rather than lose everything in future, it was better to sign and secure at least some land for themselves in law. This Treaty thus has legal value; it has historical-informational value; and, as the first of an important treaty series, it also has significant artifactual value.

Canada: Superintendent of Indian Affairs. 1871.

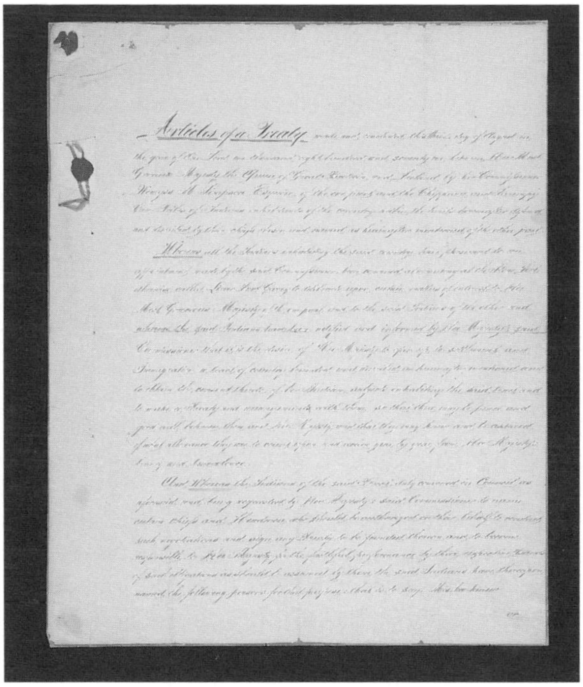

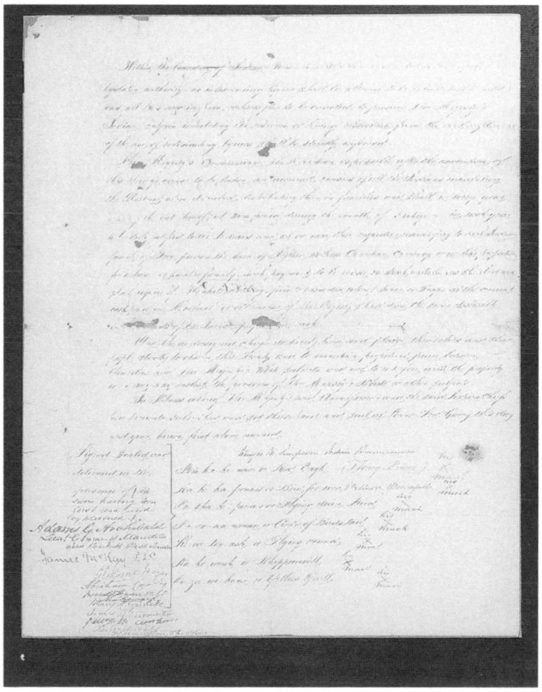

62.2 cm x 49.5 cm

National Archives of Canada,
Government Archives Division,
RG 10, Vol. 1846.

Emigration Posters

The posters displayed here informed travellers and emigrants intending to settle in the Northwest of the communications route being opened to them. They provide information on costs of the trip and on amount of luggage allowed. Much more interesting, however, is the information the posters offer on the mode of transportation and the route, the former North West Company's route into the interior.

Out of Sarnia or Collingwood, reached by rail from Toronto, steamers transported passengers to Fort William. From Fort William passengers took wagons a distance of 45 miles to Lake Shebandowan. From that point, they commenced "broken navigation in open boats" over a distance of 310 miles, a harrowing and wearisome trip over rough water and steep portages. "For convenience of transport on the portages," the poster reads, packages are to weigh no more than 150 pounds. Some convenience for the voyageurs who bore them over the portages! In a young country, brute strength was a premium.

In the final leg of the journey, passengers travelled by cart the 95 miles from the northwest angle of Lake-of-the-Woods to Fort Garry. This last stretch was the Dawson Road. Partisans of expansion into the interior had advocated such a road from the 1850s; it was finally developed following Confederation for strategic, as well as transportation, purposes. Colonel Wolseley's force, on its 1870 trek to the Red River, in fact completed the remaining work on the road.

This communications route wholly through Canadian territory was to facilitate settlement under the *Dominion Lands Act* of 1872. Modelled on American legislation, the *Act* authorized grants of quarter sections to settlers for a nominal $10.00 payment; settlers were required to meet minimal improvement norms over a period of time, such as building a house and bringing a certain acreage under the plow.

The *Dominion Lands Act* was another significant component of the Dominion government's overall policy toward the Northwest — pacification and a military presence, first in Wolseley's force and then, in 1873-1874, by the North-West Mounted Police; survey of the Dominion lands; purchase of title to land from aboriginal peoples; and then settlement through the homestead law. Only settlement of the newly-acquired Northwest could truly make Confederation from sea to sea secure. And however much government posters, such as the ones shown here, promoted the mixed wagon-and-water route, only a transcontinental railway would effectively open the Northwest to settlement and development.

Canada: Department of Public Works. 1872.

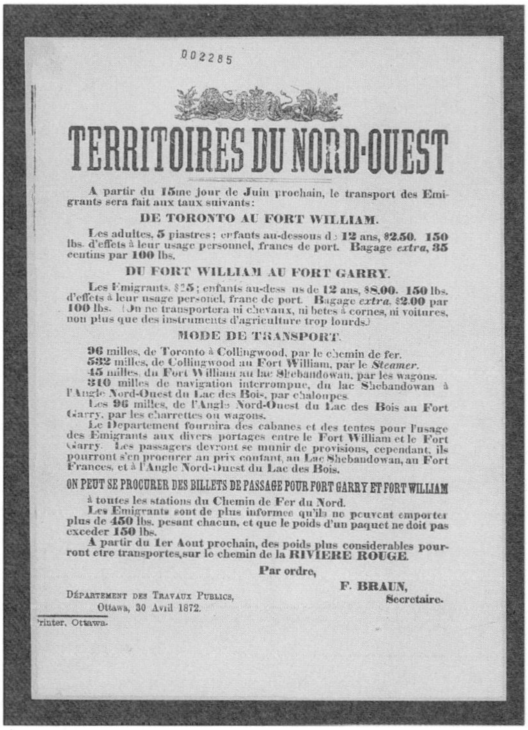

002285

TERRITOIRES DU NORD-OUEST

A partir du 15me jour de Juin prochain, le transport des Emigrants sera fait aux taux suivants:

DE TORONTO AU FORT WILLIAM.

Les adultes, 5 piastres; enfants au-dessous de 12 ans, $2.50. 150 lbs. d'effets à leur usage personnel, francs de port. Bagage *extra*, 35 centins par 100 lbs.

DU FORT WILLIAM AU FORT GARRY.

Les Emigrants, $25; enfants au-dessous de 12 ans, $8.00. 150 lbs. d'effets à leur usage personel, franc de port. Bagage *extra*, $2.00 par 100 lbs. (On ne transportera ni chevaux, ni betes à cornes, ni voitures, non plus que des instruments d'agriculture trop lourds.)

MODE DE TRANSPORT.

96 milles, de Toronto à Collingwood, par le chemin de fer.
532 milles, de Collingwood au Fort William, par le *Steamer*.
45 milles, du Fort William au lac Shebandowan, par les wagons.
310 milles de navigation interrompue, du lac Shebandowan à l'Angle Nord-Ouest du Lac des Bois, par chaloupes.
Les 96 milles, de l'Angle Nord-Ouest du Lac des Bois au Fort Garry, par les charrettes ou wagons.

Le Departement fournira des cabanes et des tentes pour l'usage des Emigrants aux divers portages entre le Fort William et le Fort Garry. Les passagers devront se munir de provisions, cependant, ils pourront s'en procurer au prix coutant, au Lac Shebandowan, au Fort Frances, et à l'Angle Nord-Ouest du Lac des Bois.

ON PEUT SE PROCURER DES BILLETS DE PASSAGE POUR FORT GARRY ET FORT WILLIAM

à toutes les stations du Chemin de Fer du Nord.

Les Emigrants sont de plus informes qu'ils ne peuvent emporter plus de 450 lbs. pesant chacun, et que le poids d'un paquet ne doit pas exceder 150 lbs.

A partir du 1er Aout prochain, des poids plus considerables pourront etre transportes sur le chemin de la RIVIERE ROUGE.

Par ordre,

F. BRAUN,
Secretaire.

DÉPARTEMENT DES TRAVAUX PUBLICS,
Ottawa, 30 Avril 1872.

Printer, Ottawa.

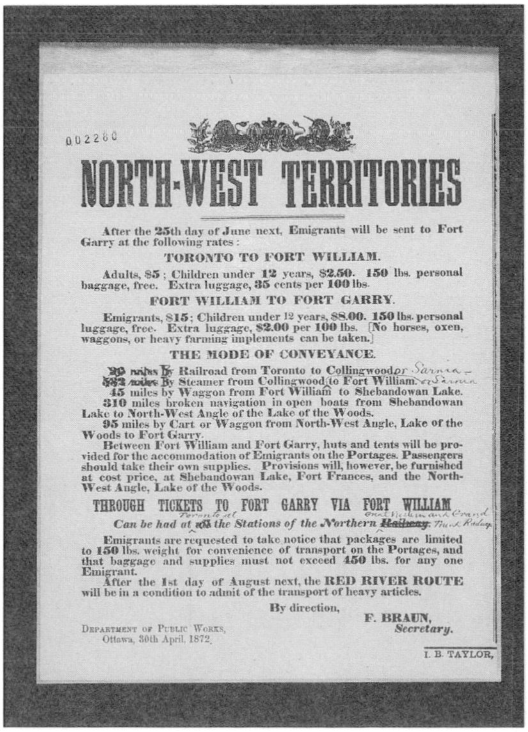

002280

NORTH-WEST TERRITORIES

After the 25th day of June next, Emigrants will be sent to Fort Garry at the following rates:

TORONTO TO FORT WILLIAM.

Adults, $5; Children under 12 years, $2.50. 150 lbs. personal baggage, free. Extra luggage, 35 cents per 100 lbs.

FORT WILLIAM TO FORT GARRY.

Emigrants, $15; Children under 12 years, $8.00. 150 lbs. personal luggage, free. Extra luggage, $2.00 per 100 lbs. [No horses, oxen, waggons, or heavy farming implements can be taken.]

THE MODE OF CONVEYANCE.

~~[illegible] miles~~ By Railroad from Toronto to Collingwood [or Sarnia] —
~~[illegible] miles~~ By Steamer from Collingwood [or Sarnia] to Fort William.
45 miles by Waggon from Fort William to Shebandowan Lake.
310 miles broken navigation in open boats from Shebandowan Lake to North-West Angle of the Lake of the Woods.
95 miles by Cart or Waggon from North-West Angle, Lake of the Woods to Fort Garry.

Between Fort William and Fort Garry, huts and tents will be provided for the accommodation of Emigrants on the Portages. Passengers should take their own supplies. Provisions will, however, be furnished at cost price, at Shebandowan Lake, Fort Frances, and the North-West Angle, Lake of the Woods.

THROUGH TICKETS TO FORT GARRY VIA FORT WILLIAM

Can be had at [Toronto at] ~~all~~ the Stations of the Northern [Great Western and Grand Trunk] ~~Railway~~ [Railway].

Emigrants are requested to take notice that packages are limited to 150 lbs. weight for convenience of transport on the Portages, and that baggage and supplies must not exceed 450 lbs. for any one Emigrant.

After the 1st day of August next, the RED RIVER ROUTE will be in a condition to admit of the transport of heavy articles.

By direction,

F. BRAUN,
Secretary.

DEPARTMENT OF PUBLIC WORKS,
Ottawa, 30th April, 1872.

I. B. TAYLOR,

36.8 cm x 26.7 cm
34.3 cm x 26 cm

National Archives of Canada,
Government Archives Division,
[French language] RG 76, p. 2285,
[English language] RG 76, p. 2280.

V

Completion of Confederation

British Columbia, Prince Edward Island and Newfoundland still remained outside Confederation following the admission of Manitoba in 1870. While the Dominion government continued to woo these colonies, the Colonial Office in Britain exercised unceasing, and not always delicate, pressure upon them to enter into the Canadian Confederation.

In 1871 British Columbia, and in 1873 Prince Edward Island, agreed to terms of entry, and became members of Confederation. In 1880 Britain formally transferred sovereignty over the Arctic Islands, over which the Hudson's Bay Company had never had any authority, to the Dominion of Canada.

The provinces of Ontario, Quebec and Manitoba continued to expand into what had been Rupert's Land. Their boundaries, as they stand today, were finally fixed in 1912. Alberta and Saskatchewan were carved out of Dominion Crown lands in 1905, and given provincial status by the federal authority. The entry of Newfoundland in 1949 completed the territorial gathering of former British colonies and territories in North America into the Dominion of Canada.

Discourse on Common Rights

In this discourse, probably read as a lecture at one of the Institut canadien's meeting halls, Alphonse Lusignan presented an interesting assessment of Canada's political and cultural climate.

It was fully in keeping with the universalist legacy of the French Enlightenment and the Positivist philosophy then reigning in Europe. His views differed from the closed "small homeland" approach of the Quebec clergy-Bleu alliance, from the too-British vision of both Maritimers and Upper Canadians. The future of Canada lay in the development and application of civil rights granted equally to all, without regard to race.

On the pages displayed, for example, Lusignan argues that expanded liberty should be the true objective of everyone in society, and that youth of all varied nationalities should strive to acquire knowledge outside national parameters. The English-French cultural dichotomy is not desirable. Like friends and equals, the youth of both English and French extraction should take what is good from both Shakespeare and Corneille, Newton and Buffon and so on, from the great men whom both England and France had produced in such abundance. Given the unparalleled opportunity which Canada's youth had to learn both languages, the future would condemn those who refused to do so, because they would deny themselves access to an instructive heritage.

In another portion of this discourse, Lusignan argues that a new nationality is in the process of evolution on the north shore of the St. Lawrence and in the Great Lakes region. Unlike the "Canada Firsters," who saw a new nationality built exclusively on the English yeoman transported to the New World, Lusignan had a more cosmopolitan vision. The new nationality would consist of immigrants to the New World from all countries of the globe, of all races, "with all their thousands of beliefs, a great pell-mell of error and truth...all pushed by Providence to this common meeting-ground to bind in unity and brotherhood the whole human family."

Arguing from American developments, Lusignan pointed out that this was inevitable, and already occurring, as evidenced by the 8,000 Chinese labouring on the great railway which would link the two oceans and make America the commercial centre of the world. (Lusignan was probably referring to the Chinese labourers completing work on the Union Pacific Railroad, the first American transcontinental railway, which would be completed in 1869.)

In this intriguing manuscript, Lusignan expresses the Enlightenment's faith in the perfectibility of society and in the equality of man, as well as unbounded optimism for the future of North American society, which will be something new, fashioned of people from all corners of the globe. Its credo will be liberty, equality and freedom.

Alphonse Lusignan. ante 1867.

A page 77-1

que j'en appelle aujourd'hui comme je l'ai toujours fait: je dis que nous devons
être soucieux, non seulement de conserver les droits qui sont acquis, mais que par
la libre discussion nous devons nous efforcer sans cesse d'en acquérir de nouveaux.
Le meilleur moyen d'obtenir cet heureux résultat, est d'appeler les jeunes & vigoureux
esprits d'élite, de toutes les diverses nationalités, à se voir, à se réunir fréquemment dans
cette enceinte, dans cette bibliothèque; dans les autres enceintes, dans les autres biblio-
-thèques de même nature. Ils s'y verront comme amis, comme égaux, comme confra-
-ternels. Ils partageront une admiration commune pour Shakespeare & Corneille, pour
Newton & Buffon, pour Coke & Domat, pour Fox & Lamartine — pour la légion des hommes
éminemment grands, serviables à l'humanité entière, que les deux nationalités anglaise & française ont produit en si grand nombre. Dans l'état de notre société, avec
la facilité d'apprendre dès l'enfance les deux langues, ce sera à l'avenir se condamner à
une infériorité marquée que de négliger de les bien apprendre également toutes deux; que
de n'être pas apte à goûter avec avidité les fruits exquis que leurs littératures ont
produit, plus abondants, & plus savoureux que ceux des autres peuples.

Non il n'est pas vrai que les dissentions politiques qui ont
été si acharnées dans les deux Canadas, fussent une lutte de races. Elles étaient
aussi âpres dans le Haut Canada, où il n'y avait qu'une nationalité, qu'ici
où il y en avait deux. Les majorités de toutes deux étaient les amis désintéressés
des droits

78

Bien aveugles sont ceux qui parlent de la création d'une nationalité nou-
-velle, forte & harmonieuse, sur la rive nord du St Laurent & des grands lacs, & qui à
tout propos ignorent & dénoncent le fait majeur & providentiel que cette nationalité
est déjà toute formée, grande, & grandissant sans cesse: qu'elle ne peut être confi-
-née dans ses limites actuelles: qu'elle a une force d'expansion irrésistible: qu'elle sera de
plus en plus dans l'avenir, composée d'immigrants venant de tous les pays du monde;
non plus seulement de l'Europe, mais bientôt de l'Asie, dont le trop plein cinq fois
plus nombreux n'a plus d'autre déversoir que l'Amérique*; composée dès lors de toutes les
races d'hommes, qui avec leurs mille croyances religieuses, grand pêle-mêle d'erreurs
& de vérités, sont toutes poussées par la Providence à ce commun rendez-vous
pour fondre en unité & fraternité toute la famille humaine.
Le grand fait est trop évident sur toute l'étendue de l'Amérique et dans toute son
histoire depuis sa découverte par Colomb; trop inévitable, pour qu'on n'y reconnaisse
point l'une de ces grandes indications providentielles, que l'homme ne peut se
cacher & sur lesquelles néanmoins il n'a pas plus de contrôle que sur les
lois immuables qui gouvernent l'univers physique.

physique

* (en note, au bas de colonne & page) Dix mille Chinois sont en ce moment sur le sommet des Mon-
-tagnes de Neige, à 8000 pieds d'élévation construisant le grand chemin qui va relier les deux
Océans & faire de notre Amérique le centre commercial du monde entier.

16.9 cm x 20.7 cm

National Archives of Canada,
Manuscript Division,
MG 29, D 27, Vol. 3, pp. 77-1, 78

V

Our New Nationality. An Address. Canada First (No. 1)

Confederation had brought a legal and constitutional unity to the British North American colonies. But it was an uncertain unity. The provinces of the new Dominion, with their own particular pasts and concerns, were more crisply defined than the centre. The outward form of Confederation required an inner substance, an intellectual, emotional and even spiritual broth that would fill all the crannies of the new vessel, and give it a philosophical cohesion and national unity. At least, so thought the Canada First movement.

This movement was founded in 1868 by a number of people like William A. Foster. They felt that Confederation was a political achievement engineered by interested elites, but not a national expression of the people. They drew their inspiration from D'Arcy McGee, from his assassination and his poetry of a new nation born. Mostly Ontarians, and representing the interests of central Canada, they set out actively to campaign and promote a "Canadian" nationalism. Because of the Red River Rebellion, and the execution of Thomas Scott, the movement gave vent to very forcible anti-Catholic and anti-French positions.

In broad outline, the "Canada Firsters" understood Canadian nationality as a British nationality; they argued for exclusively British and Protestant immigration. This immigration would people a demanding, though generous, land. In the bracing climate of boreal forest and northern plain would arise a re-invigorated Anglo-Saxon variant, better than the old. Racial Darwinism, Imperialism and a mania for geography (and geographic influences upon human development) characterized European thought in this era of empire and "the white man's burden." These characteristics manifested themselves in the thought of the "Canada Firsters," as is evident from Foster's *Our New Nationality*, the first pamphlet of a whole series of publications intended to define and inspire Canadian nationality.

The pamphlet is a paean to achievement in the past, an appeal to pride and an affirmation that, with faith and commitment, a future greatness will be secured for the "Canadian" nation. To avoid American ways, to remain loyal to Britain, and to put Canadian autonomy and interests first — these were the objectives of their program. The program's narrowly British orientation, advocated largely by Ontario interests, did not win adherents in all parts of the Dominion.

William A. Foster. 1871.

NATIONAL PAPERS. NO. 1.

There is an intellectual vivification, at last, in Canada, and there are indications that the native mind is at present awakening from the lethargy which has hitherto shrouded and dwarfed it. This is expressed in many ways, and is most observable in the large reading constituency that exists in the country, in the influence which has given the impulse to the publishing and importing of the Book Trade, and in the recognized necessity for a Canadian magazine—a vehicle of native thought and culture.

The present lecture, it is felt, will stimulate this to a further degree, and incite, it is hoped, a more hearty interest in Canadian affairs by the people of the country.

The Publishers trust to be able to issue, periodically, in the series they now initiate, a succession of papers on subjects that will prove of national importance, and their object will be gained if it aid, even in a small degree, to promote a more ambitious and healthy native literature.

THE PUBLISHERS.

TORONTO, AUGUST, 1871.

CANADA FIRST;

OR,

OUR NEW NATIONALITY;

AN ADDRESS,

BY

W. A. FOSTER, ESQ.,

BARRISTER-AT-LAW.

TORONTO:
ADAM, STEVENSON & CO.
1871.

18 cm x 11.6 cm

National Archives of Canada,
Manuscript Division,
MG 24, E 17, Vol. 3, Item 257.

Telegraphic Dispatch on Britain's Pleasure that the British Columbia Legislative Council Has Approved Union with Canada *and also* "The First Canadian Pacific Railroad and Geological Survey Parties for British Columbia, July 22, 1871"

British Columbia (the mainland colony and Vancouver Island were united in 1866) did not participate in the political process leading to Confederation. But its European population and politicians were neither ignorant of, nor immune to, the attractions of joining a North American union of British colonies. For example, in March 1867 Amor De Cosmos, editor of the *British Colonist* and member of the Legislative Council, successfully introduced a motion into the Council for future union of British Columbia with the Dominion of Canada.

De Cosmos, a talented eccentric, had a significant part in bringing British Columbia into Confederation. Born William Alexander Smith in Nova Scotia in 1825, he made his way to California in 1851. There he worked as an amateur photographer (and changed his name to Amor De Cosmos, "Lover of the Universe"). In 1858 the Fraser River gold rush drew him north. He reached Victoria, settled there and founded the *British Colonist.* In the Legislative Assembly of Vancouver Island, and later in the Legislative Council of British Columbia, he championed the cause of responsible government. He was one of the prominent members of the "Confederationist" movement.

British Columbia was a debt-ridden colony. With the gold fields in decline, and no other developed industry to replace it, the colony was losing both people and revenues — its economy was perceptibly slowing down. Confederation would, it was hoped, open markets for British Columbian lumber, fish and minerals. The inhabitants of the colony had reason to fear American expansion (although, at the same time, they valued their trade links with the United States). British governors, first Frederick Seymour and then Anthony Musgrave, adhering to stated British policy, massaged British Columbia's politicians towards Confederation.

These various pressures disposed the Legislative Council to debate union with Canada in March 1870 and to set conditions of entry into Confederation. In July 1870 Ottawa accepted British Columbia's conditions. The Dominion government agreed to assume the colony's debt and, for purposes of federal grants, to consider British Columbia to have a population of 120,000, twice the actual number. The Dominion government also agreed to a transportation link, promising a railway — British Columbia had been prepared to accept a carriage road — within ten years of union. British Columbia would be admitted with full provincial status, and with her right to responsible government guaranteed.

These terms were debated by British Columbia's newly-elected Legislative Council in January 1871, and unanimously accepted. The telegraphic despatch displayed here expresses the British government's pleasure at this outcome.

The other document shown here, Baltzly's photograph, shows the joint Canadian Pacific Railway (CPR) and Geological Survey of Canada (GSC) surveying party which went west to survey a route for a transcontinental railway through British Columbia, and to study the geology of the province. Within several days of British Columbia's entry into Confederation in 1871, Sir Sandford Fleming, appointed Chief Engineer of the CPR, dispatched ten surveying parties to lay out the transcontinental route. Baltzly was chosen to accompany the Alfred Selwyn group to British Columbia. Thus he came to photograph the B.C. survey group; seated centrally, in light suit and dark hat, is Alfred Selwyn, who succeeded Sir William Logan in 1869 as director of the GSC.

With British Columbia's admission into Confederation in 1871 the Dominion, while not yet encompassing all former British colonies in North America, did truly stretch "from sea to sea."

United Kingdom: Colonial Secretary. 1871.

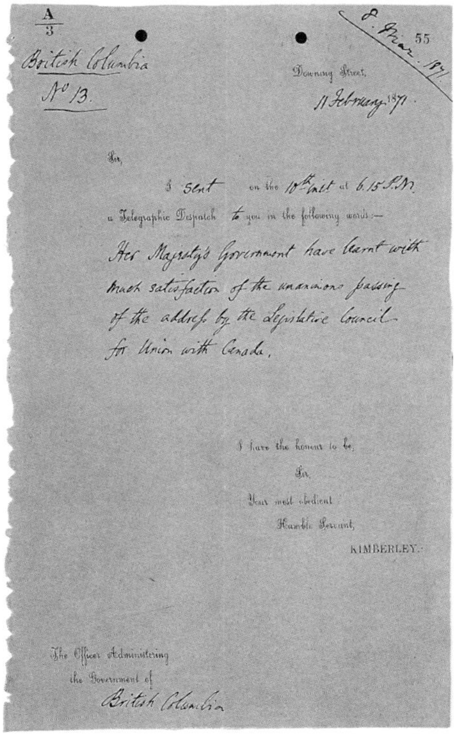

A
3

8 Mar. 1871

55

British Columbia

No 13.

Downing Street,

11 February 1871.

Sir,

I sent on the 10th inst at 6.15 P.M. a Telegraphic Despatch to you in the following words:—

Her Majesty's Government have learnt with much satisfaction of the unanimous passing of the address by the Legislative Council for Union with Canada.

I have the honour to be,

Sir,

Your most obedient

Humble Servant,

KIMBERLEY.

The Officer Administering
the Government of
British Columbia

31.5 cm x 19.6 cm

National Archives of Canada,
Manuscript Division,
RG 7, G 8, C, Vol. 18, p. 55.

17.6 cm x 23.7 cm

National Archives of Canada,
Documentary Art and Photography Division,
PA-22611.

V

Proclamation on the Admission of the Province of Prince Edward Island into Confederation

The question of British North American union manifested itself every now and then in Prince Edward Island. In 1859, for example, union with the Province of Canada was raised in the Throne Speech. But the Assembly was too concerned with other island issues — such as the schools question and the leasehold land system — to pay much attention to the matter. As the Confederation conferences were taking place Prince Edward Islanders listened; but their response to union was lukewarm. They valued their autonomy far too much to consider a union which, in their opinion, threatened them with higher taxation, decreased political power and loss of foreign trade overseas. Despite pressure from the Colonial Office, in the words of Premier James Colledge Pope in 1866, "99 out of every 100 of the people are against Confederation."

Of far greater importance than Confederation were unique domestic concerns of the Islanders, land being the most significant. The Island had been granted to a number of absentee proprietors, most of them resident in Britain. The settlers on the land were leaseholders, paying rent to the proprietors. Like the seigneurial system of Lower Canada, the land tenure system in Prince Edward Island was a relic of times past, and offended the Islanders. Successive tenant movements were organized to resist the system and demand change. A Tenants League of 1864 succeeded in withholding land rents due to the landlords; and tension rose so high that a force of British regulars was ordered to the Island in 1865 to prevent a possible uprising.

Confident in its own ability to defend itself, Prince Edward Island also ventured into independent foreign relations. In 1869 it discussed with the eager Americans a possible trade treaty, giving Americans access to its fisheries in return for free entry of Island products into the American market. The Colonial Office stiffly advised both Americans and Islanders that Prince Edward Island's foreign policy was made in London.

Proudly independent, the Islanders came to Confederation only when crushed by the financial burden of railway building. Prince Edward Island plunged into the construction of its trans-insular railway in 1871, hoping to fire up its economy. However, the burden of financing the venture became unbearable, threatening the Island with bankruptcy — and the Island petitioned in 1873 for admission into Confederation. The Dominion government promised the Island "continuous steam communication" with the mainland, made provision for buying out the remaining absentee proprietors, offered a special operating grant for the Island's legislature, gave special compensation to the Island for its lack of Crown lands and assumed the costs of the Island's railway.

The proclamation displayed here announces the admission of Prince Edward Island into Confederation, consonant with the provision in the *British North America Act* (section 146) for future admissions into Confederation. Once the negotiations with Canada were completed, a joint address from the Dominion Parliament and the Island's legislature received royal assent. On 1 July 1873 Prince Edward Island entered Confederation. The Proclamation bears the Great Seal of Canada. It is signed by Lord Dufferin, Governor-General of the Dominion, and counter-signed by Sir John A. Macdonald, in his capacity as Attorney-General of Canada.

With Prince Edward Island admitted in 1873, the gathering of the colonies into one Dominion was completed, but for Newfoundland.

Canada: Privy Council. 1873.

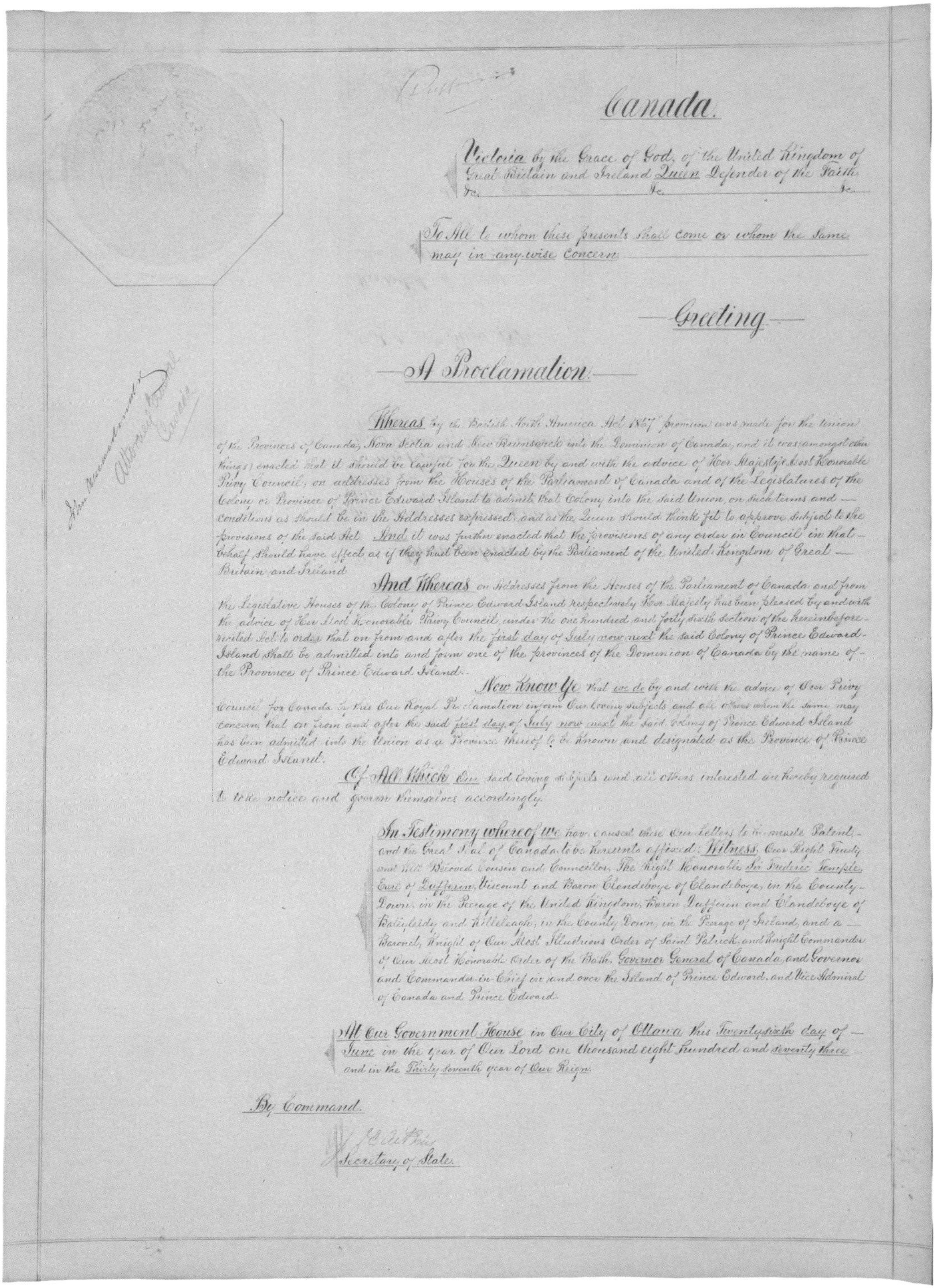

Canada.

Victoria by the Grace of God, of the United Kingdom of Great Britain and Ireland Queen Defender of the Faith &c. &c. &c.

To All to whom these presents shall come or whom the same may in anywise Concern.

Greeting

A Proclamation.

Whereas by the British North America Act 1867 provision was made for the union of the Provinces of Canada, Nova Scotia and New Brunswick into the Dominion of Canada, and it was (amongst other things) enacted that it should be lawful for the Queen by and with the advice of Her Majesty's Most Honorable Privy Council, on addresses from the Houses of the Parliament of Canada and of the Legislatures of the Colony or Province of Prince Edward Island to admit that Colony into the said Union, on such terms and conditions as should be in the Addresses expressed, and as the Queen should think fit to approve subject to the provisions of the said Act. And it was further enacted that the provisions of any order in Council in that behalf should have effect as if they had been enacted by the Parliament of the United Kingdom of Great Britain and Ireland

And Whereas on Addresses from the Houses of the Parliament of Canada and from the Legislative Houses of the Colony of Prince Edward Island respectively Her Majesty has been pleased by and with the advice of Her Most Honorable Privy Council, under the one hundred and forty sixth section of the hereinbefore recited Act to order that on from and after the first day of July now next the said Colony of Prince Edward Island shall be admitted into and form one of the provinces of the Dominion of Canada by the name of the Province of Prince Edward Island.

Now Know Ye that we do by and with the advice of Our Privy Council for Canada by this Our Royal Proclamation inform Our loving subjects and all others whom the same may concern, that on from and after the said first day of July now next the said Colony of Prince Edward Island has been admitted into the Union as a Province thereof to be known and designated as the Province of Prince Edward Island.

Of All Which Our said loving subjects and all others interested are hereby required to take notice and govern themselves accordingly.

In Testimony whereof We have caused these Our Letters to be made Patent and the Great Seal of Canada to be hereunto affixed: Witness, Our Right Trusty and Well Beloved Cousin and Councillor, The Right Honorable Sir Frederic Temple, Earl of Dufferin, Viscount and Baron Clandeboye of Clandeboye, in the County Down, in the Peerage of the United Kingdom, Baron Dufferin and Clandeboye of Ballyleidy and Killeleagh, in the County Down, in the Peerage of Ireland, and a Baronet, Knight of Our Most Illustrious Order of Saint Patrick, and Knight Commander of Our Most Honorable Order of the Bath, Governor General of Canada and Governor and Commander-in-Chief in and over the Island of Prince Edward, and Vice Admiral of Canada and Prince Edward.

At Our Government House in Our City of Ottawa this Twentysixth day of June in the year of Our Lord one thousand eight hundred and seventy three and in the Thirty seventh year of Our Reign.

By Command.

[illegible]
Secretary of State.

73.6 cm x 53.3 cm

National Archives of Canada,
Government Archives Division,
RG 68, Vol. 983.

Concluding Remarks

The purpose of this exhibition is to capture the flavour of life in its fullness in the Confederation era. It was never the intention of this catalogue or exhibition to reflect in detail the complex political story which resulted in the union of the British North American provinces. This has been done before. Rather, this catalogue and the exhibition it represents are meant to show Confederation in its human context, to re-create the background tapestry against which the Confederation drama was played out.

The selection of documents for this catalogue and exhibition may seem somewhat eclectic or incomplete. However, neither catalogue nor exhibition aspire to historical completeness. Both are venues in which the archival records and documents of the National Archives speak to us. Like windows into history, they admit us into a past age, where we can vicariously experience the lives of our ancestors and, in the process, learn about ourselves. Hopefully, the various items displayed here will do that, and allow the reader of the catalogue or the viewer of the exhibition to arrive at a better understanding of life in Canada during the Confederation era.

A careful observer will have noticed that this exhibition is not a panegyric to Confederation. As the archival records indicate, Confederation was a difficult birth and the new Dominion came into an imperfect world filled with problems. Just treatment of aboriginal peoples and their land claims, strong localisms, the role of the central government, Canada's relationship with the United States (including free trade), the place of Quebec within Confederation (and English-French tensions), the influence of geography and space upon economic and political developments — these concerns and others have been with us since before 1867.

It is hoped this exhibition will provide a historical context for Canada as we know it today. If it manages this, and does so in an aesthetically enjoyable and intellectually stimulating manner, then the National Archives will have achieved one of its chief objectives, which is to make known to Canadians the intriguing and informative archival documents of their own past.

Index

– Q U

VIEW F